The 4th Industrial Revolution is disrupting businesses and beliefs all the way to the very concept of risk and performance. Professor Steve Wyatt demonstrates with extensive insight why and how leadership, above and beyond technology, is going to be the most important asset to compete dynamically and drive enduring growth. A thought-provoking and actionable read for anyone in the business. Dip in and out, there are treasures and actionable insights throughout the book.
Alessandro Bogliolo, Chief Executive Officer, Tiffany & Co

Steve Wyatt's development of a new form of competitive advantage (for the 4th Industrial Revolution) addresses an age-old strategy issue. How can the firm most effectively compete in the present, while at the same time investing in resources and capabilities to catch the next wave of competitive advantage? It is foundational thinking, along with a practical set of easy-to-use tools, that will help shape the evolution of the field of strategy.
Professor Bernie Jaworski, Dean and Peter F Drucker Chair of Management, Peter F Drucker School of Management, University of Southern California

This is a brilliant piece of work by Steve Wyatt, skillfully balancing the strategic agility with purpose-led leadership as critical enablers to compete and win sustainably in the 4th Industrial Revolution. Steve's deep insights from emerging markets, supported by research and reflections, paint a compelling picture for change in the leadership narrative. Humanity in leadership or human-centred workforce management, which Steve has called out as one of the key elements of leadership in the 4th Industrial Revolution, will be the single biggest differentiator between success and failure of leaders. Having known Steve for a while and seen his work, there is no one better placed than him to create this masterpiece.
Atul Khosla, Senior Vice President and Global Head of Talent, Learning and Organization Effectiveness, Mondelez International

Management and Leadership in the 4th Industrial Revolution is a critical read given the current global environment and the changing expectations and responsibilities of corporations. The 4th Industrial Revolution and the shift toward purpose-driven business strategy is already having a profound impact on the global economy, businesses and people. It's imperative that leaders today adopt a more human-centred and multi-stakeholder approach to grow responsibly and better serve everyone. Steve details how values-based strategy and business growth are not at odds with one another, but required for sustainable, purpose-led growth. This book is a must-read for leaders looking to drive impactful growth in this new landscape.
Jonathan Auerbach, Executive Vice President and Chief Strategy, Growth and Data Officer, PayPal

Steve Wyatt masterfully brings together his private sector and academic careers to codify and enunciate what many managers in various industries have been dealing with as a result of the massive changes taking place as part of the 4th Industrial Revolution. The ideas and thoughts outlined in this book force a re-evaluation of strategy and management from a completely fresh perspective and spurs the rethinking of fundamental principles that many of us took for granted in leadership, talent management and technological innovation. Reflections upon the principles that Steve brings forth will help equip all leaders to embrace disruption as opportunity rather than challenge – driving sustainable growth and innovation.
Luke Kang, Executive Vice President, Managing Director, North Asia, The Walt Disney Company

A thought-provoking and game-changing book that perfectly captures the challenges and new realities of the 4th Industrial Revolution! Steve Wyatt is proposing genuine and pragmatic solutions anchored in real business transformation experiences from the most successful corporations on the planet. A must-read for anyone looking to accelerate growth, transform continuously and stay ahead!
Julien Hemard, Chief Transformation Officer, Group Sales, Pernod Ricard

Fresh thinking from an experienced strategist who has also 'rolled up his sleeves'. Steve Wyatt's analysis and insight into leadership and management for the VUCA world shaped by the 4th Industrial Revolution should be

mandated reading for those who lead businesses and those who advise and support them. 'More of the same' is not enough to survive, let alone thrive; with a clear focus on the organization and people therein, this book will help shape your strategy, thinking and approach to the world at work – a handbook for success. A consultant and academic, Steve writes with an engaging, entertaining and educational style – you'll want to keep reading, and you'll want to apply what you read!
Mark Hewett, Vice President, Capgemini Invent

Professor Steve Wyatt has a gem in writing. I highly appreciate the valuable insights and examples he provided in this book – first-hand from his work with prominent organizations around the world, particularly in Asia. In a fast-changing world with increasing complexities, being resilient and fast adapting is critical for business sustainability. Understanding dynamic capacity and how to harness it in one's organization will be critical in building the leadership and organization capabilities required for business sustainability and ongoing success. A great read with fresh perspectives.
Bryan Loo, Vice President/General Manager, Asia Pacific, Envista

Only a consultant with tonnes of experience fixing companies across the globe could possibly provide these insights. Only a professor with years of teaching experience could communicate these insights in a meaningful and easy way. Professor Steve Wyatt is both, and in his book *Management and Leadership in the 4th Industrial Revolution* he helps leaders decrease uncertainty through sensing. He helps leaders facing ambiguity to seize and replicate opportunities. He helps leaders in complex environments simplify choices by reconfiguring options. This is a playbook for every business leader wanting to navigate and lead their organization through the 4th Industrial Revolution and beyond.
Hitendra Patel, Founder and CEO of IXL Center, President of the Global Innovation Management Institute, Innovation Thought Leader and New Ventures Investor

People often say, 'Talent will trump strategy' – but why not have both! With Steve Wyatt's unique background of both strategy consulting and human capital advisory, he can really bring the best of both worlds together. As the world continues to transform at pace, it's increasingly clear that understanding how talent drives strategy is a critical component to success. Steve's experience and insight are therefore most timely and most valuable.

David Hui, Regional Managing Partner (Industrial), APAC and Middle East, CEO and Board Practice, Heidrick & Struggles

Professor Steve Wyatt's book provides an elegant and comprehensive framework to understand and address the challenges that companies face to be competitive in today's uncertain and unpredictable world. The book illustrates the challenges and how to address them with multiple practical examples, from companies coming from multiple sectors and regions. One key aspect of the book from my point of view is how clearly Steve describes what is expected of leaders in their task to help companies become dynamically competitive. I am certain it will help everyone reading the book reflect on their own experience and identify new behaviours and actions to become better leaders during the 4th Industrial Revolution.

Fernando Musa, Senior Adviser, Bain & Company, and former Chief Executive Officer, Braskem

The 4th Industrial Revolution is characterized by the major impact of advances in information and communication technologies on all the activities of the enterprise. As a result, organizational success factors will be very different in this new era. Whilst humans will be increasingly able to leverage machines and AI, what will make the difference is how well companies will unleash the power of what only humans can do. Steve Wyatt's book provides great insights on the key characteristics required by companies in the 4th Industrial Revolution – flexibility, agility, experimentation, testing and learning, constructive challenge, adaptability, creativity – not only for an individual or a small group, but at scale. As we follow through his framework of 'Sense & Make Sense', 'Seize & Replicate', being able to 'Reposition & Reconfigure', we learn from real life examples and we can draw inspiration for what to do to build better, purpose-led, future-proof organizations.

Michele Luzi, Partner, Bain & Company

Steve Wyatt's *Management and Leadership in the 4th Industrial Revolution* is an essential read for leaders trying to figure out how to respond to the relentless and rapid change in so many aspects of today's business environment. The book highlights a fundamental insight – that remaining competitive has nothing to do with the technology itself and everything to do with how organizations respond to, create and adopt technologies themselves. Building an organization that self-organizes to create and adopt technologies that build lasting competitive advantage is fundamental to success and survival in the face of accelerating change. True to the nature of the book, Steve doesn't provide a copy and paste template; instead he describes models of thought required to build an organization and culture appropriate for the 4th Industrial Revolution, encouraging readers to think for themselves while providing a roadmap to guide their thinking.

John F Diener, AgriFood Tech Entrepreneur and Investor

Many senior managers are being forced to adapt themselves and their organizations in order to embrace a new world order. Finding the right mix of pace, exploration, judgement and empathy is a tall order. So, as we all face into this 4th Industrial Revolution, I am sure that the wisdom contained within this book will be a bright 'guiding light' for a new generation of successful leaders.

Professor Veronica Hope Hailey, University Vice President, University of Bath

Since I first got to know Steve Wyatt as consultant to me in my capacity as Executive Deputy Chairman/Group CEO of PSA Port Group Singapore, he has always impressed me with his knack to drill down to the core of issues, connect dots and put in the hard work, focus and dedication to achieving the winning strategy and desired outcome.

Eddie Teh Ewe Guan, Director, RRJ Capital, and former Group CEO, PSA International

Management and Leadership in the 4th Industrial Revolution

Capabilities to achieve superior performance

Stephen Wyatt

KoganPage

First published in Great Britain and the United States in 2021 by Kogan Page Limited

2nd Floor, 45 Gee Street
London
EC1V 3RS
United Kingdom
www.koganpage.com

122 W 27th St, 10th Floor
New York, NY 10001
USA

4737/23 Ansari Road
Daryaganj
New Delhi 110002
India

Kogan Page books are printed on paper from sustainable forests.

ISBNs

Hardback   978 1 78966 682 3
Paperback   978 1 78966 680 9
Ebook   978 1 78966 681 6

British Library Cataloguing-in-Publication Data

A CIP record for this book is available from the British Library.

Library of Congress Cataloging-in-Publication Data

Names: Wyatt, Stephen, author.
Title: Management and leadership in the 4th industrial revolution:
    capabilities to achieve superior performance / Stephen Wyatt.
Description: 1st Edition. | New York: Kogan Page Ltd, 2020. | Includes
    bibliographical references and index.
Identifiers: LCCN 2020039180 (print) | LCCN 2020039181 (ebook) | ISBN
    9781789666809 (paperback) | ISBN 9781789666823 (hardback) | ISBN
    9781789666816 (ebook)
Subjects: LCSH: Industrial management. | Strategic planning. | Teams in the
    workplace–Management. | Organizational change. | Organizational effectiveness.
Classification: LCC HD31.2 .W93 2020 (print) | LCC HD31.2 (ebook) | DDC 658.4–dc23
LC record available at https://lccn.loc.gov/2020039180
LC ebook record available at https://lccn.loc.gov/2020039181

Typeset by Integra Software Services, Pondicherry
Print production managed by Jellyfish
Printed and bound by CPI Group (UK) Ltd, Croydon CR0 4YY

Whatever you do,
whether in word or deed,
do it all in the name of the Lord Jesus,
giving thanks to God the Father through him
(Colossians Chapter 3, v 17)

CONTENTS

PART SIX
Summary   227

12 Boosters and key themes   229

ABOUT THE AUTHOR

Professor Stephen Wyatt is a leading expert, thought leader, advisor and educator in the field of leadership and business. He has unique insight on the mechanisms for creating value in dynamic environments combined with a depth of experience in effecting change in organizations. A product of 30 years of curiosity and practice in these areas, he has worked with over 80 organizations and an estimated 14,000 executives. He is driven by a passion to help people fulfil their potential and adapt to the changes driven by the 4th Industrial Revolution. He adheres to the belief that insights and advice must be anchored in robust research, and provides practical, actionable support based on direct experience. Professor Wyatt is a professor of strategy and leadership at the University of Bath, Industry Associate with the University of Cambridge, and affiliated faculty with Singapore Management University. He is the founder and lead consultant of the advisory and training company Corporate Rebirth Partners (www.corporaterebirth.com). The firm focuses on supporting leaders and organizations to transform for and to thrive in the 4th Industrial Revolution.

What people say

'Since I first got to know Steve as consultant to me in my capacity as Executive Deputy Chairman/Group CEO of PSA Port Group Singapore, in December 2002, he has always impressed me with his knack to drill down to the core of issues, and connect dots, and put in the hard work, focus and dedication to achieving the winning strategy and desired outcome. I thank him for his help and support.'
Eddie Teh Ewe Guan, Director, RRJ Capital, Former Group CEO of PSA International

'Steve Wyatt's development of a new form of competitive advantage (for 4th Industrial Revolution) addresses an age-old strategy issue. How can the firm most effectively compete in the present – while at the same time investing in resources and capabilities to catch the next wave of competitive advantage?

It is foundational thinking – along with a practical set of easy-to-use tools – that will help shape the evolution of the field of strategy.'

Professor Bernie Jaworski, Dean and Peter F Drucker Chair of Management, Peter F Drucker School of Management, University of Southern California

'It is markedly impactful when one engages with a highly intellectual and relevant consultant partner. Steve Wyatt was able to plug into the reality and the root of the problems we face in the healthcare industry. Through a day of intensive questions and undivided listening, Steve was able to clearly articulate in writing the root of the problems besides a clear problem definition. Battle half won. He then gathered teams to present different scenarios and solutions. I got my leadership team to select what makes most sense for implementation, to refine further and implement. Truly helped to sharpen our thinking and provided valuable insights and examples.'

Bryan Loo, Vice President/General Manager, Asia Pacific, Envista

FOREWORD

For many years academics and practitioners have argued that business is moving into a VUCA world, one that is characterized by volatility, uncertainty, complexity and ambiguity. The challenge of how to manage in the face of VUCA has been amplified by the current pandemic, which in many industries is speeding up change. I expect that we will see a significant acceleration of the long-term trends of innovation through digitalization, the search for robust supply ecosystems, strategic control over essential supplies, an increased importance of including sustainability in decision-making and a commitment to good governance and stewardship. Many well-researched papers have been written about how to manage this type of change, and business leaders have suggested anecdotal evidence of how to cope with it. But what we missed was a good, empirically anchored, and yet practical, approach on how to respond to these accelerating trends. With his views on how to manage and provide leadership in the 4th Industrial Revolution, Stephen Wyatt offers us an excellent handbook to guide senior and middle managers alike to cope with change and the need to innovate.

Coping with fast change in technology and markets requires, of course, a good and innovative strategy. Scholars have argued that this requires companies to develop their dynamic capabilities or their ability to purposefully adapt their resource base, as opposed to the capabilities needed to exploit a firm's current strategic assets through day-to-day operations. For many practitioners this remained perhaps a bit abstract. Stephen Wyatt has and, equally important, how to make sense out of these signals for your own organization. But knowing what is going on and what is relevant to your organization is insufficient. More than ever the speed with which we can scale up our new or adjusted business models has become important. First to market as an objective has been replaced by first to scale. Seizing opportunities, replicating and reconfiguring rapidly your business models and organization are helping organizations to achieve this.

But we all know that the value of a good strategy is determined by the quality of its implementation. That is where Part Three of this book will help you a lot. I personally believe that managers and business leaders need to adopt an ambidextrous mindset, and have to develop their capacity to be at the same time driven by ruthless efficiency in the daily operations, and on the other hand be able to create slack within the organization to innovate and experiment. Innovating and experimenting in the face of uncertainty will either require a learning approach or the ability to run lots of small experiments in parallel, and being able to fail small. It requires an ability to adapt the strategy to changing contextual conditions.

Succeeding with implementation requires you to have the right crew. We used to think about getting the right people on board as a war for talent. That sort of suggested that there was a limited stock of good people, and that you had to use warlike stratagems to get them on board. It is no surprise that Stephen Wyatt, with his long experience in development of young high potentials and senior leadership, suggests a very different approach. As a former president of a university in Singapore, I am convinced that raw talent is quite abundant, but that it has to developed and groomed, and I agree with Stephen Wyatt that this is the path we have to walk. We should not go to war over talent, but take the abundant raw talent and develop it. We also have understood that the capabilities of a team are as important if not more important than an individual's capabilities to an organization. No wonder that you find in Part Four a plea for talent development and fluid teams. And, indeed, one of the strengths of this handbook is that in each chapter we get as a common thread a few suggestions about what is required from leaders to develop dynamic capabilities and implement an innovative strategy.

Stephen Wyatt enriched his own empirical observations with some of the more recent insights on strategy development and implementation. There are many real nuggets of good insight and advice in this book. For example, I loved the concepts of idea fragments, the need for an acceleration officer, the creation of fluid teams and the human-centered workforce management with duty of care. Not all of them are developed by the author, obviously, but he brought them together in a logical and appealing way.

The strength of a good handbook or manual is that it helps you to practice and hone your skills through practical examples and hints for action. Stephen Wyatt has interspersed his conceptual advice with many practical examples and short cases from all over the world. Everybody will recognize some of the examples and be able to translate the conceptual advice into their own situation.

I congratulate Stephen Wyatt on having written an excellent book that will no doubt help many managers to cope with the challenge of a VUCA world, the 4th Industrial Revolution and the disruptions created by the COVID-19 pandemic.

Professor Arnoud De Meyer

PREFACE

In naming the 4th Industrial Revolution, the World Economic Forum pointed to the profound changes taking place in how businesses operate and the inter-relationship between business and society. As profound as the adoption of mechanization in the 1st Industrial Revolution and the subsequent waves of evolution driven by science (2nd) and electronics (3rd). All the industrial revolutions profoundly change people's lives, the distribution of capital and the role of businesses and industrialists in society. Each revolution also requires adapting what managers and leaders do; the ability to deploy and leverage new technologies and to adopt new 'rules of the game'. This book is a guide for all those seeking to thrive in this exciting new environment. In particular, it is for those who understand that the 4th Industrial Revolution is not just about technology, it is about becoming more human-centred and focusing on sustainable development. As the World Economic Forum noted in 2015:

> The 4th Industrial Revolution is about more than just technology-driven change; it is an opportunity to help everyone, including leaders, policy-makers and people from all income groups and nations, to harness converging technologies in order to create an inclusive, human-centred future. The real opportunity is to look beyond technology, and find ways to give the greatest number of people the ability to positively impact their families, organizations and communities.[1]

The speed, breadth and depth of the changes being brought by the 4th Industrial Revolution (4IR) are forcing us to rethink what we mean by creating value, both social and economic, how organizations create and capture that value, and what managers and leaders need to excel at to achieve superior performance. 4IR is the era of artificial intelligence, digital automation, genome editing, biometrics, robotics, autonomous vehicles and the Internet of Things. It is the era of rapid value capture by some, matched by equally rapid value destruction experienced by others. It's the context where VUCA (Volatile, Uncertain, Complex, Ambiguous) is normal. Thriving in 4IR requires adopting new approaches to management and leadership. Competing for the future, today. Recognizing that by our actions we are creating the future. That the future we imagine is unlikely to be that which arrives so we must be ready to adapt, pivot, reinvent and reimagine, whilst building the trust and support of employees, investors and society. The 4th Industrial Revolution, it is hoped, will redress several of the damages created by the first three phases of industrialization – the sustainability of the environment, social equality and inclusiveness, physical and mental well-being – whilst further driving economic growth and increasing productivity.

Management and Leadership in the 4th Industrial Revolution identifies organizational capabilities, management processes and leadership traits that are distinctive for driving success in the 4IR. Enabled by technologies and an abundance of cheap capital, the 4IR is a dynamic environment where industry boundaries are blurred and the unknown, uncertain future is unfolding rapidly.

As the former CEO of Intel, Andy Grove, famously noted in 1988, 'Only the paranoid survive.' He was referring to the fast pace of change in the semi-conductor industry. That speed of disruption and change is now encountered in most industries and in most countries. To note emergent trends, to see how to create opportunities, to make choices and to execute quickly are increasingly key determinants of an organization's ability to survive. A proverb, reputedly from Africa, says:

> Every morning in Africa, a gazelle wakes up. It knows it must run faster than the fastest lion or it will be killed. Every morning a lion wakes up. It knows it must outrun the slowest gazelle or it will starve to death. It doesn't matter whether you are a lion or a gazelle: when the sun comes up, you'd better be running.[2]

Management and Leadership in the 4th Industrial Revolution does not explore the technologies that are enabling the revolution, nor the techniques of their adoption. Rather, our focus is on the capabilities, management processes and leadership traits that enable organizations to react and run faster than others in the 4IR.

New approaches to management and leadership are needed in 4IR

Every industrial revolution has seen an increase in the speed of business, so too with the 4th. What distinguishes this revolution is the way we think about risk. The risk of not moving fast enough, of not participating early enough in a project or venture or of not scaling big enough to become the dominant platform. The risk of losing out on opportunities that win big is eclipsing the perception of project risk associated with any one initiative. The perception of risk is changing due to two factors: the speed at which new businesses can be built (eg leveraging cloud-based solutions, fluidity in the market for talent, accessing cross-border advantages and global scale) and the availability of low-cost funding, a product of near-zero interest rates and fiscal policies of quantitative easing. In addition, in this revolution we have an abundance of data on the right here – right now. Previously we have had to do research to capture data on what was happening, then analyse it, then formulate management algorithms which were translated into procedures. This was as much the foundation of scientific management pioneered by Frederick Taylor in the early years of the 20th century as it underpinned the approaches to strategic analysis and planning pioneered by Michael Porter and Jay Barney in the 1980s and 1990s. In 4IR we can monitor in real time what is happening, ingesting data at hitherto improbable rates; and with the support of artificial intelligence and machine learning we can take timely decisions and learn. The algorithms for running 4IR businesses can be constantly evolving. Managers need to know how to employ these capabilities to enhance performance, for example adjusting the interface with customers, creating and predicting demand, flexibly adjusting operations and the supply chain, optimizing the human capital assets of the organization, etc. Leaders need to know how to compete in the new fluid, hyper-dynamic context of 4IR, where industry structure and geographic borders are of decreasing relevance and where winning in the future is increasingly valued more highly than results produced today. Reference the increasing average price–earnings ratios of listed companies and the rise and rise of 'unicorns' (young firms that are not or are barely profitable, yet valued to be worth over US $1 billion).

In this 4th Industrial Revolution we also think about the risk of corporate sustainability. Corporate valuations can rise and can fall by billions of dollars in just a few weeks – for example 'WeWork', whose valuation dropped from $47 billion to $8 billion over three months (August to October 2019). As no one knows the rapidly unfolding future, every new initiative is expected to encounter unforeseen challenges. Leadership teams, at start-ups and at big established corporations, pursue bold initiatives but must also be ready to pivot direction, aiming to disrupt marketspaces whilst also anticipating their own disruption from third parties. Sustainability requires making big bold choices in order to pivot in a timely manner, attracting and retaining talent through such changes of direction, cultivating a culture of continuous learning and driving reinvention and innovation. In 2019, the UK-based Dyson Group announced that they were relocating to Singapore and abandoned over $3 billion of planned investments in the pursuit of making electric vehicles, whilst also seeking to recycle into the wider corporation both the talent and the intellectual property developed through the initiative. As an example, Alphabet, the parent company of Google, include in their portfolio of projects some very ambitious 'moon shots', such as fully autonomous vehicles, which they hope eventually will win big. They accept that many of these projects will fail or be abandoned; however, they believe that much of the learning, even from the apparent failures (such as Google Glasses), can be recycled into other initiatives.

Every industrial revolution creates a new wealthy class, those who pioneer the changes in how businesses operate, harnessing better than others the new technologies and pushing more aggressively after their bigger vision of what could be. Bezos rather than Rockefeller or Ma rather than Matsushita are demonstrating how to lead in 4IR.

What this book covers – and what it does not

This book is a handbook of management practices and leadership competencies required to win in the 4th Industrial Revolution. It is illustrated throughout with examples and anecdotes from corporations today, as the 4IR is already here. Most of the examples are from major global corporations, often firms with significant heritage that have nonetheless responded to the challenges of managing in this accelerating and increasingly technology-enabled environment. These examples thereby are relevant both for long-established entities and for those founded much more recently. The intent is that the reader will continually ask themselves the question, 'How can this be applied in my company?'

This is a handbook for how to manage in the new environment. It is not a discussion of the different types of technology, nor of the benefits of embracing such technologies, nor indeed of how to adopt them. *Management and Leadership in the 4th Industrial Revolution* is a guidebook for winning in 4IR, but I also hope it is entertaining.

What this book is based on

The foundations of the insights in this book are based on work with global corporations as a strategy and leadership consultant, supporting their migration to embrace new management practices over the past 20 years. This was then refined through an in-depth research initiative conducted through the Singapore Management University which drew on experiences and practices at 50 corporations, together with guidance and sage advice from thought leaders such as Bernie Jaworski (Chaired Professor at Peter Drucker School of Management, Claremont University), Rajendra Srivastava (Dean, Indian School of Business) and Sir Michael Gregory (Institute for Manufacturing, University of Cambridge). The resulting insights led to the creation of an index (Dynamic Capacity) against which any firm can be assessed and which can act as a leading indicator of firm future performance. The stock price performances of corporations included in the study were tracked over a five-year period to verify the predictive effectiveness of the index. On average, those firms with a higher than average dynamic capacity outperformed their industry peers by over 31 per cent over the five-year period, whereas those firms that had a lower than average dynamic capacity underperformed their industry peers by 15 per cent over the five-year period.

How to read and use this book

This book is a handbook to support executives to successfully lead and manage their businesses in the 4th Industrial Revolution.

- **Build dynamic capacity**
  Chapters 2, 3 and 4 focus on the three sets of capabilities that enable the firm to adapt, anticipate and react to the future as it unfolds. These capabilities in combination determine the capacity of the firm to compete dynamically, ie the Dynamic Capacity, which is the index that indicates the ability of the firm to outperform its peers in the mid-term future.

- **Drive audacious growth: Be purpose-led**
  Chapters 5, 6 and 7 focus on the capabilities that support the pursuit of a purposeful vision, that can drive and sustain high growth rates.

- **Win the 4IR talent race**
  Chapters 8, 9 and 10 focus on arguably the most important asset of all in 4IR – people. Recognizing that 4IR is causes significant dislocation of jobs and requiring constant learning both of new skills and new working practices. Winning the race of developing, deploying, empowering and retaining talent is critical to the success of firms operating in 4IR.

- **Dynamic advantage**
  Chapter 11 is a guide to seizing the initiative to embrace the management and leadership practices and behaviours to win in the 4th Industrial Revolution. It includes an assessment questionnaire that will help your leadership team to identify which factors to prioritize for action.

Each of the nine core chapters (Chapters 2–10) focuses on a particular area of corporate capability. Each provides insight into the management mechanisms, the core leadership competencies, the mindsets and aspects of the firm culture required to excel in that area. Although the book provides examples of good practice in each area, reflecting experiences at over 50 global corporations, the aspiration is that the reader will be able to apply the principles and insights of each chapter to enhance the performance of their corporation, rather than mimicking the actions and examples that are portrayed in the book.

Endnotes

1 https://www.weforum.org/focus/fourth-industrial-revolution (archived at https://perma.cc/9Y5K-LK8Z)

2 Montano, D (1985) Lions or Gazelles? *The Economist*, 6 July

ACKNOWLEDGEMENTS

The journey of creating this book has not been a straight path, although the essence was always clear: how to thrive in the 4th Industrial Revolution. At times my writing deviated into consideration and classification of various disruptive forces or reviews of emergent technologies and business models. Thankfully I was guided back onto the path and able to continue. Various mentors held me to the dual obligations that whatever stayed in the book must be both proven by robust research and supported by tangible examples. Thus, this book was written with the twin pillars of support from leading academics in fields of business and executives who themselves are leading corporations in the turbulence of the 4th Industrial Revolution. In the seven years it has taken to complete this book and undertake precise research, many of those individuals have changed role, changed organization, or even retired; however, they have not wavered in the generosity of their support. In this regard, I would particularly like to acknowledge the support of the following executives: Jeffrey Hardee, Andrew Guthrie, Roland Pirmez, Eddie Teh, Bryan Loo, Julien Hemard, Hitendra Patel, Simon McKenzie, Luke Kang and Jeremy Armitage. Equally I would like to thank the following academics for their guidance, and for providing the other pillar for quality control: Bernie Jaworski, Arnoud De Meyer, Rajendra Srivastava, Philip Zerrillo and Sir Michael Gregory.

Many friends have encouraged and indeed facilitated me on the journey of writing this book; they have provided wisdom and support and at times a much-needed distraction or well-timed comment of critique. In particular I would like to thank Samantha Wong, Colin Marson, John Diener, Elisabeth Baker and Graham Wilde. Special thanks are also due to two people who painstakingly reviewed and commented on drafts of the manuscript. Their toil when I naïvely and optimistically thought I was near the final version but in fact was far from it was essential in showing me how much further I still had to travel. A sanguine comment by Toby Trotter caused me to have a major rethink when he observed that I seemed to be heading for three different books rather one integrated one. Janet Bradshaw, convalescing after an accident, invested her time in a detailed review that helped accelerate me towards the final version.

My family have been amazing in their support and love and tolerance of my hours working, mood swings and countless calls with executives and academics around the world. They have encouraged me to keep refining, to hold to the dual tests mentioned above, to never cut corners and never fall short, whilst also keeping me fed and loved. Thank you Rachel, Hannah, Sophia and Jonathan.

Over the past 30 years of my hectic professional life, I have at times been stopped in my tracks by wise words shared with good intent by people I respect. The resulting choices I own, but these people, perhaps unwittingly, made me stop and think and resulted in my making adjustments to my direction of travel: thank you Elisabeth Sam, Stephan Titze and Joseph Fuller.

I would also like to thank the executives who have written kind words of endorsement for this book. Each person a leader who has distinguished themselves by increasing dynamic capacity, equipping organizations to thrive in the 4th Industrial Revolution.

PART ONE

Introduction

As a consultant for the management consulting firm Monitor Group in the mid-1990s, I was based in Hong Kong. One year I spent over 100 nights in the Grand Hyatt Hotel in Seoul. What made that assignment memorable was not the quality of the bed linen but the resounding chorus from the Korean executives at the client that 'Korea is different... you have to interpret the data differently here'. I must have heard that refrain 30 times before I realized that 'resistance is useless'. So, instead of trying to defend our analyses, I just asked, 'How is Korea different?'

The answer was enlightening. It influenced my approach to consulting and running my own businesses over the next 20-plus years – and eventually led to this book. Korea was, at that time, indeed different from the more developed and more stable markets. It was developing rapidly and unpredictably. There was a clear opportunity cost for a firm not moving fast enough. Strategic choices were required, 'yes', but with limited insight for the future market conditions. Agility was important, 'yes', but not at the expense of operational efficiency. What western management theory started calling VUCA (volatile, uncertain, complex and ambiguous) in the mid-2000s has been 'normal' in Asia for several decades. In 2002 an executive at a global agrochemicals company wryly noted, 'A great deal of our growth has been coming from the so-called Asian Tiger economies – but Harvard didn't tell us how to ride Tigers!'

For the best part of 20 years, I worked with the Monitor Group, mainly in the Asia-Pacific region. Asia often felt a long way from Cambridge,

Massachusetts, where the founders resided. These included some of the most esteemed management thinkers of our time, such as Michael Porter, Mark and Joe Fuller, and thought leaders such as Bernie Jaworski, Roger Martin, Chris Argyris, David Kantor, Michael Jensen, Tom Copeland, Peter Schwartz and others. As a young consultant I didn't always appreciate the esteemed company I was in, yet I greatly appreciated their personal support as I worked with clients in tackling seemingly intractable problems in the fast-evolving markets in Asia-Pacific. We worked through the ups and downs of financial and political turmoil of different countries in the region. I learnt to appreciate the benefits of consultancy toolkits and the business insights inspired by the perspectives of my colleagues, drawn from their extensive business exposure mainly in the developed countries of the United States and Europe. But I also learned to appreciate the wisdom of the 6th-century BC Chinese philosopher Lao Tzu:

> Those who have knowledge, don't predict. Those who predict,
> don't have knowledge.

In unstable and accelerating business environments, the future is very difficult to predict; traditional management and leadership practices and approaches can inhibit firms from adapting fast enough or creating and seizing opportunities. Uncertainties and ambiguities, together with the speed of evolution of competitors and the rapid rate of change of customer behaviours that were then characteristics of Asia, have increasingly become the norm globally, driven not by widely differing rates of economic and social growth but by the technologies, political and social transformations of the 4th Industrial Revolution.

Today, approximately 80 per cent of the value of most western listed firms is driven by expectations of their future earnings stream. Yet past and current period results are *decreasingly* relevant as indicators of future performance as the speed of change in business, technology, trends and markets *increases*.[1] For many companies, instability is the new norm and agility and adaptation are essential capabilities.

How do big corporations create and maintain the energy to constantly adapt and compete in this new normal of accelerated, unstable business? How do they transform themselves and their ways of operating and continue to drive up their valuation? And how can we have confidence in a strategy when the future is unknown?

As Harvard Business School's Professor Clayton Christensen said:

The way the world was made for whatever reason, means that we only have data on the past or at best the present, but we have to take decisions for the future. The only way to look into the future is through the lens of a good theory.[2]

So, what 'good theory' can we use to look into the future as marketspaces are disrupted, created and the speed of business continuously accelerates? And if the strategy toolkit that evolved in stable economies with similar regulatory environments is decreasingly applicable or even obsolete, which tools should ambitious, fast-growth firms use as they venture into the unknown future?

The kernel for this book was my wish to put some structure to the insights I had accumulated on the role of the leader and the mechanisms within the corporation that most correspond to high performance in fast-evolving, dynamic contexts. I was especially interested in those firms and leaders that successfully operate across a broad set of markets and business contexts, including both the hyper-dynamic and the more stable. How do they leverage this for advantage and not become trapped with a dominant approach suited for one context but hampering performance elsewhere?

The speed of business is increasing globally, as is the rate of value creation and loss. Much has been written about models of success in relatively stable environments and for businesses whose activities in their home market dominate how they think about their strategy, culture and management practices. This book is for everyone else. It's a distillation of experiences, formal education, hands-on management and academic research into how firms consistently achieve superior performance in unstable, accelerating business contexts, where the next 'new' may come from anywhere in the world.

To formulate my experience-based insights about what makes an effective corporate leader in a rapidly changing environment, I started to interview as many of my clients as possible. I heard how they are equipping their corporations to succeed in faster-evolving, less predictable environments. Increasingly I also found focus on how many of these corporations succeed *because* they operate across a portfolio of marketspaces with a wide range of levels of instability. Instead of force-fitting the perspective of HQ onto the evolving markets they have 'reversed polarity'; they look to these dynamic markets as a source of insight into what the emerging future in more 'developed' markets might be like.

Many of the corporations that I refer to in the book are large firms operating globally. This is because I wanted to focus on and illustrate the management and organizational tools rather than the impact and personality of any one particular individual leader. Drawing on examples of these corporations across a broad spectrum of industries and markets, I present an integrated model that describes how a corporation can build its capacity to compete dynamically; to thrive, not just survive, in uncertainty and ambiguity. By focusing on developing its dynamic capacity, a corporation can achieve competitively superior performance. The executives at many of the firms in the research were confident in this, and their confidence was borne out over the following five years (December 2014–2019) of tracking the performance of their stock prices relative to those of their relevant competitors.

The book encourages a modified approach to traditional strategic planning and organization management. The firm still requires a winning and motivating strategy but against this it needs to be adaptive as the future unfolds. Purists of strategy will find solace; this book describes how to move from one position of temporary advantage to another, all the time gaining momentum and pursuing the greater mission.

Endnotes

1 https://www.dynamicadvantage.org/ (archived at https://perma.cc/MJM6-NY2T)
2 Clayton Christensen, Thinkers50 Hall of Fame Interview, https://www.youtube.com/watch?v=m4stHDQMblUUt (archived at https://perma.cc/QYS3-KDGG)

01

Competing for tomorrow, today

The future is unknown, yet strategy is about making choices – clear choices – and investing behind those choices, aligning the efforts of the organization. Strategic plans define those choices, and their clarity and communication enable managers and staff throughout the organization to take initiatives and make decisions that are aligned with the strategic intent.

Mission and vision are essential elements of a strategy, but they do not constitute the strategy. A plan is not a strategy either – although the strategy does need to be put into a plan with sequencing and prioritizing of steps. Strategy is not achieved immediately; actions and pivots are tactics, opportunistic or reactive. As professor Michael Porter often said:

> Strategy is making choices; what to do and what not to do.[1]

The right strategy sets out the middle- to long-term direction and choices. While we cannot know the future, a set of strategic choices is essential to navigate the organization forward. As much as some pundits are keen to broadcast the death of strategy, strategy is not dead – long live strategy! As the context of business accelerates, and changing technologies, regulations and non-traditional competitors cause disruptions, the past and present are decreasingly relevant as predictors of the future. Yet far from being 'dead', future-oriented strategy is increasingly rewarded by investors. Such forward-leaning firms command significant valuation premiums over others that have demonstrated historic success.

To illustrate the importance of this future orientation, at the time of writing the average price to earnings ratio for companies included in the S&P index is 20 (28 if using the Shiller formula) and the average price to book ratio is 3. In other words, on average, if the recognized assets of the companies in the index could be sold for their 'book' value then they would represent approximately 25 per cent of the current total value of the firms, because the other 75 per cent of the value is based on expectations of future earnings.

Management books such as *In Search of Excellence,*[2] *Built to Last*[3] and *Good to Great,*[4] which have sold to readers throughout the world, retrospectively analyse aspects of predominantly American corporations' approaches to 'winning' and standing the test of time. But by 2019, of the companies highlighted in these books, fewer than a handful had managed to outperform the average of the S&P 500 and several had failed or been acquired. Would their approaches have worked in different contexts or at different times or in different cultural settings? Rather than look backwards and try to explain past results, leaders need to look forwards, to peer into the murky, unfolding future. Leaders need to make decisions and take actions that will increase the future prosperity of the corporation, provide security of employment and sustain and nurture the dependent eco-system of stakeholders and the societies they are a part of.

Firms are disrupting and making new markets in this accelerating context; they are creating opportunities and abandoning old positions as much as they are also seizing and exploiting advantages in industries with what may prove to be transient business models. In 2019, Tesla, while barely having returned a profit, was valued higher than the 108-year-old General Motors Company (GM), placing it as the US's most valuable auto manufacturer. If Tesla were to deliver on the then-predicted profit for 2020, its valuation would have been equivalent to a price to earnings ratio (P/E) of 80 while GM languished at around 7, despite GM's dedication to operational excellence. No single company is immune to misfortune; General Motors itself filed for bankruptcy in 2009.[5] The point is the difference in P/E ratio, in the valuation that investors place on a company based on their belief in the ability of management to successfully navigate the corporation in the unknown, increasingly uncertain future.

Future-anchored strategic agility

Deng Xiaoping used the following metaphor to describe the process of the modernization of China at the end of the Cultural Revolution:

> Crossing the river by feeling the stones one at a time.[6]

This can also be applied to how the best-performing firms successfully deliver on ambitious visions whilst the accelerated currents of business come strongly against them and the unfolding future makes it uncertain which steps to take.

The intent is clear – to 'cross the river' – but at each step, agility and adaptation are needed.

Strategy directs decision making and points out where to go, which step to take next and when to move from stone to stone. Operational excellence is the ability to make each step without falling in the 'water', to retreat from false starts that prove unstable and to continuously learn from each step to improve the rate of travel.

It is having one's eyes down on the rushing water and semi-submerged rocks while never losing sight of, or orientation towards, the goal on the far side of the river. The skills required are those of sensing what the options are and how soon to move, being able to seize the opportunity, making a good decision in a timely manner and moving on to the next place.

The key is to keep moving so as to have equilibrium and be constantly making progress. Winning in business today, creating and capturing superior value, comes from moving forward across the river, stepping between the stones.

Rita Gunther McGrath highlighted in her excellent book, *The End of Competitive Advantage*, the need for 'transient competitive advantage',[7] noting that this requires 'strategy, innovation and organizational change all coming together'.[8]

When markets and business contexts are uncertain and dynamically evolving, corporations outperform competitors by leaning into the unfolding future. Leaders articulate and orientate the organization towards an ambitious, meaningful, purpose-led vision. They move forward into the unknown future with the expectation that their organizations will excel at achieving the vision. Yet they recognize that to be effective in achieving the vision they must also be adaptive to the unexpected and unknown challenges that will emerge.

The skills required of leaders are the capability to adapt themselves and their organizations, and the desire to constantly learn. This is particularly relevant in the 4IR as context and challenges are in flux – the business environment, the socio-political realities, technologies, economic and trade situations, exchange rates, and human capital issues inside the organization.

The greatest skill is the ability to achieve balance between the two stances – the pursuit of the ambitious future goal *and* the ability to be adaptive in a timely manner as the context evolves. Making strategic choices, good choices, in the face of uncertainty is difficult and requires leadership and courage. Change is getting faster, technologies are enabling new ways of working, engaging with customers and competing; in this context clear strategic thinking with structured choices is increasingly hard work.

These factors can lead to the perception that the situation is too complex, that strategy is too hard, and that everyone should just run experiments and see what works – what Michael Porter describes as a 'Hunt and Peck' approach.[9] This leaves the corporation rudderless and, as a result, making compromises and risking underinvestment in the areas that could most make a difference to performance today and tomorrow. To quote Porter again:

> Most successful companies get two or three or four of the pieces right at the start, and then they elucidate their strategy over time. It's the kernel of things that they saw up front that is essential. That's the antidote to complexity.[10]

My work has shown that organizations can develop and hone the capabilities that enable them to transition, in a timely manner, between subsequent positions of transient competitive advantage.

As Paul Polman (former CEO of Unilever) noted:

> The difference between average and outstanding firms is an 'AND Mentality'. We must find and create tensions that force people into a different space for thinking [...] This is not just a performance issue but a survival issue, because managing paradox helps foster creativity and high performance.[11]

It is forward looking. It acknowledges that the future is unknown and there is great uncertainty. It rallies those involved not only to overcome challenges but to celebrate adaptation. This book is a call to arms. Let's look to the future, expect unknown challenges and meet them with the skills and mindset to overcome them.

This will require learning from others (eg by embracing diversity of perspectives and experience) as well as by undertaking rapid experimentation. Most of the value of the corporation should be due to the expectations for future value – yet the future is unknown. The executives leading the firm will need to be robust and adaptable. Executives will be risk takers and improvisers. They will be hearing, seeing and making sense of the weak signals as they peer into the 'fog' of uncertainty of the future.

Competing for tomorrow, today

In sports, the skill of predicting the trajectory of an oncoming ball and coordinating your movement to intercept it is called *coincidence anticipation timing*. It is pivotal in dynamic sports like tennis or soccer. Top players have excellent coincidence anticipation timing; they seem to have more time to get into the right position.

The same is true for businesses in fast-moving, dynamic markets. The outperforming firms are those that are able to sense where the market is going and reconfigure their capabilities and assets to be in the right place at the right time, to make the right strategic plays.

The skills required for coincidence anticipation timing in sports are known as *dynamic capabilities* in business. To illustrate the efficacy of the analogy, consider this quote from Steve Jobs, founder and former CEO of Apple, who was a proponent of dynamic capabilities:

> There's an old Wayne Gretzky [the ice-hockey great] quote that I love. 'I skate to where the puck is going to be, not where it has been.' And we've always tried to do that at Apple. Since the very, very beginning. And we always will.[12]

So, what are the skills required of businesses to 'skate where the puck is going to be'? In 2009, Helfat and colleagues defined a dynamic capability as the ability 'of an organization to purposefully create, extend, and modify its resource base'.[13] Dynamic capabilities enable a firm to move from one position of 'transient competitive advantage' to another, as noted by Rita Gunther McGrath.[14] David Teece grouped dynamic capabilities into routines and processes of supporting sensing, seizing or reconfiguring, noting that such capabilities are 'difficult to develop and deploy'.[15] Building on these perspectives, my work with corporations has identified specific ways global firms are unlocking advantages of their extensive networks of operations to advantageously develop their capacity to act dynamically.

The capacity of a firm to adapt to and to influence the evolution of its competitive context is increasingly important as the speed of business accelerates.

The ability of the corporation to be adaptive to the future as it unfolds whilst also pursuing a consistent winning and motivating strategy is its dynamic capacity. The dynamic capacity enables the firm to move in a timely manner from one transient competitive advantage to another – repeatedly. From one 'stone to another stone', as it 'crosses the river' towards its longer-term objective. The dynamic capacity is the product of three sets of capabilities, as shown in Figure 1.1.

FIGURE 1.1   The dynamic capacity of a corporation is the product of three
                sets of capabilities

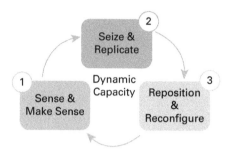

- **Sense & Make Sense**
  Explore possibilities, note weak signals and develop greater insight. Anticipate the evolution of the marketspace. Question existing assumptions. Refine the vision for how to act in the unfolding future.

- **Seize & Replicate**
  Adjust offerings and business models to create and capture value through newly identified opportunities. Propagate insights and redeploy resources across the organization in a timely manner to extend advantages.

- **Reposition & Reconfigure**
  Adjust the scope of activities conducted by the firm and its relationships with others in the eco-system. Morph the portfolio of offerings and the choice of marketspaces in which to compete.

A great athlete requires prowess at all three capabilities: to 'Sense & Make Sense', to 'Seize & Replicate', and to 'Reposition & Reconfigure'. It is much easier to watch the TV broadcast of a sporting event, with perhaps an advantageous camera angle, and see where your favourite player should move to on the field (or court). You might even be right in how you call the shot that they should play and call it out in a timely manner. But only they have the ability to see the emerging opportunity, move to the right location and execute the perfect shot.

   The overall skill of the player is determined by the multiplication of the three dynamic capabilities. Similarly, the ability of the corporation to achieve superior performance is the product of the three dynamic capabilities; if any one of the capabilities is 'zero' then the overall ability of the player (or corporation) to win is zero, irrespective of the strength of the other two capabilities.

Just as a professional athlete, when playing at the top of their game, is rarely static, in the 4IR businesses need to be in a near-constant state of flux and change. Somewhere in the organization there will be changes or adjustments taking place (eg integrating new acquisitions, carving out new business units, adopting new fluid relationships with external partners or changing the internal organization). The more practiced the corporation is at managing changes, large and small, the greater its ability to act in a timely and meaningful manner.

For the corporation, a key question is, 'What are we doing today?' An important part of the answer should be that we are preparing for greater success tomorrow. This requires the corporation to be making the right investments for tomorrow while ensuring strong competitive performance today. For without confidence-building results today, tomorrow may not come.

There is a premium, as with the valuation of the firm, on navigating to the future. In 4IR we move away from traditional approaches of resource management, whereby organization design reflects specialization, and instead we emphasize mobility of resources, fluidity of insight and collective responsibility for performance both today and tomorrow. Mobility and fluidity are value destroying without moving in the right direction, therefore understanding how the future is unfolding is critical. This requires integrating insights from across the organization and taking decisions that are unbiased by projections of prior assumptions about the market or winning tactics, which may no longer be valid. Each initiative is an opportunity for learning, for probing and experimenting. Thus, the cycle initiated in Sense & Make Sense, applied in Seize & Replicate, and then established through Reposition & Reconfigure, continues on from Repositioning and Reconfiguring to feed into Sensing & Making Sense.

The long-term strategy is of fundamental importance because of the uncertainty and ambiguity of the unfolding future. It enables firms to look beyond current turbulence and to make more consistent, aligned decisions for investments and refinement of activities that improve their performance towards those goals. To succeed in achieving its objectives, the corporation must navigate the uncertainties of the future as it unfolds – it must adapt and adjust, *in service* of the long-term strategy, not *as* the strategy.

An indicator of future performance

It is the expectation of future earning streams that defines the value that investors place on a corporation. This expectation increases with greater confidence in the combination of the capabilities that enable the corporation to simultaneously deliver results today and prepare for better performance tomorrow. Thus, the measure of the dynamic capacity of a corporation, in comparison to its peers, is an indicator of its future performance compared to those peers.

Dynamic capacity describes the move from over-dependence on past proven knowledge of the marketspace and previously successful techniques to a forward-leaning, future orientation. The higher the level of dynamic capacity, the better able the corporation is to learn, to adapt to seize and make opportunities in a timely manner. The measure of the dynamic capacity indicates the ability of the corporation to become better, not only more practiced at the processes and approaches that are bringing it success currently but also to evolve further; to thrive, not just survive, in the unknown future.

The global financial crisis (GFC) of 2008 was a watershed moment for the world's economies and stock markets. Since the GFC, the differences in valuations achieved by different types of company have increased dramatically. 'Unicorns' (young companies achieving valuations in excess of US $1 billion) are increasingly common, with investors attracted primarily by the promise of future growth and future earnings – they may have never yet generated any profit. Additionally, the questioning of the continuing relevance of traditional approaches to strategy has intensified, as non-traditional firms with non-traditional strategies are achieving the fastest growth in value – recall the earlier discussion comparing Tesla with General Motors.

In their book, *Built to Last*,[16] Jerry Porras and Jim Collins profiled companies that had long histories (many were established in the 19th century) and yet remained household names. As I indicated earlier, most of the companies that they profiled have, since 1994, survived but have not thrived. As a portfolio, they have underperformed the S&P 500 index. By rights, many shareholders could have divested for better returns elsewhere. But inertia and the fact that several remain large corporations means they provide a steady base for investments of large pension funds and others.

Size and tradition may indicate potential stability, but not always. This was famously demonstrated by Kodak. Founded in 1888, it had a peak valuation of over US $31 billion in 1996 and accounted for over 90 per cent of all film sales in the United States; yet it collapsed and was bankrupt by 2012. Kodak was famously unable to adapt. Neither the age nor the size of a corporation is a factor that determines its ability to survive.

FIGURE 1.2 Dynamic capacity is more important in less stable marketspaces

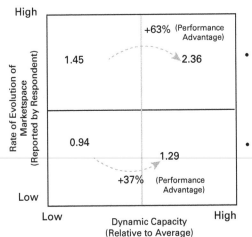

5-year stock price performance December 2014–2019

- Companies with *high* (defined as higher than average) dynamic capacity on average outperformed their relevant peers by **31 per cent** over the five-year period

- Companies with *low* dynamic capacity on average underperformed their relevant peers by **15 per cent** over the five-year period

I conducted my own survey into the relative performance of companies compared to their peers. The results are shown in Figure 1.2. All firms with a relatively high capacity to behave dynamically outperform those firms with a lower capacity. However, the difference is particularly important for those corporations competing in faster-evolving or less stable contexts.

The results shown in Figure 1.2, indicating the higher level of competitive advantage (performance superior to competitors), whilst important, were based on a single point in time and were reliant on the inputs of the participating executives. Therefore, a further analysis was made of the performance of the stock price of the corporations compared to their sector peers over a five-year period from December 2014 to December 2019. The result of the comparison between the share price movement of the participating companies and the stock price movement of their relevant peers is as follows:

- **Companies with *high* (defined as higher than average) dynamic capacity on average outperformed their relevant peers by 31 per cent over the five-year period.** However, it should be noted that within this group two companies underperformed their peers.

- **Companies with *low* dynamic capacity on average under performed their relevant peers by 15 per cent over the five-year period.** However, it should be noted that within this group two companies over-performed compared with their peers.

FIGURE 1.3 Three capabilities enable a corporation to thrive in the dynamic context of 4IR

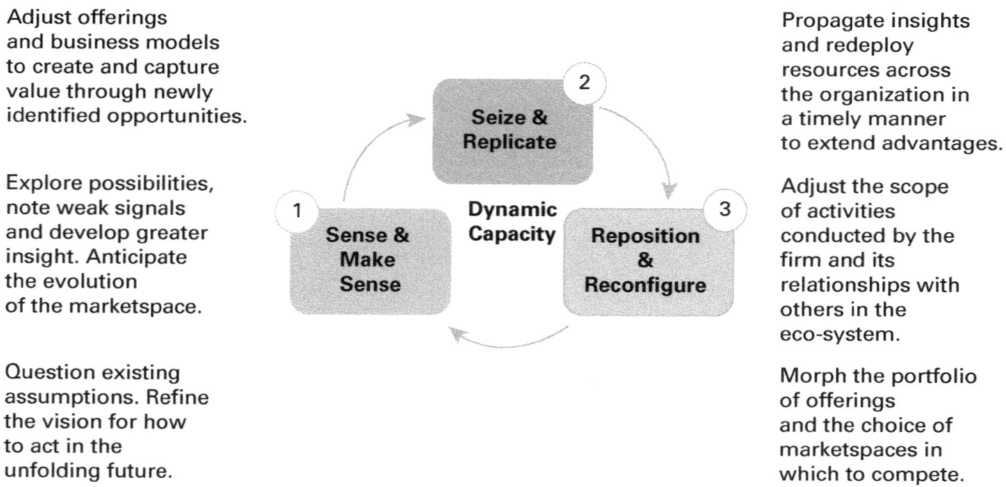

Adjust offerings
and business models
to create and capture
value through newly
identified opportunities.

Explore possibilities,
note weak signals
and develop greater
insight. Anticipate
the evolution
of the marketspace.

Question existing
assumptions. Refine
the vision for how
to act in the
unfolding future.

Propagate insights
and redeploy
resources across
the organization in
a timely manner
to extend advantages.

Adjust the scope
of activities
conducted by the
firm and its
relationships with
others in the
eco-system.

Morph the portfolio
of offerings
and the choice of
marketspaces in
which to compete.

1 Sense &
Make
Sense

2 Seize &
Replicate

3 Reposition
&
Reconfigure

Dynamic
Capacity

Not all the companies that completed the survey and interviews could be included in the stock price analysis as some of those companies (eg Cargill) are privately owned and others (eg Syngenta) were bought over and thereby delisted from the stock market during the five-year period. Additionally, two of the firms undertook several initiatives that significantly enhanced their dynamic capacity during the period, which moved them from being classified as 'Low' to being classified as 'High'.

The stock price performance of both groups of companies (high dynamic capacity and low dynamic capacity) over the five-year period December 2014–2019 validates the original findings and demonstrates that the measure of dynamic capacity can be used as a leading indicator of future performance.

As the management saying goes, 'If you can measure it, you can improve it', so how do we measure the dynamic capacity of a firm? It is the product (multiplication) of the strengths of the three sets of capabilities (introduced above). A questionnaire for assessing these strengths is provided in Chapter 11.

KEY CONCEPTS: CHAPTER 1

As the world of business accelerates and it becomes decreasingly relevant to peer into the future by projecting from the past, firms need to adopt new mechanisms for strategic planning and managing the resources of the organization:

- Future-anchored strategic agility:
  - transient competitive advantage: crossing the river one stone at a time;
  - strategy is making choices.
- Competing for tomorrow, today:
  - coincidence anticipation timing: skate to where the puck is going to be;
  - dynamic capacity:
    - Sense & Make Sense;
    - Seize & Replicate;
    - Reposition & Reconfigure.
- Dynamic capacity as a measure is an indicator of future performance relative to peers.

Endnotes

1 Hammonds, K (2001) Michael Porter's big ideas, *Fast Company*, 28 February

2 Waterman Jr, R H and Peters, T (1982) *In Search of Excellence*, HarperCollins

3 Collins, J and Porras, J (1994) *Built to Last: Successful habits of visionary companies*, William Collins

4 Collins, J (2001) *Good to Great*, William Collins

5 Bigman, D (2013) How General Motors was really saved: the untold true story of the most important bankruptcy in US history, *Forbes*, 30 October

6 South China Morning Post (2002) Crossing the river by feeling the stones, 22 July, https://www.scmp.com/article/385907/crossing-river-feeling-stones (archived at https://perma.cc/6JZK-84TK)

7 Gunther McGrath, R (2013) *The End of Competitive Advantage: How to keep your strategy moving as fast as your business*, Harvard Business Review Press

8 Ibid

9 Hammonds, K (2001) Michael Porter's Big Ideas, *Fast Company*, https://www.fastcompany.com/42485/michael-porters-big-ideas (archived at https://perma.cc/U79M-Q34S)

10 Ibid

11 Lewis, M W, Andriopoulos, C and Smith, W K (2012) Paradoxical leadership to enable strategic agility, *Industrial and Organizational Psychology*, June

12 Gallo, C (2012) Apple's unique website tribute to Steve Jobs, *Forbes*, 5 October

13 Helfat, C E et al (2009) *Dynamic Capabilities: Understanding strategic change in organizations*, John Wiley & Sons

14 Gunther McGrath, R (2013) *The End of Competitive Advantage: How to keep your strategy moving as fast as your business*, Harvard Business Review Press

15 Teece, D J (2007) Explicating dynamic capabilities: the nature and microfoundations of (sustainable) enterprise performance, *Strategic Management Journal*, 28 (13), pp 1319–50

16 Collins, J and Porras, J (1994) *Built to Last: Successful habits of visionary companies*, William Collins

PART TWO

Build dynamic capacity: Thrive in 4IR

Build the capacity to thrive in the dynamics of the 4th Industrial Revolution. The dynamic capacity of the firm is the product of the interaction between three sets of capabilities: Sense & Make Sense, Seize & Replicate, Reposition & Reconfigure – enabling the organization to adapt and pivot in a timely manner, moving from one position of transient competitive advantage to another.

FIGURE II.1 The dynamic capacity is the product of the strength of three capabilities

02

Sense & Make Sense

IN BRIEF

The capability to Sense & Make Sense: to be sensitive and detect emerging trends and weak signals that are leading indicators of how the marketspace or competitive dynamics are evolving. The extent of the scope of the network with which the corporation operates and the diversity of the markets within that network can increase its opportunity to sense. However, the capability needs to be nurtured in order to overcome tendencies such as the dominant perception coming from the corporate centre or depending only on designated research or development teams. Making Sense of the multiple signals and idea fragments requires the ability to 'connect the dots', ie to make connections between separate pieces of data and insight. Four key mechanisms can significantly enhance the capability to Sense & Make Sense.

FIGURE 2.1 Sense & Make Sense: The first set of capabilities forms dynamic capacity

1 The ability to harvest idea fragments globally, without cognitive or selection biases. To organize and effectively interrogate the growing database of idea fragments, with or without the support of AI (artificial intelligence), ie crowd-source as 'everyone' is smarter than anyone.

2 Access unique external insight: obtain independent data and insight on customers and the marketspace, generate new insights, enhance internal beliefs and points of view.

3 The propensity to demonstrate the validity of insights and to generate more through rapid, low-cost experimentation, ie test and learn.

4 The culture to expect and ask colleagues to share deeper thinking. Making it safe (or even celebrated) to share partially formed ideas rather than a culture that makes them feel vulnerable or attacked, ie adopting the habit of asking '... and what else?'.

Skate to where the puck is going to be

Let us return for a moment to that well-known saying attributed to legendary ice-hockey player Wayne Gretzky and quoted by Steve Jobs (former CEO of Apple):

> 'I skate to where the puck is going to be (not where it is)', and that is what we have always tried to do at Apple.

Under the leadership of Steve Jobs, Apple inspired a generation of users to adopt technology into their lives in ways that they had never imagined previously: the iPod (personalized music), the iPhone (smartphone), the iPad (tablet computers), iTunes (streaming and legally downloading music and movies) and the ever-expanding cosmos of applications and games available from the App Store.

Steve Jobs led Apple to 'skate to where the puck would be', not where it was. Of course, not everything was a success – remember the Newton? – but under the leadership of Steve Jobs, Apple was undeniably an outstanding example of a company leaning forward into the unknown, unfolding future with a high capability to Sense & Make Sense of trends and weak signals.

There are other great leaders who also look beyond what is known, who imagine future markets and competitive plays, and who start 'skating' to reach the position the 'puck' will be in before it gets there, before there is the possibility of market assessment and data. They move in anticipation of the market and before competitors. This is the skill of being able to Sense what is happening (what are the movements, what are the trends, what are the other players doing, how fast or slowly is the future unfolding?) and to Make Sense, to distinguish between noise and signals, to focus in on the scenario that they think is going to unfold, and to then act decisively – to actually 'skate to where the puck is going to be', in order to make a difference.

In 1959, Soichiro Honda, the founder and driving force behind the Honda Motor Company, decided to try to export his new line in motorcycles to the United States. Honda was at that time still a young company, with limited experience in and no recognition outside of Japan for making motorcycles. Soichiro dispatched a couple of containers full of his small-engine, unglamorous motorcycles, with the goal of at least recovering the costs of the vehicles and the initiative. At that time, the US market was dominated by large-engine motorcycles by manufacturers such as Harley-Davidson and Triumph, each with passionate, loyal followings and iconic branding cemented in popular movies.

The motorcycle users that the sales team interviewed confirmed what the motorcycle distributors and retailers were saying: no one would want to ride (or be seen on) small motorcycles from Japan.

Without being able to sell even a handful of the bikes the mission was set for disaster, but the team was determined to at least recover their costs. Out of desperation more than inspiration, one of the team suggested offering the Honda as the 'opposite' to the way other motorcycles and their manufacturers were competing. They decided to appeal directly to the non-motorcycle 'biker' community.

They developed the slogan 'You meet the nicest people on a Honda', which stated the opposite of the 'biker gang' rebel image that was later epitomized in films such as *Easy Rider*. They bypassed traditional distribution channels, instead selling directly to retailers. Soichiro Honda and his team had 'Sensed' the changes happening in society, and they 'Made Sense' of how these changes were (or could be) coming together. They made a decision on how to position, where to go, that no other motorcycle company was doing at that time.

(Note: If you have the time I suggest you enjoy watching a couple of the original Honda USA commercials, eg https://www.youtube.com/watch?v=ck9wBHW2160.)

We don't need to look to the past only to see people who are sensing the signals of things changing in their markets and seeking to spot and exploit emerging patterns, implications and opportunities. However, it is only when the future becomes the past that we can know for certain that what they believed to be unfolding was proven correct.

I recently polled 18 venture capital firms (together covering much of the globe, although with less insight in Africa and Eastern Europe); taken together, they estimate that they had seen over 6,000 requests for early stage funding in the two years of 2017 and 2018. I don't pretend this is a complete list, but it is directionally indicative of the large number of new ideas that are being pursued. Established firms are also being innovative, preparing themselves for the unfolding future, coming up with new offerings and business models. The 4IR is increasing the speed of business and pace of innovation – peering into the future and being able to Sense & Make Sense of what is unfolding is therefore of increasing importance.

Corporations with global reach and activities are present in a large number of markets. These markets have a diverse range of dynamics in terms of innovations, the evolution of demand and the actions of competitors, etc. If the global corporation is sensitive to these differences and can fluently communicate the wide array of insights from the different markets, then they have an advantage in the Sense & Make Sense capability over firms with smaller networks.

Entrepreneurial or founder-led firms are often able to retain high sensitivity to the signals in the markets in which they participate. However, these smaller companies may have more limited marketplace exposure. The dichotomy of greater sensitivity associated with a smaller sensory network versus a much more extensive sensory network with dulled sensitivity is now changing. Information technology support is increasingly being deployed to greater effect to gather and interrogate vast amounts of data, across all activities and all peripheries.

Communications technology increasingly enables executives and team members to interact with one another, irrespective of the physical distances or time zone differences between them. Technology can enhance the ability of corporations to Sense & Make Sense of weak signals – to peer into the fog of the unfolding future.

Whilst this technology is applicable to large and small corporations, my research indicates that the impact advantages are disproportionately enhancing larger corporations with global operations. Technology is more effective in capturing and bringing primary data to life for a large global corporation than in creating data or insight from secondary data. Large corporations are deploying technology to good effect to increase their sensitivity. They are leveraging their structural advantage of global reach and their scale advantage to support investment. Smaller companies succeed in democratizing data and insight by ensuring informal networks and discussions complement the formal (eg through personal interactions and the use of social media and group chats).

Crowd-source: everyone is smarter than anyone

Making sense and deriving insights from data is different to amassing data, although both are essential for value creation and capture. Making sense requires engagement with the context from which the data is drawn. Hence, no matter where someone is in the organization, at a Research and Development (R&D) centre, in HQ or in a remote sales office or production site, they should be encouraged and enabled to both contribute data and to interrogate the global data lake for insights. A Unilever executive characterized it as the democratization of data:

> Everyone can and should seek to capture and contribute data, without regard or foreknowledge of how the data may be used. We call it a 'data lake'. Everyone who needs it can have access to this data lake, interrogate the data and look for insights.[1]

FIGURE 2.2 Sense & Make Sense: Crowd-source

Key Mechanisms	Examples

• Involve everyone in capturing data and looking for new insight.
    o Invest in data capture, always; don't be restricted by thinking about what the data will be used for.
    o Dismantle the mindset and behaviours that lead to siloes or that 'power and influence' come from withholding information.
 • Actively pursue depth of understanding of customer behaviours, drivers of behaviours, trends, influencers and context.
    o Learn from competitors, but don't copy.
 • Enable and encourage everyone to interrogate the data and contribute new ideas.
    o Provide tools and support for analytics. Invest and continue to invest in AI.
	Alcohol: 'The region is quite huge, people are sharing knowledge and insight with each other, we are all learning all the time.'
	 Media: 'We have a futures team who spot ideas globally and they share and discuss, they spot trends and activities that are very future-looking. Not just the next few years, but much further out.'
	 Heavy Equipment: 'We have really smart guys and gals. Their job includes finding out what else of relevance others are doing and what the future may look like, they look everywhere inside and outside the industry.'

Google dominates the internet search industry, which gives it the ability to interrogate billions of search queries daily and provides the company the opportunity not only to spot emerging trends but also to identify specific companies and individuals who are active in particular fields. This ability to see the aggregation of queries enables the corporation to move before other firms are aware of an opportunity or trend as well as to reduce the risk of its seemingly pre-emptive moves. Google emphasizes global reach and future market sense by highlighting its insight into emerging business models and technologies, often before they become widely known.

Idea fragments

Hitendra Patel, the founder of the innovation consultancy and training company IXL Center, describes using 'idea fragments'. Idea fragments, he argues, can and should be contributed by anyone, anywhere, in any form. Idea fragments cannot be judged for their value, as every idea fragment has the same value – that is, nothing. Idea fragments can be combined in myriad ways to create innovative concepts, potential solutions and insights. These can be judged and compared. They can be tested, they may succeed or fail. Even if the concepts fail the idea fragments remain and can be recycled in other combinations.

IXL Center had been or was a partner of several of the corporations in my research and is mainly appreciated for its impact on raising the innovation capabilities of executives and staff. Its training and combined consulting support resulted in accelerated growth, and heightened the agility of the client corporation.

When I interviewed Hitendra he elaborated: while everyone in an organization should contribute 'idea fragments', to instil the discipline to do so often requires conducting periodic exercises at local market or operating company levels (eg as part of the quarterly business review meetings). He suggests conducting idea fragment 'harvesting' sessions as a team activity, running quickly through different lenses that stimulate thinking and recall. These could include:

a initiatives undertaken by iconic brands not in the industry;

b pick an iconic business leader and think what they might do in your industry;

c run through competitor intelligence and learnings from external partners and initiatives within the firm conducted elsewhere.

Hitendra recommends always starting and finishing these harvest sessions with reflection on customers and their changing behaviours, contexts and desires.

Other corporations have similar approaches to democratizing data and innovation. Airbus Group, active in over 35 countries globally, has intentionally set out to gather idea fragments from across the globe to give direction to the firm's technology development. They believe their reach gives them a strong advantage of knowing what is happening around the world within their industry. They do this by deliberate investment in several key activities:

- Share and develop ideas with a network of partners: 'Like pieces of a jigsaw being put together, we may have some pieces, they may have others; together we can come up with new solutions.'
- Robustly pursue feedback through collaboration and intimacy with customers.
- Float and promote new thinking and concepts externally, through initiatives such as 'Fly Your Ideas', which engages universities.

Caterpillar has built an enviable reputation through the design and manufacture of excellent, robust power generation, construction and mining equipment. Their machinery holds its value well and meets or exceeds the most stringent health and safety and other regulatory requirements. However, their global reach and listening network picked up on an important signal: competitors from emerging markets, in particular China, were effective at challenging Caterpillar's assumptions about customer needs and behaviours and their approach to market.

These efforts can be supported well within a framework such as Design Thinking. Many of the firms in the research have adopted some form or other of Design Thinking. In 2005, Stanford began teaching Design Thinking through its D-School and the approach quickly became widely known, with many companies adopting the principles and adjusting the process to fit their needs and culture. The Design Thinking process is interactive and easy to understand and apply, as such teams within companies can quickly come together and run through the process. Jake Knapp and colleagues at Google Ventures adapted the Design Thinking approach into a five-day process which they named Sprint: 'How to solve big problems and test new ideas in just five days.'

The first step of innovation processes such as Design Thinking is to understand the customer's context and their relationship with the product or service that is being considered. This sentiment is echoed by titans of business such as Alibaba's Jack Ma, who advises, 'Forget about your competitors, just focus on your customers. You should learn from your competitor but never copy. Copy and you will die.'[2] Or in the words of Jeff Bezos: 'If you're competitor-focused, you have to wait until there is a competitor doing something. Being customer-focused allows you to be more pioneering.'[3]

Understanding customers more deeply than just their use of the product or service offering is essential to be able to obtain insights that can spark fresh thinking for how to meet their needs.

In 2002, the consultancy Monitor Group popularized the use of the term 'Customer Portrait' to describe the relationship between a customer and the offering. The elements of a customer portrait – which is applicable in both business-to-business (B2B) and business-to-consumer (B2C) contexts – are:

a the setting (purchase and usage environments);

b the desired experience (what the customer wants from their relationship with the offering);

c their beliefs and associations with the offering (their emotions, past experiences etc); and finally

d what the customer (or potential customer) actually does with the offering.

Whichever approach a company adopts, my research shows that the outperforming companies not only have a deep understanding of their customers, but they combine this with innovation techniques embraced by teams across the organization, simultaneously reinforcing a culture of internal collaboration and external focus.

Access unique external insight

A high ability to Sense & Make Sense can be a source of competitive advantage. Hence it is important to take deliberate steps to connect with flows of knowledge and insight beyond the organization itself and beyond industry and professional associations that share knowledge openly with all members. A particularly productive path is for firms to partner with (eg by making investments into) appropriately focused venture capital funds. The funds themselves are scanning for, and being approached by, early-stage entrepreneurs with ideas that could be game-changing and that could scale up to have a significant impact. The bigger the partnership the corporation has with a fund, the more start-ups they may see, as they may receive briefings on companies that the fund may be reviewing but has not yet invested into.

Another tactic, which several executives describe as both eye-opening and energizing, involves guided trips in global locations famed for innovation (eg New England Research Triangle, Silicon Valley, Cambridge-Oxford, Shanghai-Hangzhou). Such trips involve purposeful, targeted visits with start-ups, technology and research centres at leading universities. These are particularly productive if organized around a particular theme or challenge that the corporation is seeking to innovatively address.

Another innovative approach is to crowd-source ideas using an external platform such as that provided by Innovation Olympics. In this platform teams of MBA students, sourced from over 120 business schools globally, work for several weeks to find solutions to challenges posed by corporations. The teams scour the knowledge universe for relevant data, idea fragments and examples, and then create multiple potential solutions.

Well-known approaches that are consistently productive also include commissioning unique research to be conducted by research agencies. Online mobile panel-based research has proven to be particularly effective in developing markets where traditional approaches to gain customer insight have struggled to achieve sufficient market coverage and consumer segment penetration. Data mining tools already have immense power and with the coming of age of artificial intelligence are stepping far beyond the capabilities of human-driven analysis of mega data sets. Corporates with access to large data caches should be resubmitting them to the newer analytical tools in the attempt to uncover hidden insights, particularly on customer behaviours and needs.

Open access

Unilever has invested tremendous energy in accessing and analysing data. CIO Jane Moran describes the new environment:

> At Unilever, we have the enormous opportunity to predict the future. These [AI] tools now help remove those siloes and democratize the data. It allows us to streamline and automate the data ingestion into our environment [...] We are trying to put data in the hands of our employees. This really gets us a step closer to automated and augmented decision making; to be an insights-driven organization [...] The data lake actually makes it possible to put the data in the hands of the employees that need to use the data.[4]

Unilever is also using artificial intelligence to influence more of its marketing, from processing insights to finding influencers. AI is now used to synthesize insights from both structured and unstructured data from sources such as social listening, customer relationship management (CRM) and traditional market research. The intent is to move away from mass-reach marketing channels towards more personalized communications that are also cheaper to produce and localize at scale.

AI has helped identify new opportunities, for example a range of cereal-flavoured ice-creams under the Ben & Jerry's brand. It was inspired after Unilever found that there were around 50 songs that featured lyrics on 'ice-cream and breakfast'. The insights came at the same time as the advertiser commissioned research into the ice-cream category, which found businesses like Dunkin' Donuts were already serving ice-cream for breakfast. One of the AI algorithms Unilever worked with then sifted through those different data sets and revealed an opportunity for creating sweet treats in the morning. Two years later, the Ben & Jerry's range launched a range of cereal flavours including Fruit Loot and Frozen Flakes.

AI has enabled Unilever to build better and more effective advertising campaigns, adding scale, reach and personalization, for example Close-up toothpaste in Asia. Using search analytics, Unilever discovered that the second most-searched-for term for their website users was 'learning how to kiss'. Using this insight, the team created a three-day campaign for the brand around Valentine's Day, deployed in six key Asian markets. To make the campaign a success, they needed to resonate with a target audience that spanned culturally diverse areas across Asia. To do it, they analysed trending social media data to optimize their marketing assets in real time and created culturally relevant content that spoke respectfully to each region and consumer individually. The campaign touched nearly 500 million people and generated positive uplift in brand engagement and consideration.

Unilever's LiveWire product provides business functions with insights into how products and business lines are performing globally. This was previously done via business analysts having to pull data from disparate sources but is now in the hands of the users via a simpler interface, providing brand sales and performance insights, blending together sales and market share data from internal and external sources. It shows whether the Unilever brands are winning competitively, comparing in-market execution and innovation performance.

The democratization of data through the creation of the universal data lake and enabling self-service analysis is transforming how Unilever does business whilst revealing new insights for action throughout the business.

Experiment: test and learn

Almost all of the executives who participated in the research believe the diversity of markets in which the firm operates is an advantage for sensing how their industry is evolving. Such a range of perspectives increases the visibility of emerging threats and opportunities, enhancing their frames of reference and helping them to make better decisions earlier, which accelerates their knowledge creation, particularly through marketplace experimentation. An executive at Syngenta noted:

> The real world is the test lab.

With a mindset of driving the business results locally whilst retaining coordination across the network, the corporation can undertake marketplace initiatives that are regarded as experiments. The new knowledge so created can lead to new business model and market discoveries.

Experiment to learn

Syngenta, the agribusiness company, is a prolific innovator seeking ways to improve the effectiveness of its products to boost crop yields whilst improving the sustainability of agriculture and the environment. Like many leading research companies, Syngenta is often concerned about low-priced competing

FIGURE 2.3   Sense & Make Sense: Experiment, test and learn

Key Mechanisms	Examples

• Create a bias for action: 'Show me – don't tell me.'
  o Adopt experimentation behaviour and mindset throughout the organization.
  o Establish guidelines and the discipline to ensure proposals and options are considered through the lens of practical tests and reaction to prototype.
• Experiment to learn, to test hypotheses, not only prototypes.
  o Probe for market, channel, regulator or competitor reactions.
  o Encouraging rapid experimentation to either scale or fail fast!
• Simultaneously conduct partial experiments across geographies and markets to accelerate learning.
  o Collaboration, not rivalry between country or regional executives.
	Media: 'We do quite a lot of experimentation now, particularly to new customers and with customer offers. But that wouldn't have been true a few years ago. We are growing so fast, we experiment with content, content creation formulae and business models all the time.'
	
	Entertainment: 'The Japan team showed the powerful impact of discovery about consumers through experimentation as research, as we really didn't know how to grow the business; the approaches from Europe and the US simply weren't delivering. I now do more such discovery experimentation globally.'

products offered by makers of generic products. These often come from firms with lower investment in sustainability and agronomy.

However, research laboratories making advances in compounds and basic chemistry can only progress at a certain speed. Their pace is dictated by regulatory requirements for testing and approvals. Syngenta has been effective at using its presence in multiple markets to accelerate learning in product and application development.

An executive describes how they make a deliberate choice to simultaneously experiment with different aspects of new innovations (eg a reformulation of a product range) in different countries. Their approach is to experiment in order to learn, not only to pilot test fully fledged concepts.

For example, they will experiment with new packaging with proven products in certain markets. They will try new branding and marketing approaches in some markets and test new product formulation in others. They have also tested countries' new channel (route to market) offerings in two different countries.

> Simultaneously conduct partial experiments across geographies and markets to accelerate learning.

In this manner, they learn simultaneously about the effectiveness of multiple different aspects of the intended new product range. The integration of all these learnings from experimentation then enables a faster and more successful roll-out. An executive noted that conducting simultaneously dispersed experiments also makes it much harder for competitors to understand what the real thrust of the initiative is.

In Japan, a global media and entertainment company was struggling to get the traction it was used to elsewhere in the kids and youth segments. Without strong precedent elsewhere of developing new revenue streams in other segments, they decided to experiment locally with alternative approaches. Their experimentation with different character-branded merchandising led to the discovery that there was great affinity with the young and young-at-heart adult segments. As these segments have strong purchasing power, the company had discovered an opportunity to significantly increase their sales of merchandise.

Through experimentation they found a way to grow with the older age groups without alienating the kids and youth segments. The resulting commercial success and new insights about these older segments could be leveraged in other geographies, in Asia and globally.

In the aforementioned Design Thinking process, teams are encouraged to interact with potential customers early and often throughout the innovation process. Engaging with potential customers with the explicit objective of involving them in the creation process, not with the intent of selling them on the emerging new concept, yields very different findings.

A quick way to do this may be to take simple sketches or drawings of five or six significantly different potential solutions to customers, seek to explain to them the thinking and intent behind each sketched solution, and then listen to their thoughts and comments. This step would be followed by integrating the insights from all the feedback and then synthesizing to one potential design or solution. The fourth step in the Design Thinking process is then to create a physical prototype as quickly and cheaply as possible, often as simple as a non-functioning mock-up. This is then taken to the potential customers and once again their feedback is solicited, thus enabling further refinement – and an ongoing iteration.

This process is easy to understand and apply, it typically energizes the team, and it creates momentum and provides opportunities to deepen relationships and understanding with customers. However, there are also detractors who note that it may be more suited to B2C-type environments rather than B2B. Other concerns are that it tends to favour 'small i' innovation (ie more incremental-type improvements), that it fails to highlight or address potentially big barriers such as technical feasibility, and that there can be a very long 'tail' to the process of repeated iterations between potential customer and designer. As mentioned, Google Ventures and the broader organization widely use a version of Design Thinking.

However, Eric Schmidt, the former chairman of Google and Alphabet, describes the 'big I' innovative programmes (which Google calls 'moon shots') the corporation decides to fund as being those that:

a address a huge potential market;

b have some new thinking that would provide a radically new approach to serving the potential market;

c have technical strength and unique capabilities that have a high likelihood of achieving the solution.

Part of the espoused approach to 'big I' innovation is to try to fail as quickly as possible – to address what are thought to be the hardest problems first, rather than to build up to these through tackling others first and perhaps by so doing find new insights and alternatives.

IXL Center uses the Eureka process as a robust stage-gated innovation process. It uses the principles of Design Thinking but embeds them into a formal process that ensures progress and consistently delivers results. Cross-functional teams then draw on the idea fragments, making connections so as to be able to describe distinctly different ways in which the challenge could be addressed. In the first iteration, these potential solutions represent alternative 'fields of play' (marketspaces), and each team is required to produce five alternative potential fields of play.

After evaluation with the clients (internal or external), one field of play is selected, which may be a refinement from one or more of the five that were presented. In the next iteration, the team produces five potential business concepts, each within the selected field of play. Once again, through interaction with the clients, one business concept emerges to be developed further. The final step is to develop business models and make the case for the team's preferred solution.

As with Design Thinking, the process is iterative, with customer input at each step and cross-functional teams. However, the Eureka process formalizes the diverge-converge process steps to ensure progress through stage-gates and creates a database of idea fragments, capturing all the insights developed by the team, which can be leveraged throughout the process and in the future.

Building up personal knowledge of customer needs and empathy for their context is critical and, although it has long been discussed, remains an elusive goal in many organizations. Organizations are usually more comfortable looking inwards. Innovative ideas that don't fit with the established view of 'how we work and what we do' do not get the support from management even if the individuals who came up with them were closer to the customer.

The Eureka process is more robust than pure Design Thinking as it has several teams working in competition with one another. I have seen very robust processes employing five teams working in parallel, each team producing five fields of play and five business concepts. Even if all the resulting 25 business concepts are rejected by the client, the process doesn't have to start again. They can go back and revisit the 25 fields of play, perhaps being more conservative and aiming for closer adjacencies the next time around or deliberately being more adventurous.

This approach reduces uncertainty at the launch of the final solution because of the customer involvement throughout the stages of development.

It also helps to ensure poor ideas are dropped early on, before significant investment of time or resources. I often describe this approach as Ready-Fire-Aim.

Ready-Fire-Aim

Rather than the conventional approach of 'Ready-Aim-Fire', 'Ready-Fire-Aim' is faster to 'firing' (ie launching) more concepts. 'Ready-Aim-Fire' assumes that you know before launching exactly what you are aiming at.

If a product or service is truly innovative, there will be no market or operational data available until it is launched. While the 'Ready-Aim-Fire' approach can give a false sense of accuracy as well as slow down the launches, is the market research data gathered before the launch predictive of how behaviours will change?

After any innovation process that arrives at the commercial launch of a new product or service or business model, there will then be more innovation, refinement and adjustments required. Market learning and discovery are the most important forms of market research. Test and learn in order to be able to test and learn many more times, and in each cycle to be scaling the size of the business.

Personally, 'Ready-Fire-Aim' is one of my favourite concepts. It echoes one of the projects I worked on almost 30 years ago for a defence contractor, making ammunitions and tasked with improving the accuracy of ship-borne naval artillery. My idea, at that time, was simply to increase the firing rate from the 'guns' despite the roll of the ship in the ocean. Once the shells are in flight, sending microwave signals to small detonators on the spinning shell would be able, crudely, to slightly redirect the shell onto the target. 'Ready-Fire-Aim' is so much more 'fun' (for innovation and business projects) than 'Ready-Aim-Aim-Aim some more...' and then 'Oops the target has moved'.

Ask... and what else?

Challenges exist in ensuring the sensing skills of the corporation and the ability to generate and act on insight are not dulled by the policies and culture. A senior executive at the Hong Kong headquarters of a major conglomerate summarized the challenge they are facing as follows:

We have over 30 operating companies, most actively engaged in markets across the [Asia Pacific] region and several active globally; taken together there is a huge wealth of experience and insight. Across this portfolio, digital disruption or empowerment is impacting everyone, everywhere; some sooner and some later. We should be at an advantage with our scale and scope; but we are not. If every company does its own thing, what's best for its business, then we repeat errors and learning and duplicate efforts; alternatively, if we centralize and coordinate we move too slowly, we prioritize and deprioritize. Centrally we can't match the insight across all the operating companies, but individual OpCo initiatives and local market solutions are sub-optimal.

The solution to this dilemma, at least in part, is to create a culture of constructive challenge. This can be enhanced by training and formal adoption of techniques such as:

- establish the discipline of asking 'why' and 'what if';
- elicit new joiners' perspectives;
- celebrate ideas – as Peter Drucker once noted, 'Nothing is more dangerous than having one great idea.'

FIGURE 2.4   Sense & Make Sense: Enquire... and what else?

Key Mechanisms	Examples

• Create a culture of constructive challenge to assumptions and practice.
 	
  o Establish the discipline of asking 'why?' and 'what if?.'
 	
  o Elicit new joiners' perspectives.
 	
• Encourage and facilitate dislocated networks of experts and interest groups combining internal AND external.
 	
  o Ensure collaboration and communication whilst fighting against group-think.
 	
  o Create more perspectives, reflecting different contexts.
 	
• Build the mindset and capabilities of innovation throughout the organization.
 	
  o Provide the tools, encouragement and reinforcement to innovate, share and collaborate.
	Technology: 'It is an advantage for the thought leaders to be based in the markets which are evolving most quickly as we need to be connected to the customers that are pioneering.'
	
	Entertainment: 'Before the expert was the person who knew the data numbers or a specific number, "Wow, you're really smart." Now it's the people who are able to take all those data points and observe trends that become really valuable and the insights of the team members. Sense makers, they are the new experts.'

Networks of dislocated experts

Encourage networks of dislocated experts (eg interest groups) to develop and draw on their energy and insight for operational and strategic decisions. These dislocated groups should remain flexible and adaptive, focusing on sharing insight and experience and active in ensuring they do not succumb to 'group think' or adopting a 'one-size-fits-all' mindset (one approach or solution works everywhere).

IBM has designated thought leaders whose role is to contribute industry-leading insight in their topic area. These leaders publish internal and external papers as well as gleaning insight and information from IBM's knowledge system. As one executive noted, this knowledge gathering needs to be structured in a global way: 'It is an advantage for the thought leaders to be based in the markets which are evolving most quickly as we need to be connected to the customers that are pioneering.'

Over the past 10 years, many researchers and authors have shared insights on the benefits, pitfalls and remedies of working effectively in virtual teams. My research did not seek to repeat, extend or refute such a body of work; however, some important themes did emerge.

The need to battle against 'group think' is certainly not limited to virtual collaboration, but neither are virtually collaborating teams immune to group think. Group think is fuelled by norms of behaviour that can seemingly enhance the efficiency of interactions (we are all 'on the same page' and understand how to interact virtually), but also dull sensitivity to market (business context) diversity.

Remote working may provide convenience for some, but it can also limit debate, particularly if there is significant diversity of insight. This can reduce opportunities for the collection and contribution of idea fragments. An executive at a major transportation provider put it like this:

> We operate globally and so we often have 'calls'* to share insights on customer trends and competitors' actions. Collectively we try to see patterns and to define and prioritize coordinated initiatives [...] We don't spend much time sharing things that may not be important to others [...] It can feel like each person [is] simply providing a one-way update, there is little lateral discussion in these calls [...] we all listen carefully to each other. The problem is that more often than not we end up with a centrally defined and coordinated initiative that proves to be of limited relevance in many of the markets.

*This firm uses a range of video, voice and collaboration technologies to assist virtual collaboration.

Dispersed leadership

We can see from these examples that even well-established corporations with global reach can succumb to the pitfalls of organization and group think. The solution to this dilemma, at least in part, is to distribute the senior leadership across markets rather than having the entire team collocated at the group headquarters. Unilever placed their global COO in Asia, thus ensuring insight and follow-through to impact in the key growth markets in the region. Standard Chartered Bank has members of the senior leadership team located in London, Hong Kong and Singapore.

CASE STUDY
Schneider Electric

Schneider Electric, the global electricity distribution equipment manufacturer originally headquartered in France, has annual turnover in excess of US $26 billion. However, the CEO, Jean-Pascal Tricoire, is based in Hong Kong, as the corporation has adopted a decentralized management structure, with approximately equal numbers of the senior management team based in Europe, Asia and the United States. In an interview Tricoire said:

> Corporate decisions should be made close to our customers [...] we make our decisions based on the business we see on the ground [...] our leaders are visible to our employees so that they are not in the ivory tower. With us, one can have global responsibilities while staying in one's place of origin. For example, our head of China operations used to be the boss of a line of business internationally. Our senior managers have to manage transcontinental teams that have a balanced world view in decision making while taking into account the local realities.[5]

This decentralized model relies on communications technologies which enable executives to be always contactable and equip them with productivity tools that run on mobile devices.

One way of forming and deriving value from global networks of dislocated experts is to create a platform for partnering externally. In 2000, then-new CEO of Procter and Gamble (P&G) A G Lafley set about driving a major rebirth of the corporation. He knew that his objectives could be achieved only by challenging traditional approaches throughout the enterprise and driving growth.

This would require focused strategies in each market and product category accompanied by rigorously aligned follow-through. The scale and scope of the corporation needed to be redefined and remodelled, turning complexity and bureaucracy into focused market power and innovation dominance. 'Big I' innovation – that which enables the creation and capture of significant new value – usually happens at the intersection of different teams, internal and/or external.

Scaling up internal R&D departments was neither an option nor expected to deliver the growth required. Hence P&G launched 'Connect + Develop', a platform for collaboration with external individuals and institutions globally, which aims to find good ideas that are relevant to P&G's focused strategies and to enhance them by leveraging P&G's internal capabilities. Critical to the success of Connect + Develop is the ability to build and leverage large global networks.

Leadership traits: Sense & Make Sense

Harvest idea fragments

A critical skill in 4IR is the ability to look outside the organization and see what is happening. The more people observing a broader horizon of the external environment, the greater the ability of the firm to sense the changes taking place. In particular it is critical to sense how customers' needs and behaviours are evolving. In addition to in-depth research and analysis of data, every member of an organization should contribute idea fragments (ie observations of actions or initiatives). Harvesting idea fragments happens only if there is an explicit encouragement, a process and discipline established. For example, weekly team meetings start off with a round of everybody sharing something new that they have noted. Many of the idea fragments may not be of known relevance at the time of sharing, so there should not be judgement of the value of the individual idea fragment – the significance may be revealed over time as more pieces come into view and the team members start to join the dots. Spotting emergent behaviours and acting in a timely manner is a source of competitive advantage.

Data driven, digitally enabled

To sense well requires the ability to be open to the emergent data, actively guarding against interpreting it through biases of previous assumptions of trends and interpretations of behaviours. This requires building a culture in the firm that insists discussions are based on relevant, recent data that is understood in context, challenging biases that can result from precedence, practice or positional power. The ability to make sense of what is happening is dependent on not only seeing the unfolding data but also sharing and combining that data with others. Digital analytics (and machine learning) can help aggregate data from multiple sources and interrogate it, but executives also need to be asking the right questions. Executives in 4IR companies need to demonstrate the ability to use technology effectively and productively, updating their skills and knowledge to stay current with the tools available.

Experiment: Test and learn

Ideation (creative thinking) is a critical skill as the speed of business accelerates. Ideation is the ability to connect the dots, ie the items of perhaps seemingly disparate data and information, to create a new insight that can lead to an action with meaningful benefits. Having an idea is of no value unless it is acted upon. Leaders need to evolve the reflex to test and get feedback as quickly as possible, with minimal cost and time invested. The objective is to test and learn in quick cycles so as to be able to inform decisions and shape larger initiatives. Accelerating the cycle of ideation-experimentation-feedback builds momentum and agility. In the 4IR there is an increased premium from creativity and action, as the speed of business and the dynamics of marketspaces increase. Adopting a culture of 'ready-fire-aim', ie insight-experiment-refine, increases the momentum and helps to energize the organization.

Mindset: Curiosity

A desire to learn from others and the expectation that there will always be surprises and something new. Developing the skills of listening, learning, and being open to change. The capability to ideate, to 'connect the dots' of idea fragments. Acknowledging ideas are concepts requiring exploration, to be refined or rejected through rapid experimentation.

KEY CONCEPTS: CHAPTER 2

The ability to Sense & Make Sense of emergent signals can be a source of advantage; seeing and understanding leading indicators of trends and forces that could significantly reshape the marketspace and competitive dynamics. The key mechanisms and behaviours to foster are:

- Crowd-source: everyone is smarter than anyone:
  o idea fragments;
  o unique external insight;
  o open access.
- Access unique external insight:
  o partnerships with unique access to insight;
  o AI support for mining existing data caches for new insight;
  o open source/open access.
- Experiment: test and learn:
  o experiment to learn;
  o ready-fire-aim.
- Ask... and, what else?
  o networks of dislocated experts;
  o dispersed leadership.
- Leadership traits:
  o harvest idea fragments;
  o data-driven, digitally empowered;
  o experiment: test and learn;
  o mindset: curiosity.

FIGURE 2.5 Sense & Make Sense: Key management practices

Explore possibilities, note weak signals and develop greater insight. Anticipate the evolution of the marketspace. Question existing assumptions. Refine the vision for how to act in the unfolding future.

Crowd-source: Everyone is smarter than anyone

- Involve everyone in capturing data and looking for new insight. Invest in data capture, always; don't be restricted by thinking what the data will be used for. Enable and encourage everyone to interrogate the data and contribute new ideas. Provide tools and support for analytics. Invest and continue to invest in AI.

- Actively pursue depth of understanding of customer behaviours, drivers of behaviours, trends, influencers and context. Learn from competitors, but don't copy.

Access unique external insight

- Gather external data and carefully interrogate it seeking new insight, particularly on customer behaviours and needs. Seek out non-conventional data sources that can provide early indication of changes.

- Counteract biases in data interpretation and blind spots by challenging existing dominant perspectives and assumptions.

Experiment: Test and learn

- Create a bias for action. Adopt experimentation behaviour and mindset throughout the organization.

- Experiment to learn, to test hypotheses. Probe for market, channel, regulator or competitor reactions. Simultaneously conduct partial experiments across geographies and markets to accelerate learning.

Ask... and what else?

- Create a culture of constructive challenge to assumptions and practice. Establish the discipline of asking 'why' and 'what if'.

- Encourage and facilitate dislocated networks of experts and interest groups combining internal AND external.

Sense & Make Sense

Endnotes

1 A similar set of comments is reported in the *Diginomica* article 'Unilever teams up with Microsoft to deliver AI-assisted decision making to users' by Derek du Preez, 24 May 2018

2 Jack Ma speaking at the Gateway 2017 conference, https://www.inc.com/kaitlyn-wang/jack-ma-alibaba-tips-for-success.html (archived at https://perma.cc/TSN3-N33U)

3 Tabaka, M (2019) Amazon's 4 Keys to Success, According to Jeff Bezos, Inc, https://www.inc.com/marla-tabaka/jeff-bezos-says-these-4-principles-are-key-to-amazons-success-they-can-work-for-you-too.html (archived at https://perma.cc/UJX5-KPQZ)

4 Du Preez, D (2018) Unilever teams up with Microsoft to deliver AI-assisted decision making to users, *Diginomica*, 24 May

5 South China Morning Post (nd) Schneider Electric opts for global management structure, https://www.scmp.com/business/companies/article/1070667/schneider-electric-opts-global-management-structure (archived at https://perma.cc/U5F4-ZN7B)

03

Seize & Replicate

IN BRIEF

The second capability is to Seize & Replicate. This is the capability to quickly determine a response to an emerging opportunity (or threat); when an initiative in one part of the network is gaining traction, to be able to quickly disseminate the insight and knowledge to other markets or business units where a similar approach may also be beneficial. Corporations with dispersed networks need to work particularly hard to ensure the rapid transfer and application of knowledge and experience, which may be most effectively achieved by the movement of people. Corporations with dispersed networks may also have more opportunities for reapplying insight created elsewhere, thus they may be able to multiply the benefits achieved.

Management mechanisms that differentiate the capability to Seize & Replicate include:

1 Move people, to access expertise. The fastest way to replicate (or create initial application of) success of an innovation (eg from one location or business unit to another) is through moving the people who were intimately involved with the first application or with the concept generation. This minimizes hand-offs, whilst promoting sharing knowledge and allowing adaption for the new context. The repeated application also deepens experience, further accelerating results.

2 Organization design: clusters not regions. The mobility of people and knowledge is fastest when the design and policies of an organization accentuate the sense of being on the same team. Regional or business unit structures and allegiances can mitigate the desired mobility. Cross-silo team memberships and new organization designs aligned with common themes (eg marketplace dynamics) are replacing

traditional approaches and matrices defined by geographic and business unit or functional boundaries.

3 Shape the future: as marketspaces are increasingly in flux, there is increased attention on the role of the institution/corporation as an actor that shapes the future that unfolds. This ambition energizes stakeholders, attracting investors and high-quality talent. As momentum builds, other members of the eco-system are drawn in and media attention multiplies, which increases the influence of the corporation to shape the unfolding future.

FIGURE 3.1   Seize & Replicate: The second set of capabilities that form dynamic capacity

It can be hard for organizations to build the capability to Seize & Replicate but doing so is fundamental to creating the capacity of the organization to act dynamically. To illustrate the point, I share a story from a particular client, a government agency, with responsibilities for domestic security; they are big believers in and users of scenario planning. Like many organizations, sometimes they use consultant support, sometimes they do not. A review involving one of my colleagues was undertaken after the devastating September 11 terrorist attacks on the World Trade Center in New York. The key question to answer was why had such a form of attack (targeting important high-rise buildings with airplanes) not been predicted? When the recriminations settled down, one of the staff members produced a list of the outputs from the scenario planning sessions that had been previously run. There was a bone-chilling moment when they reached the scenario describing the potential for a hijacked airplane attack on a high-value target. Of course, the scenario was not city or building specific (or indeed that there could be multiple attacks), but the description of the scenario was there. Clearly, there was demonstrated its ability to Sense &

Make Sense. Equally clear was the need to 'Seize', to act in a timely manner on the insights.

In the previous chapter, we learned a bit of wisdom from legendary ice hockey player Wayne Gretzky, and I would like to add another wise notion attributed to him: 'You miss 100 per cent of the shots you don't take.'

Jack Ma, founder of Alibaba, expresses a similar sentiment when he says, 'If you don't give up, you still have a chance. Giving up is the greatest failure.'[1]

Having the greatest ability to Sense & Make Sense of what is unfolding, to have insight and understanding beyond other firms, is of no value if we do nothing with it. If we don't 'take the shot' or we are not prepared to commit resources, time and energy to see our ideas become reality, we create no value. We don't win competitively – and indeed we may lose out to others.

Move people

Moving people is a highly effective mechanism both to move knowledge (for reapplication) and to create new insight. Despite all the advances in communications technologies and repositories of knowledge, when people are in physical proximity and able to collaborate effectively, there is greater transference of knowledge and greater creativity. Breaking down silos and encouraging people to work across boundaries can also increase efficiencies, alleviating some 'capacity' that might otherwise be trapped.

Many organizations today still operate by principles that were articulated by Frederick Taylor in *The Principles of Scientific Management,*[2] which was published in 1911. Why do they use 100-year-old principles? Because this is how most people have experienced organizations throughout their lives.

At school we had teachers separated into subject-specific departments, which were separated from the administrative and pastoral care functions and admissions etc. Most schools did not have a customer-centric organization that focused on your on-boarding, monitored your development and your experience and adapted for your differentiated rate of learning and development, which then saw you off into the world as an exceptional human being.

Rather, we condition our children by feeding them through a system that is divided and dissected by department and function, where the only constant is themselves, impacted by the production line of interventionist experiences.

This is 'scientific management', and most people have been conditioned to see the world and every organization in a similar compartmentalized way. This approach is designed for internal efficiency rather than an integrated experience that is adaptive to maximize outcomes.

If the optimizing lens is internal efficiency, then the organization is designed around its own cost drivers and constraints, rather than the evolving needs of the market and expectations of the customer.

Frederick Taylor proposed that by optimizing and simplifying jobs, productivity would increase. He promoted the following approach:

1 Carefully study the work activities to determine the most efficient way to perform specific tasks.

2 Match workers to jobs based on capability and motivation, and train them to work at maximum efficiency.

3 Monitor worker performance and provide instructions and supervision to ensure they're using the most efficient ways of working.

4 Separate the duties between managers and workers so the managers spend their time planning and training, ensuring the workers perform their tasks efficiently.

The scientific management approach produces specialists who reside in specific units within the organization. A clear example of this type of organization can be seen in military forces in many countries. Military units have specific specializations and roles, and commands and communications travel up and down the chain of command. Only the most senior officers see across the entire array of resources available – those deployed and those actively engaged. Each specialist unit is drilled and trained to perfect execution of its mandated function under a variety of challenging conditions.

This approach, whilst leading to robust specialists, can in turn breed a culture of silos that inhibit communication and mutual understanding. Despite the proliferation of media and means for communicating and sharing data and insight, the 'truth' of human behaviour remains that we learn most through experience. This is not new; the famous Chinese philosopher Confucius, who lived between 551 BC and 479 BC, is noted for saying, 'Tell me and I forget. Show me and I may remember. Involve me and I will understand.' There is no better way to broaden understanding, combine insights and generate new ideas than working together, in person.

FIGURE 3.2 Seize & Replicate: Move people

Key Mechanisms	Examples
• Move people between teams and locations in order to apply knowledge and experience quickly, whilst also deepening insight and learning. • Fire bucket brigade and flying doctor models both enable flexible role adjustment as capacity required changes or colleagues are drawn into alternative teams and activities or to address problems or capacity constraints. • Fluid teams that can be quickly formed, drawing resources from across the organization. Each individual member knowing how teams operate in 'this' corporation so collectively to be productive as quickly as possible.	**Alcohol**: 'Supply chain... We have the flying doctors based in Vietnam because it is cheap to be located there. We have five people based in Vietnam not reporting to the region. Reporting to the global. One manager needs a flying doctor. He goes directly to global, says, "I need two flying doctors"... the region is not involved.' **Finance**: 'We end up moving resources, people around and assigning them to projects. We are doing a lot of this, actually. This is what we end up doing. We say, "X, you know more about this than anybody. Put three people together and figure out what we're going to go and do in country Y."'

Enabling people to be mobile is critical to the adaptive strength of an organization. To clarify, people mobility here refers to the fluid coming together and dispersal of groups of individuals within and across an organization to work on projects together. This facilitates the direct exchange and application of knowledge and insight between them. This type of mobility enables teams to address the changing challenges and opportunities the organization continuously faces.

Fire Bucket Brigade and Flying Doctors

In the pursuit of greater flexibility, most corporations have adopted management practices that increase flexibility. This allows them to adjust to swings in output demand and offers greater labour cost efficiency. When it is necessary to add resources, labour output can be increased by creating overtime for the existing team. Alternatively, the labour force can be supplemented by labour from within the company or with short-term contract labour. This model remains aligned with Taylor's scientific management principles even when corporations venture into even lower levels of fixed internal resources, increasing the reliance on short-term (even 'zero hour') contract workers. Mega-companies such as Amazon and Microsoft are often criticized for such working practices, because of the vulnerability of the incomes and employment rights of these workers.

Other current steps to increase workforce flexibility, which also remain in the shadow of Taylor's scientific management, include the concepts of 'Fire Bucket Brigade' and the 'Flying Doctors'. You may have seen the 'Fire Bucket Brigade' concept at work at your local Subway sandwich store. Your sandwich is created with a certain sequence of steps, which does not vary. However, depending on demand intensity, fewer or more individual staff may be involved in creating the sandwich. If one person's activity set becomes the bottleneck that limits the overall rate of flow of the sandwiches down the line, then the people either side of that individual may start to take on some of the activities that individual is performing. In this example, the tasks have been scientifically defined, and within this specific production unit the individuals can flexibly cover all the tasks. Which tasks they do and how many people work on the line is determined by the demand intensity and the work rate of the other individuals on the line.

The 'Flying Doctor' model distinguishes between individuals engaged in 'business as usual' activities of the operations and the periodic, or on-call, internal consultant support required from specialists who may 'fly in' (from another department, part of the company or even further afield). In some cases, the 'flying doctors' may represent or report into the corporate headquarters, as a group-managed resource. The 'flying doctors' may also have specialist skills (eg Production, Supply Chain, Legal, etc) and when they are deployed to support the operating unit, they are expected to share their insight and knowledge. They also have the opportunity to learn from the context, challenges and ideas of the staff at the operating company. Appropriately motivated internal consultants can therefore increase knowledge transfer and the agility of a corporation in ways that exceed the practices previously described that may only enhance flexibility.

Let's consider an example. A European beer company has evolved its global organization that blends in-country operations teams with several regional and global 'flying doctor' supporting teams covering functions such as Supply Chain, Production Expertise and Product Innovation. In addition, they have global reporting lines of in-country Finance and HR. In combination, this form of organization allows a degree of localization whilst maintaining global standards and control. Furthermore, it allows a degree of learning from market engagement that can then be reapplied elsewhere – in other words, Seized & Replicated.

Examples of the effectiveness of this mechanism to Seize & Replicate include:

- the rapid and successful introduction of new packaging formats (slim cans) into the Asia market (initially into Vietnam, an important market for the brewer in APAC) after successful innovation of the format in Europe;

- the successful introduction of flavoured beers (under the range name 'Radler') into Asia, leveraging successful growth of non-traditional beer drinker segments in Europe through the development and launch of such beers.

These APAC local market successes did not depend on local innovation but on human resource mobility. Through fluid deployment of people involved in the initiatives in Europe to work with the local market teams, the company was able to Seize & Replicate the successes achieved elsewhere.

Adaptive teams

Google and Cisco (and others) have pioneered human resource management models that increase mobility beyond those described above. The core of these models is the recognition that the team is the unit of performance of the corporation. Teams may come together for a short or long period of time. An individual may be a member of a single team or simultaneously a member of other teams.

In 2004, Google founders Larry Page and Sergey Brin introduced the guideline that 20 per cent of each employee's time (up to one full day a week) could be spent working on a Google-related passion project of their own choosing or creation, the goal being to increase creativity and enthusiasm. There is an internal platform where anyone can post their project and invite individuals to offer their time to join the team, and where employees can browse the available projects requiring resources and offer their services.

The 20 per cent model could easily be abused by employees who contribute little during their self-directed project time. So, the system is first founded on a decision to trust that employees want to be productive during the project time, and secondly is enforced through the culture of the organization. This reflects an explicit doctrine of teaming and contributing to the performance of the team and the firm. As to be expected in a data-driven company, there are also metrics that track performance and collaborative contributions of individuals. These metrics provide insight and the opportunity for feedback, in support of the trust and teaming doctrine rather than being the primary tools of control.

Other notable firms that have adopted 'team-based' approaches and share the intent of increasing resource mobility, employee engagement and rate of innovation include LEGO, UTC, Unilever and JAL, amongst many others. I highlight these four firms to illustrate that there is no limitation to sector or national identity.

Adopting a team-based model can have very significant benefits for the overall performance of the organization, both directly – eg increasing agility and innovation – and indirectly – eg quickly identifying over-performing and underperforming talent that may have remained relatively unnoticed in a traditional organization, John Diener, the COO of AgriProtein, noted:

> Increasingly I see everything we do as being suitable for a team-based approach. I am establishing SPRINTS and SCRUMS all the time as I transform this organization and speed up – well, 'everything' that we're doing.

Note: The topics of teams and teaming are explored in more depth in Chapter 9.

Clusters not regions

Competitive advantage can be derived from quickly disseminating and applying insight between markets with similar demand or competitive dynamics – the capability to Seize & Replicate. However, geographic proximity does not necessarily imply similarities in market dynamics, stage of development, cultural or regulatory framework. Administering together as a cluster markets with similar conditions and dynamics can help accelerate the development, transfer and reapplication of relevant insight.

Organize by customer type

Syngenta, a leader in global agrochemicals, with a strong heritage as a science-based organization, defined their products by the chemical formulation and the crop diseases they were designed to cure. They later saw the need to realign their organization, adopting a structure defined by crop type and a product range matching to the life stage of the crop. As well as serving the farmers better, this approach enhanced the exchange of insight between the in-country staff and global HQ teams on farmer needs and product effectiveness, as the global team was able to share experiences and solutions that may have worked elsewhere in the world with a similar climate and the same crop type. Local-global communications increased and created the opportunity to refocus roles and staffing in regions. To quote a senior executive:

> We now look to 19 'territory clusters', whereas we used to have four geographically defined regions. This helps us move knowledge and respond more quickly to marketplace developments and competitor moves. Our resources are now more simply defined and managed as either being 'in-territory' or 'above-territory'.

All global companies face the familiar tension between allowing local flexibility and adaptation versus maintaining global consistency and control.[3] An approach to manage this tension is the concept of 'anchored agility', which was described by a Syngenta executive using the analogy of playing tennis:

> Each player knows the rules of the game, the size of the court etc; this is what the global team sets for all the country and cluster leaders. But within that set of rules the country managers decide how to play the game, what tactics, what is the game strategy, and which shot to play when.

FIGURE 3.3   Seize & Replicate: Clusters not regions

Key Mechanisms	Examples
• Quickly disseminating and applying insight between markets with similar demand or competitive dynamics. • Improvements in communications technology and virtual collaboration have reduced the advantages or necessity for proximity in managing across geographic markets. • A corporation's ability to Seize & Replicate insight and actions across its network is enhanced if markets with similar dynamics are clustered administratively together. • Corporations are also realizing efficiencies by reducing (or entirely removing) regional headquarters going straight from global to local.	**Agriculture**: 'Transformation has connected Local to Global and removed Regional. Now look to 19 "territory clusters", whereas we used to have 4 regions. Resources are defined and managed as either "in-territory" or "above-territory".' **FMCG**: 'We now operate with 11 clusters of countries and territories. The product mix thought to be most relevant for the countries within any one cluster is determined by global and cluster leadership. The cluster also provides guidance for brand activation, investment and channel management. The country management team is responsible for actual selection of the product mix, activation and operations.'

An executive at a major beverage company expressed similar views on the transformation of the organization that they had carried out:

> We now operate with 11 clusters of countries and territories. The product mix thought to be most relevant for the countries within any one cluster is determined by global and cluster leadership. The cluster also provides guidance for brand activation, investment and channel management. The country management team is responsible for actual selection of the product mix, activation and operations. The cluster approach [rather than the regional] is more focused as the markets are more similar to one another.

Organize by market dynamics

Several of the firms that participated in the research divide the markets in which they participate globally into developed and developing markets, this distinction being an overlay of the regional administration of supporting services that enhances coordination and knowledge exchange between markets with similar dynamic conditions. The developing markets cluster includes some markets in Africa, Asia, the Middle East and Latin America; the developed markets may also include other countries in some of these same regions, the Japanese 'developed' market being clustered with Australia-New Zealand, but not with geographically closer markets such as China. The intent of this clustering is both to increase the movement of relevant knowledge and to seek operational efficiencies when possible.

Although said with intentional humour, this statement from a global executive at an alcoholic beverage company conveys an important insight:

> One of my last tasks before moving to the global role [at the global HQ] was to close down the regional HQ; over the preceding years we had been reducing the role of the regional office to the point where pretty much the only responsibility left was to tell the operating companies at what level to set their air conditioning. Every other decision had been moved to either in-country or to global.

Shape the future

Take deliberate actions to influence the evolution of the market – customer behaviours, regulation, competitive dynamics, distribution channels. To quote Abraham Lincoln (16th President of the United States of America): 'The best way to predict the future is to create it.'

- Globally apply insights from experience in any one market in order to seek to influence the evolution of other markets, either to pre-emptively mitigate negative dynamics or to recreate positive outcomes previously achieved. Pursue the most advantageous competitive structure for the market, which may be three to four players in an oligopoly.

- Lobby regulators enthusiastically, according to the legal framework in each territory, to shape the future market conditions that will most benefit your corporation's competitive position and unique strengths.

The largest financial institutions in the world are not always household names but manage tens of trillions of US$. They operate at a scale that enables them to have tremendous influence in many national economies yet equally they are exposed to highly fluid situations and contexts of great ambiguity and uncertainty due to shifting regulation and technology. Because of their stature and size, they are very often both a respected discussion partner and an effective lobbyist with government finance ministries and central bankers. Senior officers in the company place a high priority on leveraging their global networks to identify and share insights from one jurisdiction to another. As one executive noted:

> We may have more experience and insight than the people setting the national policies; we see so many experiments, changing and tweaking policies, that we are often invited to have a say or at least it is likely that we will be given the opportunity to dialogue. This is both a responsibility and can also be an advantage for us. Yet, as the contexts are in flux we also need to have an approach of 'feeling the way across the river, one step at a time'. We are always learning everywhere and sharing and whenever possible integrating new insight.

Influence regulation

In the research, pharmaceutical companies particularly emphasized the importance of influencing purchasing and usage practices and policies in the medical sectors of the markets in which they operate. Their ability to do so would inform how they then decided on the rate and sequencing of the introduction of newer on-patent formulations.

Similarly, the heavy equipment manufacturers pointed to their efforts to encourage the adoption of stringent regulations for machine operator health and safety requirements and emissions controls in developing markets. The 'developed markets' machinery already adhered to more stringent regulatory codes whereas local competitors may not yet be operating at such standards.

FIGURE 3.4   Seize & Replicate: Shape the future

Key Mechanisms	Examples
• Deliberate actions to influence the evolution of the market: 'The best way to predict the future is to create it.' • Globally apply insights from experience in any one market in order to seek to influence the evolution of other markets. • Engage regulators and competitors to enhance evolution of industry structure, whilst benefiting the customer. • Winner-takes-all approach to dominate the ongoing evolution of the marketspace. • Establish eco-system alliances to enhance the overall value proposition for customers. Move to platform-based competition.	**Semiconductor**: 'We have the opportunity in some markets to move from demand-fulfilment to demand creation; this has happened in many developed markets but in younger markets this is a change that we help to influence, which is to our advantage over more locally focused players who may not have the resources and eco-system partnerships to compete so effectively in creating "demand creation" markets.' **Financial**: 'We are very active in trying to influence the evolution of the industry in different markets, working with the regulators. Very often, we would be one of a very small number of industry experts on particular issues.'

Lobbying of government representatives, members of the judiciary, policy and law makers by corporations occurs everywhere in the world and has happened throughout history. Each territory has its own regulations and form of the practice. What is considered illegal bribery in some countries is acceptable in others. Access and influence are sometimes granted to domestic companies at the expense of overseas-based firms. Some overseas corporations and their governments perceive this approach as unfair trade practices although in their own home territory these same corporations may be the beneficiaries of similar practices and behaviours.

Special interest groups using money and other tactics of persuasion to influence policymakers to make decisions in their favour is prevalent everywhere, whether overt or covert, legal or illegal. Lobbying is particularly visible in the United States, not only because of the scale but also as lobbyists can be officially registered and their spending reported.

However, in 2014, *The Nation* reported that lobbying was 'Officially, shrinking – unofficially, exploding',[4] there being approximately 12,000 registered lobbyists in 2013 (fewer than in 2002). *The Atlantic* reported the scale of official lobbying to be bigger than the total budget for the operations of the House of Representatives ($1.18 billion) and the Senate ($860 million) combined: 'Corporations now spend about $2.6 billion a year on reported lobbying expenditures.'[5] However, according to *The Nation*, unofficial and official lobbyists number closer to 100,000 in total and spending is approximately $9 billion per year.[6]

If these numbers are even directionally correct, that equates to a lot of people actively seeking to shape the future!

Seize today to make tomorrow. The external context has a future that is contingent on the actions of multiple parties and factors – including the corporation's own actions. What we do now shapes the tomorrow that we compete in.

Winner-takes-all strategy

In situations where the belief is that a significantly dominant player reaps disproportionately high profits, a strategy known as 'Winner Takes All' can prevail. For example, Netflix vs Disney+, Xbox vs PlayStation, Android vs iOS, Uber vs Lyft. Across many industries, but particularly evident in the born-digital industries, there is an evident separation in scale and market influence between those giants that command a dominant platform and everyone else who participates in, or accommodates, that platform. A winner-takes-all strategy has the objective of one firm owning the platform and dominating the ongoing evolution of the marketspace.

This phenomenon is not new or limited to digital: in the 1970s and 1980s there was a battle between Betamax (from Sony) and VHS (from JVC) in home video recording.[7] Similarly, Starbucks launching in the United States employed the tactic of over-populating key street intersections and malls with outlets in order to deny competitors access. The strategy is similar also in mature industries where big companies buy up multiple smaller companies in order to achieve a long-term, stable and highly profitable position – for example, the tobacco industry.

Strategically, rather than consolidation to achieve greater efficiency or scale advantages, the winner-takes-all goal is to provide dominance in steering the evolution of the industry in the future. This will be a growth-hungry company prepared to sustain long periods of losses and pouring in cash to continue to expand, with no certainty about future earnings.

Winner-takes-all strategy has been particularly evident in 'network platform' businesses, where scale and reach beget greater scale and reach. In the past, network effects were hard to reverse in industries that relied on physical networks such as railways and telephones. In the present, the popularity of Uber or Airbnb increases with the number of cars or properties they have available on their platform. However, increasingly, network effects aren't as durable as they used to be. Challengers may also have enormous capital that they can deploy to establish their own challenger network, potentially resulting in long, drawn-out, loss-making battles. Consider this example of the ride-hailing business in China.

In 2016, Uber agreed to sell its business in China to rival Didi Chuxing for US $35 billion – not bad for a company that had been in the market for only two years and was losing an estimated US $1 billion per year.[8] The two firms had been fierce competitors, but Didi Chuxing dominated the Chinese market with up to 90 per cent share. Both firms were spending huge sums to subsidize discounted fares in their battle for dominance. It is estimated that Didi was losing up to US $8 billion per year as it fought ferociously to retain its position. Didi Chuxing was able to sustain such huge losses as it is backed by Chinese internet giants Tencent and Alibaba, which understood the importance of a 'winner-takes-all' strategy in a network platform market. Within just a few weeks of the merger, fares on the Didi Hitch service rose by 20 per cent in Beijing, and customers in other major cities such as Chengdu and Xi'an reported spending more for the same distance. Didi also reduced its subsidies for drivers in Beijing, with weekend subsidies totally cut. With China dominance assured, Didi Chuxing and its investors are expanding regionally and globally in pursuit of unassailable dominance of the platform. It has an alliance with India's Ola, Southeast Asia's Grab and US firm Lyft. It has launched in Mexico and entered Brazil through acquisition of a local operator. Uber, meanwhile, pulled out of more international markets, selling its operations in eight Southeast Asian countries to rival Grab in 2018.

Winner-takes-all is a growth strategy dependent on an abundance of cheap capital, deeper reserves than others and the ability to scale operations quickly – and continuously – until the others are forced to concede. Once established as the 'winner' of the platform, then prices may rise, and other value-adding services and revenue streams may be added. The winner-takes-all strategy requires having the vision of the contingent future; if I win the scale race, then I can determine the future rules of competition in the marketspace.

Collaborate: form and maintain alliances

Systems thinking may be seen in situations where firms act in a collective manner; whilst there is competition between them, they also act in such a way that a profitable and relatively stable industry structure is maintained, which benefits them all.

One of the most stable competitive structures, which enables all players to achieve higher than expected returns, is when there are three (or four) companies competing in the market. The stability doesn't result from overt collusion but from an ability to read and understand each other's intents and actions, thus enabling each individual firm to take actions to maximize its own interests, which include avoiding self-destructive competitive tactics. These structures can be particularly enduring if one of the companies is significantly smaller than the other two.

The smaller company may become the more innovative company as it struggles to win market share, but its actions may be easily mimicked by the others, which can also leverage greater scale advantages if the initiatives are shown to be successful. For such oligopolies to mature, there may be a prior period of consolidation between many more companies that were previously sub-scale and suffered from insufficient profitability or over-capacity. The survival of such oligopolies, then, requires some degree of barrier to entry by potential new entrants, which may be the result of licensing requirements (eg telecoms providers or full banking licences) within a certain geographic territory. It may also be reinforced through aggressive defence against the new entrant from each of the incumbents, acting collectively through the adoption of similar marketplace responses.

Executives often mention their awareness of the challenges to profitability in highly competitive marketplaces where there are multiple parties competing in different ways, reflecting that there are advantages for the consumer and for firm profitability of an oligopoly structure. When they think about the current attractiveness of the markets they are in, they also consider what action they could take (or might seek to avoid) in order to enhance or maintain attractiveness of the structure. Pharmaceutical companies, for example, consider the number of dominant players for a disease category, whereas alcohol players consider the intensity of competition in certain market segments or drink classes in specific markets and the like.

CASE STUDY
Ag Gateway Consortium

Another example is the Ag Gateway Consortium, which is a non-profit consortium of more than 200 businesses with many players.[9] Collaboration across the sector enables all players to share data with the common intent to obtain greater insights on how better to address and shape customer needs. This is performed through an industry-wide initiative, known as the Agricultural Data Application Programming Toolkit (ADAPT).

Syngenta (agrochemicals) and John Deere (machinery) are both key members, as are many software companies, other equipment builders and others. The goal of ADAPT and the Ag Gateway Consortium is to improve the productivity of farmers, farmland and water usage in farming, to 'revolutionize precision agriculture', which is in the interests of everybody involved in the sector. With ADAPT, 'Manufacturers can still use their proprietary software, but they can also build plug-ins that allow their systems to translate between their own format and a common data model.' 'ADAPT is a translator that allows growers to speak with the rest of the world,' explained a systems architect with Syngenta.[10]

Syngenta is keen to support the growers to use the correct amount of each of their products at the optimal moment and applied in the most effective manner. This will reduce wastage and maximize crop productivity. But in order to achieve such accuracy, the machinery, the soil conditions, the weather and the crop conditions all must be measured in real time and the application guided with support from the data analytics. Similarly, John Deere's focus is to make smart machines and support smart decisions that enhance the overall productivity of the farmer and farmland.

To be effective, across the consortium, there needs to be coordinated and collaborative development of:

- Machine optimization – solutions that will get the most out of machines using the Internet of Things (IoT), precision technology and wireless, mobile data networks for higher levels of productivity and increased uptime.
- Logistics optimization – managing logistics and machinery use from remote locations through fleet management solutions and increased machine-to-machine communication.
- Ag decision support – user-friendly monitors, sensors and wireless mobile networks to provide easy access to machinery and agronomic data essential to making proactive management decisions.

To increase momentum of building out the network for innovation, John Deere opened up its initiatives to third parties. Developers can integrate telematics machine data into their applications through the Machine Monitoring resources in the John Deere app. The John Deere API enables developers to build apps that provide machine locations, fuel levels and other data points such as soil moisture and weather. Through analysing aggregated data, all members of the consortium can increase their insight and support further gains in productivity. For example, fuel usage of different harvesters can be analysed and correlated with their performance. By analysing the data from hundreds of farms, it is possible to fine-tune operations for optimum levels of production.

Leadership traits: Seize & Replicate

Rapid Scale-Up

Innovation is one of the most important capabilities of firms moving at the speed required by 4IR. Driving innovation requires the combination of strategy, capacity and discipline. I would like to lay to rest the notion of blue-sky innovation; impactful innovation comes from identifying and seeking to solve a need – as the proverb states, 'Necessity is the mother of invention.' Innovation Strategy is the choice of what to focus on – the priorities, the scale of outcome required and the timeframe. Innovation Capacity is created by ensuring the development of the innovation management and ideation capabilities of the team. A suitable framework of such is provided by the Global Innovation Management Institute.[11] Skills alone are insufficient – there must be the decision to align commitments of time and resources with the strategy. Innovation Discipline is created when establishing and enforcing metrics, both leading metrics such as number of team members certified or number of team members or of projects initiated, and trailing metrics such as pass rate through stage gates or percentage of revenues that are from innovation in past three years.

Personal accountability

Executives and their teams need to drive the implementation of the innovations and solutions from one part of the firm to others. As they do so they may have to transcend organizational boundaries, forming collaborations to attain the desired benefits. Across the management cadre each individual must have a strong sense of personal ownership for achieving the best overall performance. They should eagerly look across the organization for innovations and ideas that they can bring into their area of direct responsibility as well as proactively push innovations and insights from their area into others where they think it could bring benefits. If innovation application occurs only as a result of centrally driven initiatives, the entity will not be moving as rapidly as it could be. In 4IR businesses executives need to have a sense of individual responsibility for the dissemination, application and improvement of innovations throughout the firm. They should be accountable to one another for ensuring everyone aligns with this culture.

Collaborate across boundaries

For ideas and innovations to flow across the organization individuals must be skilled in collaborating across boundaries, working in multi-functional teams. The effectiveness of such teams is dependent upon all team members sharing a common overall objective (eg the performance improvement results to be achieved through the application of new innovations and insights) whilst bringing their different specializations and perspectives. Team members need to be respectful and curious about each other's perspectives. To enhance their ability to be understood and to understand one another they should share their thought processes and support logic, not being defensive but acknowledging that others may not know why they have arrived at the insight or observation they are making. During their work together there will be new discoveries, such as identifying ways to amplify the benefits, which may require the vision to be adapted.

Mindset: Sense of urgency

A high energy to improve firm performance by applying innovations and insights. To share and apply knowledge quickly and broadly across the organization. Given the ambiguity and uncertainty of the dynamic context, executives may be tempted to wait on the collection and analysis of more data to reduce risks of taking poor decisions. However, this tendency must be weighed against the need to act as the future is unfolding so as to be able to seize opportunities and shape the evolution of the marketspace. Hence, the approach of Ready-Fire-Aim can help to ensure there is momentum, energy and increased adaptability.

KEY CONCEPTS: CHAPTER 3

The ability to seize on successful initiatives in one location or business unit and to quickly scale them up or to replicate them elsewhere can be a source of advantage. Knowledge turns into action fastest when there are fewest hand-offs between individuals and departments. Hence moving people across boundaries and adopting an organization structure defined by the core theme determining business outcome will accelerate results. The key mechanisms and behaviours to foster are:

- Move people:
    - fire bucket brigade and flying doctors;
    - fluid teams.
- Clusters not regions:
    - organize by customer type;
    - organize by market dynamics.
- Shape the future:
    - influence regulation;
    - 'winner-takes-all' strategy;
    - collaborate: form and maintain alliances.
- Leadership traits:
    - rapid scale-up;
    - personal accountability;
    - collaborate across boundaries;
    - mindset: sense of urgency.

FIGURE 3.5   Seize & Replicate: Key management practices

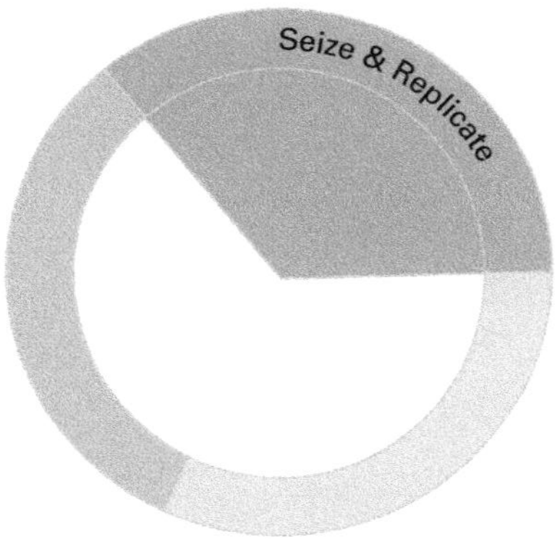

Adjust offerings and business models to create and capture value through newly identified opportunities. Propagate insights and redeploy resources across the organization in a timely manner to extend advantages.

- **Move people**
  - Move people between teams and locations in order to apply knowledge and experience quickly, whilst also deepening insight and learning.
  - Fire Bucket Brigade and Flying Doctor models both enable flexible role adjustment as capacity required changes or colleagues are drawn into alternative teams and activities or to address problems or capacity constraints.
  - Fluid teams that can be quickly formed, drawing resources from across the organization. Each individual member knowing how teams operate in 'this' corporation so collectively to be productive as quickly as possible.

- **Clusters not regions**
  - Administratively cluster markets with similar dynamics together, to deepen insight and accelerate knowledge dissemination.
  - Disseminate insight between markets with similar demand or competitive dynamics. Apply insights from experience in any one market in order to seek to influence the evolution of other markets.
  - Reduce (or entirely remove) regional headquarters: Go straight from global to local.

- **Shape the future**
  - Deliberate actions to influence the evolution of the market, 'The best way to predict the future is to create it.' Winner-takes-all approach to dominate the ongoing evolution of the marketspace. Move to platform-based competition.
  - Engage regulators and competitors to enhance evolution of industry structure, whilst benefiting the customer.
  - Establish eco-system alliances to enhance the overall value proposition for customers and/or create platform-to-platform competition.

Seize & Replicate

Endnotes

1   The Silicon Review (2018) 'If you don't give up, you still have a chance. Giving up is the greatest failure,' says Jack Ma Yun, https://thesiliconreview. com/2018/05/if-you-dont-give-up-you-still-have-a-chance-giving-up-is-the-greatest-failure-says-jack-ma-yun (archived at https://perma.cc/FX8D-MY7C)

2   Taylor, F W (1911) *The Principles of Scientific Management*, Harper and Brothers

3   Prahalad, C K and Doz, Y L (1987) *The Multinational Mission: Balancing local demands and global vision*, Free Press

4   Fang, L (2014) Where have all the lobbyists gone? *The Nation*, March

5   Drutman, L (2015) How corporate lobbyists conquered American democracy, *The Atlantic*, April

6   Fang, L (2014) Where have all the lobbyists gone? *The Nation*, March

7   Smith, C (2018) Betamax vs VHS and three more hard-fought high-tech format wars, BT, https://home.bt.com/tech-gadgets/tech-features/betamax-vs-vhs-and-three-more-hard-fought-high-tech-format-wars-11363979948999 (archived at https://perma.cc/FJ3F-RUUL)

8   Newcomer, E (2016) Uber to sell China business to rival Didi Chuxing, *Independent*

9   https://www.aggateway.org/ (archived at https://perma.cc/F27Q-K2E5)

10 Ehlers, M (2017) New technology will merge farm-management data, *Thrive*, https://www.syngenta-us.com/thrive/research/farm-management-data.html (archived at https://perma.cc/KK4R-UJK5)

11 https://www.giminstitute.org/ (archived at https://perma.cc/3BSM-CEA2)

04

Reposition & Reconfigure

IN BRIEF

The third capability is to Reposition & Reconfigure. This is the ability to be always reflecting on how the firm is operating and on what changes can be made to improve performance, both incrementally and significantly. This capability requires the ability to be questioning and challenging the assumptions about what the firm is doing and why. Asking if the practices, assets and activities are still relevant; if it is still relevant for the firm to conduct them itself or if they are better done by others; if inside the firm, how can they be changed and performance improved?

Management mechanisms that differentiate the capability to Reposition & Reconfigure include:

1 **Define new marketspaces**

   Blue oceans are described as marketspaces where competitors are not present, where a company can chart its own course and configure its offer and activities as it sees fit. However, sailing in the uncharted waters of a blue ocean can be daunting for managers, requiring skills of exploration rather than exploitation. This may require honing skills of managing the environment (operations, supply chain and channel partners), an increased sensitivity to feedback and the ability to adjust, and the expectation that unforeseen risks and competitors may unexpectedly emerge.

2 **Glide, don't jump**

   Large corporations can leverage their scale to reduce risk whilst facilitating the smooth adaptation of their scope of activities and portfolio of offerings. They can venture into new marketspaces in a competitively substantial manner, without destabilizing or compromising the activities of the core. Similarly, they can sustain trailing positions as they reduce focus in other areas, harvesting value and maintaining strategic flexibility rather than abruptly exiting, which may create a platform for emergent competitors.

3   Choiceful duplication

In dynamic unstable contexts, binary choices can increase exposure to risk. If the global supply chain is designed to optimize efficiency with large orders placed in overseas suppliers, then it becomes vulnerable to international trade disputes, supplier production interruptions, currency fluctuation, etc. Deliberate choices of duplication can help to mitigate risk through providing flexibility. For example, maintaining competing ranges of products under different brands, at different price points, mitigates risk should the market swing either towards premium or to economy product preferences.

FIGURE 4.1   Reposition & Reconfigure: The third set of capabilities that form dynamic capacity

Let's build on the analogy of the tennis player. The first set of capabilities – 'Sense & Make Sense' – enables the player to anticipate where the ball is going and how quickly, and to intuit where the opposing players may be most likely to move. The second set of capabilities – 'Seize & Replicate' – enables the tennis player to make timely decisions about what shots to play to return the ball. The third set of capabilities are those that enable the tennis player to move into position, not only to the right part of the court but also with the right configuration or body positioning, so that they can execute the desired shot well. For a firm with high *dynamic capacity*, it is possible to move quickly with a smooth flow, to bring maximum execution prowess at the desired moment of impact, and then to follow through, whilst positioning for the next play, always in motion.

Before digging into the factors that define our third mechanism of dynamic capacity – 'Reposition & Reconfigure' – let's consider two examples of the kind of adaptive mindset that facilitates this aspect of strategy. W. Chan Kim and Renée Mauborgne of Blue Ocean Strategy explain their fundamental approach:

> Blue ocean strategy is the simultaneous pursuit of differentiation and low cost to open up a new marketspace and create new demand. It is about creating and capturing uncontested marketspace, thereby making the competition irrelevant. It is based on the view that market boundaries and industry structure are not a given and can be reconstructed by the actions and beliefs of industry players.[1]

As CEO of Honeywell (from February 2002 until March 2017), Dave Cote led a determined transformation of the organization, including a spree of buying and exiting an estimated 100 businesses. He morphed Honeywell to align with his three priority themes: Energy Efficiency, Energy Conservation and Safety. 'I believe in placing lots of bets on lots of businesses,'[2] he said. He also recognized that many smaller deals might be safer than a few big ones, as he said, 'A big deal that goes bad can ruin a company.'[3]

Honeywell's shopping spree under Cote was successful. On average, Honeywell paid around 12 times earnings for the acquired companies and tripled their profits. That improvement owes a great deal to Cote's relentless focus on integration. For all deals over $50 million, he reviewed the integration plan's progress after closing for the following 30, 60 and 90 days, and quarterly thereafter for at least a year.[4]

These anecdotes exemplify some of the key mechanisms that enable a corporation's capability to 'Reposition & Reconfigure'.

Define new marketspaces

New marketspaces

Many of the executives stretch or create entirely new definitions of the marketspace that they compete in. In so doing they are able to find or create 'blue ocean' where they focus more on shaping customer demand and less on the actions of competitors. An executive at a media conglomerate reflected:

> We are expanding into new business areas. We bought the global businesses of A** and now B**. You could argue they are similar businesses to what we were in, that it is a sheer expansion, but they have also confirmed our thinking of ourselves as a consumer products and experience business – that is a better

definition of how we think about ourselves now, not confined to media and entertainment. Another good example would be C**, the multi-channel [online video streams] network that we bought.

In exploring potential blue ocean, the corporation leverages existing core assets, thus providing advantage in being able to explore and expand into the new space. Global reach provides both additional insight on opportunities and a broader range of markets in which to experiment with the 'new' ones (often with lower risk for the core).

An executive at Coca-Cola company described their expansion of scope up the coffee value chain, leveraging the advantage of the scale of their business to capture greater value by backward integrating:

> Our coffee businesses used to buy the roasted coffee beans [...] What we have now done is gone back into the supply chain and basically looked from the green coffee beans forward [...] we are now in a position where we can start to manage the different steps ourselves, even sometimes back to buying the green coffee beans ourselves rather than have a supplier do this at all [...] We never used to think that we could reconfigure the supply chain and we probably wouldn't have seen the opportunity if we hadn't changed the structure and the culture.[5,6]

FIGURE 4.2   Reposition & Reconfigure: Define new marketspaces

Key Mechanisms	Examples

• Establish unique definition for the space to compete in; unconstrained by existing definitions of industries and sectors.
 	
   o Focus on a set of needs of the target customers.
 	
• Continuously explore adjacencies, adjust the offering and refine the business model. Act incrementally rather than with dramatic step-changes.
 	
   o Probe new opportunities. Harvest existing positions that become less relevant.
 	
• Create options. Identify potential marketspace opportunities that can be pursued in a step-wise manner. Determine the value of creating an option for future expansion, or the cost of withdrawal.
	Agriculture: Maintains two go-to-market models: the traditional pharmaceutical approach to markets presenting products by chemistry and targeted to disease types, plus a new range of products that correspond to the specific life stages of crops and is supported by crop-based teams.
	
	Metals: We decided that we want to have a global supply chain, but we have to be more nimble – and we can do that by coordinating across the global network and having options through leveraging multiple previously semi-independent plants.

An executive at a medical devices company reflected on the advantages of their global reach in morphing the portfolio of activities:

> This is an advantage of being a global firm, we can be in a new line of business somewhere, with scale and learning a lot yet without having to fully commit the organization. We are heading towards a big transformation, by divesting a lot of businesses, and investing in new ones.

Jeff Bezos' acquisition of Whole Foods can also be seen as a morphing by Amazon, adjusting its position and redefining its marketspace. Despite the size of the transaction – $13 billion – this is still small relative to Amazon (at the time of the deal Amazon's market capital was approximately $950 billion).

Steve Jobs is quoted as saying:

> Some people say, 'Give the customers what they want.' But that's not my approach. Our job is to figure out what they're going to want before they do. I think Henry Ford once said, 'If I'd asked customers what they wanted, they would have told me, "A faster horse!"' People don't know what they want until you show it to them. That's why I never rely on market research. Our task is to read things that are not yet on the page.[7]

Under Steve Jobs' leadership, Apple was famous for defining new market-spaces, creating products that people didn't know they wanted and achieving outstanding success. He definitely was masterful at sailing in blue oceans, although not everything he launched was a success. When defining the new marketspace he relied on insight and understanding which came from observing behaviour (figure out what they're doing) and listening to comments and opinions from users of products in adjacent spaces. This kind of insight combined with intuition is a key skill for leaders that differentiates firm performance and distinguishes great business leaders.

Create real options

'Real options' refers to the choices a company's management makes to expand, change or curtail projects based on unfolding economic, techno-logical or market conditions. According to Investopedia, 'Using real options value analysis (ROV), managers estimate the opportunity cost of continuing or abandoning a project and make decisions accordingly.'[8] The analysis takes into account the expected probabilities of outcomes for the choices to be made at decision milestones in the future.

Investopedia also explains that 'Investing in a new manufacturing facility may provide a company with real options of introducing new products, consolidating operations or making other adjustments to changing market conditions. In the course of making the decision to invest in the new facility, the company should consider the real option value the facility provides.'[9]

Some manufacturing companies and telecoms operators describe how, in response to the uncertainty about market evolution, they will often think in terms of creating options, by first taking a small step. If the conditions become increasingly favourable they can accelerate scaling up, building on the existing presence they have established. If the conditions turn negative, they can delay or withdraw without too great a financial penalty.

Jack Ma of Alibaba has described a key ingredient – the business leader's 'entrepreneurial mindset' – which he says is defined by 'taking the first step without knowing the final outcome, nor even the fourth step'. With this mindset, one can participate in the market with the goal to learn more about the dynamics and to always be reviewing options for pivoting and course adjusting. Future steps may only be possible if the first step is taken.

Real option valuation identifies economically the value of flexibility such that in situations of high uncertainty, the decision is not only informed by a 'go/no go' net present value (NPV) calculation of a cashflow forecast.

CASE STUDY
A global medical devices company

The client was considering the importance of establishing a presence in Myanmar. At the time, the market was tiny, but with a population of almost 55 million people, many of whom had not previously had access to high-quality medical care, and with the possibility of normalizing trade and political relationships with the rest of the world, it had the potential to generate significant demand – possibly quite quickly. Working with a willing local distributor would provide a toe-hold in the market and mitigate potential problems in the prevailing trade and political environment of direct participation. The company considered what else could be done to better lay the foundations for potential participation in the market and provide a competitive edge, should the market be open. They needed to determine what the cost of those options would be and what the potential upside could be.

To structure their thinking, they used a simple decision tree and the real options approach. In the end, they opted to make two types of limited investment that could quickly be scaled should the market open but could also be pulled away from should the political and trade climate deteriorate. One of the options they took up was investing in the small distributor, providing training and preferential trade terms that would allow the distributor to invest their own funds in upgrading their facilities. The other option was a training partnership with the ministry of health, aimed at supporting the poorer rural communities. Neither option required the injection of funds. In time, it will become evident how prudent these actions have been, yet in the meanwhile both are building goodwill and deepening the company's understanding of the operating context inside the country.

Glide, don't jump

Don't be afraid to rebuild

'Dare to rebuild' is one of the axioms of the 'Ferguson Formula'[10] – a set of eight axioms of management that were espoused by Sir Alex Ferguson, the former (highly successful) manager/coach of Manchester United Football Club, a top soccer club in the English Premier League. Several of the firms with higher-performing corporations in the research have developed fluency in reshaping the portfolio of their businesses. These firms have established prowess at managing transactions, both acquisition and divestment, as well as in integrating new businesses and separating out business activities intended for divestment.

FIGURE 4.3 Reposition & Reconfigure: Glide, don't jump

Key Mechanisms	Examples

• Determine the portfolio (business lines, offerings, geographies, customer segments) required for the vision of the future.
  o Will the portfolio provide the robust platform required for the future?
  o Is the portfolio aligned with the strategic roadmap and mission/vision?
• Develop expertise at identifying, negotiating, acquiring and integrating new acquisitions as well as birthing new businesses from existing business units.
• Develop expertise at preparing businesses for exit. Harvest businesses before exit, maximize strategic advantages.
• Retain and recycle key talent from legacy businesses.
	Technology: Sold out legacy core hardware businesses to focus on existing software and to develop a major new business division in cloud-based services and AI.
	
	FMCG: Bought and sold over 40 companies during an eight-year period. Sold out of core business lines that were synonymous with corporate brand but which were deemed to not be aligned with the new mission and growth strategy of the corporation.
	
	Industrial products: Bought and sold approx. 100 businesses within seven-year period. Focused on excellence in integration of new acquisitions, driving significant improvement in profitability.

An advantage for many of the firms in the research is their global network, which enables them to see more potential opportunities. For example:

- Google uses its global reach to find the most attractive teams and companies before they are widely known. Google's dominance in search has enabled it to build up a huge cash pile that it is using to fund expansion into areas such as content creation, education and autonomous transportation. Google's wealth has also enabled it to acquire companies in the areas of robotics and artificial intelligence. Among the companies recently bought are Schaft, a Japanese team developing a humanoid robot, and HUBO robots from South Korea. Google has also purchased Boston Dynamics and US start-ups such as Industrial Perception, Meka, Redwood Robotics and Bot & Dolly.

- When EADS announced its new strategy and rebranding to Airbus Defence & Space in 2013, it clarified that it would be focusing on commercial and defence aviation. The speed of the implementation of the Airbus Defence strategy has been aided by its global network, particularly in identifying suitable acquisition targets and opportunities for selling companies. A senior executive noted, 'We see what is happening in markets globally so we can reach out to partners in whichever location and explore collaboration with them; it's our reach that makes a difference.'

Harvest before exiting

The most successful firms often harvest rather than abruptly exiting existing positions that become less relevant. Harvesting can help to block competitors from gaining a foothold and can maintain customer confidence and overall customer reach. Several global firms highlighted that they seek to extend the life of products (and assets) by continuing with them in less demanding markets or segments. Harvesting may enable them to offer a 'fighting brand' version that a new premium offering can stand atop of. Another benefit of harvesting rather than abandoning is that it can reduce the space for disruptive competitors to gain significant share.

Harvesting may bring reduced but sustainable profits and revenues – hence it is important to have the right set of financial performance metrics, matching the strategic objectives. McGraw-Hill is an example of successful harvesting, as retold in an article by PwC:

> In 2011, McGraw-Hill was a broad and scattered media and information services provider under fire from activist investors. The company leaders knew they had to sell off the businesses that didn't fit, particularly the large education publishing business. But rather than hurriedly dismantling the company, they mapped out a multi-year programme in which they restructured costs, put new management in place [...] and transformed their operating model. The divestitures, when they happened, contributed strongly to the bottom line. The resulting company [...] increased its market value by $23 billion.[11]

Choiceful duplication

Similar but different

The dilemma for senior leadership is how to pursue overall efficiency whilst being flexible in the face of uncertain, evolving market contexts. Corporations need to resist a drift towards 'one size fits all' situations. How have some of the most successful corporations with global reach achieved this?

FIGURE 4.4 Reposition & Reconfigure: Choiceful duplication

Key Mechanisms	Examples
• Intentional choices to increase adaptability through maintaining alternative options (products, services, market presence and capabilities) whilst recognizing the cost penalties, eg of excess capacity. • Design supply chains with a degree of redundancy (eg dual or triple sources of components) in order to be robust under the influence of volatility in logistics context (eg exchange rates, logistics delays, etc). • Increase flexibility in human resources by maintaining capabilities in-house whilst also seeking external support. Maintain relationships with key talent that rotates through the firm, so that they can return if needed in the future.	**Agriculture**: Maintains two go-to-market models: the traditional pharmaceutical approach to markets presenting products by chemistry and targeted to disease types, plus a new range of products that correspond to the specific life stages of crops and is supported by crop-based teams. **Metals**: We decided that we want to have a global supply chain, but we have to be more nimble – and we can do that by coordinating across the global network and having options through leveraging multiple previously semi-independent plants.

As introduced earlier, Syngenta, the Swiss-based agrochemical company, was formed in 2000 through the merger of the agribusinesses of Novartis and Zeneca. Starting in 2012, Syngenta reorganized into crop-based teams and formulated a range of products that correspond to the specific life stages of those crops. Across the wide range of countries, cultures and climates that Syngenta serves there is an equally wide variety of farmers. Syngenta has discovered the benefits of maintaining two approaches – the traditional chemistry/disease model and the new crop/life-stage model – which provide the solutions required to best serve the diversity of its customers.

> Maintain competing product/service line ranges within the portfolio so as to be able to capture changes in the nature of customer demand.

Whilst developing a range of lower-priced products under a separate brand, Caterpillar has had to manage the tension of resisting the temptation to seek overall group efficiencies between the new and traditional brands. Recognizing the value of flexibility, Caterpillar already invested in developing alternate supplier networks, which enables them to adapt when faced with currency swings or supply interruption due to political, terrorist or natural disasters. Jim Owens (former chairman and CEO of Caterpillar) noted, 'In our industry, the competitor that's best at managing the supply chain is probably going be the most successful competitor over time. It's a condition of success.'[12]

An executive at a global asset management company describes the need to be flexible with the interrelationships with other global financial institutions on a territory by territory basis:

Sometimes we are competitors, but most frequently we are suppliers and customers of each other; in some places we might be the supplier of services to our global peers, in others or at other times we might be the customer of the same services from these same global peers. We always need to adapt and leverage each other's strengths, and of course this changes depending on where and when we are.

Similar, but different, parallel approaches are required because of differences in the dynamics of the evolution and the changing nature of demand in different markets. The opportunity is to have distinct alternative solutions that complement or could replace each other – such as online retail sales as well as physical stores; both solutions are often required. Unanticipated events and volatility may drive the market to be better served by one model over the other; the diversity of solutions provides the firm with the needed agility to 'win' in either scenario. Over time, the firm will be introducing new business solutions to address emerging needs and conditions but also retaining existing offers that may or may not be harvested eventually. Parallel models equip the firm with flexibility but do not maximize efficiency. The ability to adapt to fluid conditions in the contexts in which a corporation operates is enhanced by maintaining alternative, potentially competing, offerings or supply chains and product offerings. This results in business units that, to some extent, compete with one another for similar customers. Let's turn to some examples.

A challenge with evolving alternative solutions, product ranges or sourcing options is to manage the resulting complexity. Left unattended, the complexity of multiple options and alternatives will create significant inefficiencies, consume production capacity and choke the performance of the corporation. Hence, the key is to be attentive to 'choiceful' duplication, weighing the advantages sought from increased optionality with the systemic costs and consequences of that duplication. A simple discipline is to insist that every deliberate duplication that is introduced is balanced by an equal or greater step to simplify; removing costs, improving speed, reducing downtime etc – ie reducing complexity.

CASE STUDY

A global woven polypropylene fibres manufacturer

A client in the polypropylene fibre and fabrics sector prided themselves on their engineering quality and being able to manufacture to each customer's performance requirements. This had led over the years to a dramatic proliferation of product variations, matched by the commitment of the client to be always able to support their customer with re-orders in the future. Although the quality of the product delivered merited the industry-leading price premium and the factory was one of the biggest globally, it barely returned a profit. I supported the client in a detailed review of the full costs of serving each customer and each product variation (using Activity-Based Costing methodology). With the details of the full costs available, they then engaged with each of their customers, presenting them with options of price increases to match the full cost of serving them with the existing product lines and ordering patterns, or switching to alternative product variations, which would be within the new core product range of my client. Most customers chose to switch as they would benefit from lower prices and shortened order-deliver cycles. The factory reconfigured to have a specialist shop for bespoke orders, and the main production team produced the core product range. The resultant jump in overall efficiency was matched by increased throughput, facilitating both a spurt in growth of market share and a return to healthy profitability.

Although the above example does not need to be seen in the light of 4IR, it did in fact play a significant part in the evolution of the corporation to 4IR. The specialist part of the factory provided an environment suited to experimentation with new products and new processes. This proved effective not only for my client but also for their customers, enabling deeper partnerships in co-creation and rapid experimentation.

Internal and external talent

The mechanisms of talent management (internal and external) are outside the scope of this book and the underlying research. However, research did highlight the increasing focus and dynamism in talent management, accompanied in several cases by elevation of the position of Chief People Officer within the corporation.

In highly dynamic corporations the skills and capabilities required for success are frequently reviewed, together with active discussions on whether the required talent should be within or outside the firm. The CHRO (Chief Human Resources Officer) reports increasing flux, flexibility and dynamism in how internal talent is recruited, developed, retained and deployed. The adoption of HR analytics is enabling significant changes to talent and performance management.

Many CHROs also commented that the increasing dynamism of internal talent management is being mirrored by the changes in attitude and mechanisms of engaging external talent. This includes greater dependency on short- and long-term individual contractors, engaging a wider variety of consultants and interim managers, as well as outsourcing of supporting functions and services. Additionally, some made reference to increased 'insourcing' – contracting with expert facilitators to support internal initiatives such as accelerating innovation.

Highly adaptive corporations have embraced the notion that good talent may rotate through the firm, then out – and then may return, depending on the priorities of the firm and the priorities of individual talent at any particular moment. Deliberate effort is required to stay relevant to key talent when they are outside the formal structure of the corporation or are engaged as contractors, consultants or advisors. Firms with high dynamic capacity foster relationships with key talent that are collaborative rather than exploitative, promoting their development and well-being whilst recognizing that their tenure with the firm is uncertain.

Leadership traits: Reposition & Reconfigure

Simplify: reduce complexity

As the company evolves and seeks to increase its ability to adapt (eg creating options and including choiceful duplications) there is the risk that complexity will increase. Complexity (eg organizational, operational or product line) slows the business down and undermines performance. Therefore, managers must vigorously seek to simplify, ie to reduce complexity whilst pursuing greater adaptability. For example, as positions are harvested, the product range or service offerings may be reduced. As experience accumulates with established processes, the managerial levels may be reduced. As new options are explored, the teams are empowered to demonstrate results rather than required to seek permission to experiment. Responsibility for reducing complexity can be pushed deeper into the organization through reducing the resources available, forcing choices of what to retain, merge or abandon. For further reading on this topic I refer you to the book *From Complexity to Simplicity* by Simon Collinson and Jay Melvin.[13]

Persuasion and influence

Individuals in dynamic organizations need to be effective in implementing changes through working with others often across boundaries or in fluid groupings. They are often unable to rely on positional power or subject matter expertise, instead having to have effective skills of persuasion and influence. As people use short-cut heuristics in assessing a situation and making decisions, understanding these and using them in communications helps to make a leader more effective. Robert Cialdini explored six such heuristics in his book *Influence*.[14] Influence, he argued, can be significantly enhanced by leveraging the principles of Scarcity, Authority, Commitment, Social Proof, Liking and Reciprocity. Framing is another approach that can enhance the ability to influence others. The way people choose between alternatives that involve risk, where the probabilities of outcomes are uncertain, is influenced by the way the proposition is presented (ie framed). In general people have a bias to avoid potential losses and they tend to discount potential upside benefits. Therefore, if a choice is framed as loss avoidance then there is a greater likelihood of acceptance. This insight, known as Prospect Theory,[15] was created in 1979 and developed in 1992 by Daniel Kahneman and Amos Tversky.

Global vision

A Global Mindset is the ability to form high-functioning relationships, to communicate clearly with and to absorb information and insights from around the world, bridging cultural differences. The global mindset is important for understanding and appropriately responding to the complexities and nuances of the global environment. A global mindset enables a globally operating firm to make better operational and strategic decisions, for example: being able to spot and take advantage of emergent opportunities; making better decisions between local adaptation and global standardization; being better able to reconfigure and manage global supply chains and outsourced support; and passing, combining and applying knowledge between countries. In 4IR companies a global mindset is particularly important as there is heightened importance in embracing perspectives and insight from around the world, informing insightful choices and acting with precision. Individuals develop a global mindset in different ways but the most important is direct personal experience, particularly if tasked with resolving a complex challenge. Success in such situations requires the manager to understand the nuances and details of the local situation, and to work closely with local staff (and with external parties). These assignments may expose executives not only to different cultural, social and political contexts but also to markets with very different levels of dynamism or stability.

Mindset: Adaptability

To heighten the ability of the corporation to Reposition & Reconfigure, executives need to operate with awareness that performance is optimized by aligning operations behind clear strategic choices whilst retaining the capacity to adapt as the future unfolds. Allowing low-cost (or no-cost) optionality to exist whilst still pursing maximum impact with the chosen strategic thrusts. Decisions to adjust or adapt are the result of learning from closely observing and experiencing the emergent reality of the marketspace.

KEY CONCEPTS: CHAPTER 4

The key to Repositioning & Reconfiguring is fluidity – to flow through change, to flex and morph in a timely manner, instilling greater confidence in and expectation of what will be achieved in the future. The meta-capability to Reposition & Reconfigure rests on three practices:

- Define new marketspaces:
  - o   new marketspaces;
  - o   real options.
- Glide, don't jump:
  - o   don't be afraid to rebuild;
  - o   harvest before exiting.
- Choiceful duplication:
  - o   similar but different;
  - o   internal and external talent.

The leadership traits most supporting the capability to Reposition & Reconfigure are:

- simplify: reduce complexity;
- persuasion and influence;
- global vision;
- mindset: adaptability.

FIGURE 4.5 Reposition & Reconfigure: Key management practices

Adjust the scope of activities conducted by the firm and its relationships with others in the eco-system. Morph the portfolio of offerings and the choice of marketspaces in which to compete.

- **Define new marketspaces**
  - Establish unique definition for the space to compete in, unconstrained by existing definitions of industries and sectors. Focus on a set of needs of the target customers.
  - Continuously explore adjacencies, adjust the offering and refine the business model. Act incrementally rather than with dramatic step-changes.
  - Probe new opportunities. Create options. Determine the value of creating an option for future expansion, or the cost of withdrawal. Harvest existing positions that become less relevant.

- **Glide, don't jump**
  - Determine the portfolio (business lines, offerings, geographies, customer segments) required for the vision of the future.
  - Develop expertise at identifying, negotiating, acquiring and integrating new acquisitions as well as birthing new businesses from existing business units.
  - Develop expertise at preparing businesses for exit. Retain and recycle key talent from legacy businesses. Harvest businesses before exit, maximize strategic advantages.

- **Choiceful duplication**
  - Intentional choices to increase adaptability through maintaining alternative options (products, services, market presence and capabilities) whilst recognizing the cost penalties, eg of excess capacity.
  - Design supply chains with a degree of redundancy (eg dual or triple sources of components) in order to be robust under the influence of volatility in a logistics context (eg exchange rates, logistics delays, etc).
  - Increase flexibility in human resources by maintaining capabilities in-house whilst also seeking external support. Maintain relationships with key talent that rotates through the firm, so that they can return if needed in the future.

Reposition & Reconfigure

Endnotes

1 https://www.blueoceanstrategy.com/what-is-blue-ocean-strategy/ (archived at https://perma.cc/ML9J-X86P)

2 Tully, S (2012) How Dave Cote got Honeywell's groove back, *Fortune*, May

3 Ibid

4 Ibid

5 Morton, A (2016) The Coca-Cola Co moves into coffee bean market in Brazil, Just-Drinks, https://www.just-drinks.com/news/the-coca-cola-co-moves-into-coffee-bean-market-in-brazil_id120802.aspx (archived at https://perma.cc/KW4U-JQ6V)

6 Laursen, L (2018) Here's why Coca-Cola is buying Costa Coffee for $5.1 billion, *Fortune*, August

7 https://www.applegazette.com/steve-jobs/steve-jobs-quotes-the-ultimate-collection/17/ (archived at https://perma.cc/BWT9-8VBG)

8 https://www.investopedia.com/terms/r/realoption.asp (archived at https://perma.cc/2E3D-U2KL)

9 https://www.investopedia.com/terms/r/realoption.asp (archived at https://perma.cc/2E3D-U2KL)

10 Elberse, A (2013) Ferguson's Formula, *Harvard Business Review*, October

11 Kent, A, Lancefield, D and Reilly, K (2018) The four building blocks of transformation, *Strategy + Business*, Winter

12 McKinsey (2010) McKinsey conversations with global leaders: Jim Owens of Caterpillar, November

13 Collinson, S and Melvin, J (2012) *From Complexity to Simplicity: Unleash your organization's potential*, Palgrave Macmillan

14 Cialdini, R (2008) *Influence: Science and practice*, 5th edition, Pearson

15 Kahneman, D and Tversky, A (1979) *Prospect Theory: An analysis of decision under risk*, Econometrica

PART THREE

Drive audacious growth: Be purpose-led

Drive audacious growth in pursuit of a purposeful vision. This requires commitment to a meaningful and motivating purpose, developing a cadre of managers who are able to think and act ambidextrously, resolving dilemmas and overcoming seemingly conflicting goals. It requires establishing the expectations and the mechanisms that facilitate continuous evolution.

Part Three explores the three factors that are essential for the pursuit of high rates of growth: scaling fast in pursuit of a vision that is meaningful and motivating for the many that will need to lend their support; overcoming the challenges that will frequently emerge as the market and competitive contexts evolve; the need to be constantly adjusting and adapting both within the organization and across the evolving network of relationships in the eco-system. These *factors* are embodied in the attitudes and behaviours of the management cadre:

1 **Purpose-led**
   Establish a forward-leaning strategic posture, strengthened by the pursuit of a meaningful purpose and adoption of audacious goals. Think about possibilities not probabilities.

2 **Ambidextrous**
   Require and enable managers to individually and collectively think and act ambidextrously; to overcome, resolve or dissolve dilemmas of competing goals; exploring, testing and challenging existing assumptions,

constraints and practices with others, in order to find new ways forward. Ambidextrous: adopting a 'both, and' mindset.

3 Continuous evolution

Establish the expectation of and mechanisms to enable the organization to continuously evolve; adopting new technologies, adapting processes and structures, morphing scope of activities, pivoting direction, whilst striving for new levels of performance.

FIGURE III.1 Drive audacious growth: Be purpose-led

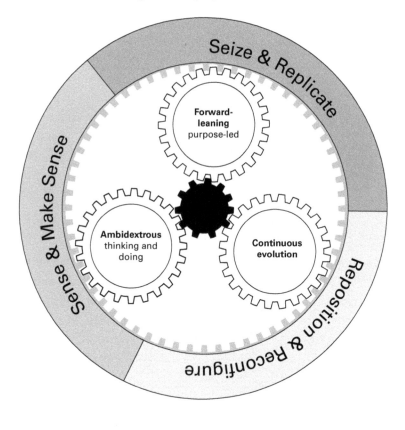

05

Purpose-led, forward-leaning

IN BRIEF

The 4th Industrial Revolution is in progress. Whether and how to act or react is something each leadership team must decide for themselves. Whether they perceive themselves as 'gazelles' or 'lions';* whether they have ambitions to shape the unfolding future, or to survive whilst others do so, are questions of strategy. Firms that lean into the future (adopting a strategy that embraces the changes of the 4th Industrial Revolution and implementing the management mechanisms and leadership practices of managing 4IR) outperform their peers. This is proven in terms of both perceived competitive advantage and comparative stock price movement (over a five-year period).

Management mechanisms that enable leadership teams to adopt a strategic posture that leans into the future include:

1 **Being purpose-led**
   Organizations that proudly and authentically adopt a purpose to positively impact society attract and keep highly engaged top talent. They weather difficult times better than their contemporaries, score higher on trust indexes, and also attract investors seeking ethical investment opportunities. The pursuit of purpose is not an alternative to the pursuit of profit; to 'do good' they have to 'do well'.

2 **Pursuing possibility not probability**
   As technologies enable the speed of business to accelerate and the contexts become increasingly dynamic, the future is increasingly difficult to predict. Disruption is increasingly accepted as a norm, as are 'bubbles and crashes' and black swan events. The antidote to the inherent uncertainty is to lean more forwards into the future, adopting the maxim (ascribed to various

visionary figures such as President Lincoln, Peter Drucker or Nobel Prize winner Dennis Gabor) 'The only way to know the future is to create it.'

3 **Adopting adaptive strategic planning**
Strategic plans and choices still need to be made in contexts that are fast changing and uncertain. On the basis of those choices, investments are made and resources deployed, in order to make competitively winning moves. However, strategic analysis and choices cannot be made in absence of recognition of the inherent uncertainty and ambiguity. Leaders need to create a balance between formal (eg periodic) and informal (eg episodic) planning processes and between developing a point of view about the future but not holding rigidly to forecasts.

*Note: There is a reputedly African proverb that says 'Every morning a gazelle wakes up and knows that to survive it must outrun the lion and other gazelles. Every morning a lion wakes up and knows that it must outrun the gazelles and choose wisely in order to survive. Whether you are a gazelle or a lion, each morning you must wake up, choose wisely and run faster than others.'

Purpose-led

Organizations that do not become purpose-led in the next 25 years will cease to exist. I know this is a provocative statement, but I believe it to be true.

In 4IR, expectations of investors, employees, consumers and other stakeholders around the role and impact of corporations on society and the environment are changing significantly. In response, organizations need to see themselves existing for the good of society, not just their shareholders, customers and employees.

Note: This section has been co-authored with Simon McKenzie of the Bridge Institute (http://www.bridge-institute.org/mac-mckenzie).

What does it mean to be purpose-led?

Aristotle offers an excellent definition of purpose. In short, it is a focus on objectives and social goals bigger than ourselves. It is about looking after all of society, not just one's immediate stakeholders (shareholders, employees and customers). 'Wherein your talents and the needs of the world lie, therein lies your calling' – Aristotle.

FIGURE 5.1 Why, how, what of being purpose-led

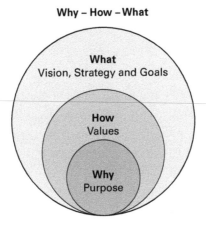

It is also important to define what having a sense of purpose is not. It is not a short-term promotion or initiative (eg 'day of service'); it is not something that is siloed with a single person or department rather than embedded across the organization; it is not belief in a silver bullet to solve all your problems; it does not involve putting the financial health of your company in jeopardy.

A clear and meaningful purpose (*why* the organization exists) provides the foundations to shape the vision, strategy and goals of the organization (*what* the organization does). It is also important to be clear on the organization's values (*how* we do things). In short, your purpose is your North Star, and your values are the ground you walk on.

The benefits of being – or becoming – purpose-led are profound and significant. For one, purpose-driven firms perform much better financially. According to Raj Sisodia, author of *Conscious Capitalism*[1], purpose-driven firms in the United States produced an outstanding aggregate return of 1,681 per cent over the first 15 years of the 21st century, compared to 118 per cent for the S&P 500.

Purpose also sparks innovation but acts as an antidote to short-termism. According to Simon McKenzie of the Bridge Institute:

[Purpose] is the greatest motivator (more important than compensation); it attracts and retains the best talent, it boosts the brand, increases well-being and empowers women. Women are more purpose-led on average, and hence much more likely to join purpose-led organizations.[2]

In short, organizations that are purpose-led can outperform, on multiple different measures, those that are not.

CASE STUDY
Southwest Airlines

Herb Kelleher, founder of Southwest Airlines, built the airline for the purpose of giving people the freedom to fly. This has built a remarkable business, based around creating friendly, reliable, low-cost air travel. In 2018, it reported its 45th year of profits in a row.

Not only has Southwest Airlines done incredibly well, but Kelleher's initial move inspired a purpose movement that would change the course of how visionary companies would treat their employees, their stakeholders, customers, vendor partners, communities and their nation.

TABLE 5.1   Stock price of Southwest Airlines compared to Dow Jones Industrial (December 1999 vs December 2019)

	December 1999	December 2019	Increase	Compound average per annum
Southwest Airlines	US$ 10.7	US$ 54.6	510%	8.5%
Dow Jones Industrial	US$ 1421	US$ 3221	227%	4.1%

Discover and embed purpose

To discover purpose requires the organization to find the overlapping point of these three questions:

1 **Talents and strengths:** Where does your organization's potential for greatness reside?

2 **Passions:** What motivates the people that make up the heart and soul of your organization? What do they care deeply about?

3 **Societal need:** What problems is the organization equipped to solve? What differences do the people of the organization aspire to make in the world?

Because buy-in and engagement are critical, it is essential to begin this discovery process at the top of the organization with structured discussions in the leadership group and with key stakeholders. The process needs to be

FIGURE 5.2   The sweet spot of purpose

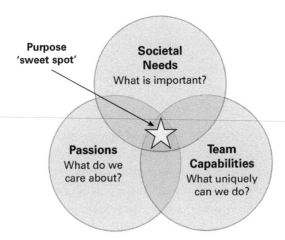

collective and encompassing, engaging broadly before then structuring choices and distilling out the essence of the purpose for the organization. The final stage is to understand the needs of the world that the organization could potentially serve. This involves research into the whole eco-system, including appropriate NGOs, the government, the civil society actors, the customers and the supply chain partners of the organization.

The data from these processes is synthesized into potential themes and purpose statements. These then need to be tested globally, to ensure the words and meanings translate well across the world. All of this groundwork is essential, as it needs to be embraced and championed by the organization thereafter.

Once discovered, the purpose needs to be activated.

Activate purpose

MISSION-CRITICAL PRINCIPLES
There are some mission-critical principles one must consider when activating purpose. These are headlined below:

- In order to truly live and embed a newly defined purpose, the purpose must be viewed primarily as a driver of growth and profitability and therefore of the long-term sustainability of the organization. This requires significant discipline in assessing all aspects of the business through the lens of the new purpose and this should inform all key strategic and operational decisions.

CASE STUDY
Lifebuoy

Globally, 6 million children die before they reach the age of five, many due to preventable infections. Handwashing with soap, particularly after using the toilet, can reduce diarrhoeal diseases by over 40 per cent and respiratory infections by 30 per cent. The Lifebuoy 'Help a Child Reach 5' handwashing behaviour change programme was launched in 2013 – to move the needle on child mortality. The programme created a significant impact, with mothers reporting reduction in incidence of diarrhoea from 36 per cent to 5 per cent, and 26 per cent more children washing their hands before meals. The programme has been scaled across India and other countries. Simple low-cost interventions have been shown to reduce child mortality by up to 44 per cent.

The programme shows the power of finding the sweet spot of purpose: the organization's strengths (eg marketing soap), the passions of the organization (eg cleaning hands) and addressing a societal challenge (reducing the high cases of child mortality across the world).

- Building the story to inspire employees and other stakeholders is integral to this journey, but it must be done in light of the above or else the purpose will be another 'nice to have' that is hard to disagree with but will not define and drive the business on a daily basis. As importantly, if this is not followed up by clear actions consistent with our stated purpose, it may create credibility issues in the business, and there is mounting evidence that it will in fact do more harm than good.

- Leadership advocacy is key, especially from the executive leadership and CEO. Every employee needs to be shown how the purpose can be central to the long-term business success. It is a process of education and inspiration, not merely engaging communication and branding. The goal is to make the purpose relevant at multiple levels in the organization. Ultimately, there needs to be a clear line of sight between the purpose and the front-line team members of the organization. What does this mean for me in my role – what can I do to make this real in my business?

- Enhanced attractiveness as an employer and reputation are undoubtedly important benefits too; these should be at the forefront of consideration in decision making across the organization.

CASE STUDY
CVS Pharmacy[3]

In September 2014, CVS Health became the first national retail pharmacy chain to stop selling tobacco products in all of its stores because it conflicted with its purpose of helping people on their path to better health.

Though this decision amounted to a loss of $2 billion in annual sales, the drugstore giant's overall sales increased in the following years thanks to new business and new innovations the business created for itself, including growing a pharmacy benefit management division and growing their medical services businesses. This demonstrates the power of purpose in helping create innovative businesses.

It also demonstrates the importance of living purpose from the very beginning, embedding it into every decision, and doing so with great courage.[4]

- Rapid momentum and a sense of creating a movement for change are important to the success of this effort. Demonstrating significant and visible early examples of the purpose being lived are crucial to building credibility. These become the most powerful platforms against which to build the internal story and shape the wider engagement of people across the organization.

The key steps to become purpose-led

There are three key pieces of work to be done, to activate the new purpose. These are set out below.

1 Build a governance team

The governance team provides oversight of the purpose activation, ensuring focus and alignment across the organization. They are responsible for the company-wide issues (eg how the board and executive leadership team make decisions according to the purpose, reporting, company-wide policies, etc). The governance team also decides on the purpose metrics of success. A strong team is required with the right levels of institutional power, credibility and expertise so that informed, intelligent decisions are made. Key functions and businesses should be represented, and each member should be committed personally to activating the purpose globally. Determination of the right members of this team is the first step needing attention.

CASE STUDY
8 Islands

Nikoi[5] and Cempedak[6] private islands are part of a group (eight islands) dedicated to achieving the highest standards of sustainability in the tourism sector globally.

The leadership have set an inspiring purpose and vision to be a beacon to the world on how businesses can be run, which leaves the planet in a better place and provides profound life and economic opportunities for the most vulnerable people they employ.

They have activated their purpose in everything they do – from the way they grow their food sustainably to the way they employ and develop their staff. They have partnerships with NGOs to maximize their positive impact in the region where they operate. Their measures of success are aligned around culture, conservation, community and commerce.

This story shows that purpose is as important for small organizations as well as global multinationals.

---

2   Activate purpose in the businesses and function

Each business needs to be supported through the same journey to activate the purpose in their respective areas. These are the six outcomes that each leadership team will need to achieve:

a   Identification of the big opportunities – what possibilities emerge from the new purpose? What are the activities in the business already under way that we can amplify?

b   Alignment of process, objectives, culture and performance – how do these need to be aligned to be congruent? What does living our purpose mean for our future strategy and for the culture of our organization?

c   Determining the measures of success – what will success look like? How will we know we have been successful?

d   Transforming of mindset – what shifts in mindset will be needed if we are to be successful?

e Purposeful partnerships – what government, business and civil society partnerships do we need to cultivate to bring our purpose to life?

f Identification and celebration of quick wins – what quick wins can be found to generate momentum and credibility? What might be two to four strategic experiments we can make in the organization that are relatively low-risk rapid prototypes of living our purpose?

Empowering delegated teams to shape and deliver the big purpose opportunities enables a significant proportion of the leaders and employees to get involved and inspired. It is also helpful to coach the senior leaders on how to become purpose-led, including areas such as visionary leadership and system thinking.

3 Launch purpose to the organization
This is where we inform, inspire, and engage the whole organization. This includes making short films sharing the story of the new purpose and purpose immersion events for all the employees to get informed and involved. Each event immediately creates an opportunity for every leader and employee to see its relevance and commit to a few actions they can take in the short term to bring the purpose to life in their part of the organization.

It is profoundly important to do all these key steps well and rigorously. It is also essential to do all of this with authenticity; recent research illustrates companies that 'purpose-wash' actually do more harm than good. For instance, this could involve running an advertising campaign on a social issue, without living the purpose holistically inside the organization. Employees will see clearly the disconnect between espoused values and lived values and the unambiguous lack of integrity, and either become increasingly disengaged or leave.

CASE STUDY
Coca-Cola

Coca-Cola's heritage, dating back to 1886, and their global renown for marketing excellence, gave them confidence and operational excellence that had delivered strong growth and profitability. By 1998 their price/earnings ratio reached a peak of almost 60[7] with stock trading above $42 per share. But the market had been changing for several years; by 1999 the movement away from high sugar-content carbonated soft drinks to more healthy alternative beverages was in full swing. Coca-Cola initially struggled to adapt to the changes in the market, lacking the required level of dynamic capacity. In

FIGURE 5.3 Coca-Cola (KO) share price December 1989–2019

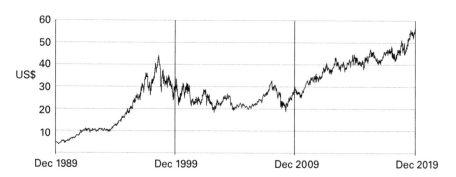

1999, maintaining their reliance on their marketing excellence and their focus on the core product suite, they achieved a new volume record (16.5 billion cases) and pushed revenues up 5 per cent over 1998 to $19.8 billion. However, they also reported a 31 per cent drop in net income.

Undaunted, Doug Daft, a 30-year veteran of the company and then chairman and CEO, opened the annual report of 1999 with the statement:

> Around the world, the history of the Coca-Cola Company is one of great brands, tremendous consumer enthusiasm and innovation. Even more than that, it is a history that reveals to us today the core attributes that, properly heeded, nurtured and applied, are just as important to our success in the 21st century as they were in the beginning.[8]

By March 2000 the stock price was down to $22. Over the next 10 years, Coca-Cola had to reinvent itself, acknowledging the changed market context and trying new approaches. An apparent recovery in results in 2007 was reflected in the stock price finally breaking back above $30 per share at the end of that year, only to once again collapse to just above $20 per share by February 2009. Whilst this collapse was impacted by the general market sentiment there was also enduring concern over whether and how the company would turn around its long-term performance. However, this also ushered in an era of rebirth, making deliberate choices on the priorities for the long term, aligned with a new sense of purpose. In 2010 the company embraced a vision for 2020, saying 'we must get ready for tomorrow today'.

FIGURE 5.4 Coca-Cola mission and purpose statement[9]

Our Mission

Our Roadmap starts with our mission, which is enduring. It declares our purpose as a company and serves as the standard against which we weigh our actions and decisions.

- To refresh the world...
- To inspire moments of optimism and happiness...
- To create value and make a difference.

Purpose-aligned societal initiatives embraced by Coca-Cola as part of its rebirth included the following:

- **'5by20'** which supported the economic empowerment of 5 million women entrepreneurs globally by 2020, and an initiative to make Coca-Cola the first Fortune 500 company to replenish 100 per cent of its global water use.

- In 2013, the company added **'Framework for Action'** to tackle key human rights risks (child labour, forced labour and land rights) in the agricultural supply chain, through collaborating with suppliers, bottlers and other stakeholders. The goal was to complete initiatives in 28 countries by 2020.

- In 2018, Coca-Cola announced the start of a new initiative to collect and recycle the equivalent of 100 per cent of its packaging by 2030.[10] 'The world has a packaging problem – and, like all companies, we have a responsibility to help solve it,' said James Quincey, President and CEO of the Coca-Cola Company. 'Through our World Without Waste vision, we are investing in our planet and our packaging to help make this problem a thing of the past.'[11]

FIGURE 5.5 Growth of $10,000 invested in Coca-Cola stock 2009–2019 (with dividends reinvested)

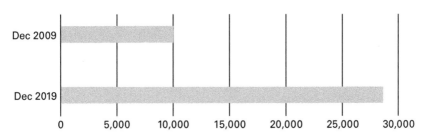

Since the rebirth of the company, Coca-Cola has created significant value for stockholders (see Figure 5.5), as well as positive impact in the societal issues aligned with the purpose of the firm (note: there was a stock split in 2012). It took 10 years from the collapse of performance and stock value in 1999 for Coca-Cola to truly embrace a new vision, mindset and way of operating. Now that they have been on the new trajectory for 10 years, the question is whether they are able to adopt a new vision and whether the pursuit of the purpose will continue to drive outstanding returns.

Possibility not probability

The leadership team of the corporation will tend to 'lean forward' into the unfolding, unknown future when they are motivated to do so in pursuit of a bold, inspiring mission and they are convinced they have identified a winning strategy.

All firms require some degree of forward momentum as the executive seeks to incrementally improve performance. What differentiates those that build a higher level of dynamic capacity is a dissatisfaction with the status quo and the desire that they will 'put a ding in the universe' (to apply Steve Jobs' description of the mission at Apple).

The degree of dynamism that the leadership team seeks to drive the corporation to adopt is a function both of the marketspace that the company is engaged in (some sectors have been evolving rapidly, eg cloud-based services, whilst others have been more stable, eg rail transportation) and of the strategic posture of the firm (eg to be a 'path finder' in the sector or a 'follower').

Consider the following examples of firms determining the appropriate strategic posture:

- Tata Communications, the India-based, global telecommunications company, is operating in a 'dynamic' sector and they have adopted a forward-leaning strategic posture.

- Conversely, Heraeus, the German-based globally operating trader and supplier of rare metals, operates in a relatively 'stable' sector and does not describe itself as leaning forward.

- US-based, global beverage company Coca-Cola, on the other hand, operates in a sector that, although clearly evolving, is regarded as being moderately 'stable' and yet as a firm, Coca-Cola has adopted a forward-leaning strategic posture.

> The sector or market doesn't determine the strategic posture: that is the job of the leadership.

As the data demonstrates, a forward-leaning posture is an important motivator for a firm to build up its dynamic capacity, which leads to it outperforming its competitors. Increasing the dynamic capacity of the corporation requires work to nurture and invest in strengthening the three meta-capabilities discussed in Part Two. The motivation to do so requires that the leadership is leaning forward into the future.

Firms that have adopted a bold and motivating *purpose* tend to have a forward-leaning posture and to evolve higher levels of dynamic capacity. Executives are committed to achieving the mission; the purpose motivates and engages them. The goals linked to the mission are inherently future-oriented, and the leadership and staff strive to attain meaningful societal goals rather than settling only for period-by-period incremental improvement in operating results.

Jack Ma, founder of Alibaba – a firm that is both in a highly dynamic marketspace and has adopted a very strong forward-leaning strategic posture – makes several observations (note, these and other well-known quotes by Jack Ma are easily found online).

> 'If you want to be a great company, think about what social problem you can solve. It's about solving the social problems.'
>
> 'You cannot unify everyone's thoughts, but you can unify everyone through a common goal.'
>
> 'The world will not remember what you say, but it will not forget what you have done.'

In adopting a meaningful societal purpose for the organization, it is important to focus the unity on the goal and not on 'everyone's thoughts', as Ma points out. The leadership should cultivate diversity of skills and perspectives within their organization, so that different ideas and ways of thinking can be brought together in the pursuit of the one unifying goal. This sentiment is echoed by Céline Schillinger, Head of Quality Innovation & Engagement at Sanofi Pasteur:

> With the purpose-based movement we have triggered, people from everywhere in the organization are co-creating the change, and they're proud to do so. You see amazing natural leaders emerge from deep within the company. They're bringing their colleagues with them. There's a totally unprecedented amount of engagement and energy. This is a fantastic human asset for our culture and our performance.[12]

But having a sense of purpose or mission is not enough – as Jack Ma's final quote, above, makes clear. The organization must also take actions – lean forward into the future, take risks, take steps to act, and *do*. It is these actions and accomplishments that will keep re-energizing the company and sustain the forward-leaning posture.

Analysis of the survey data shows a significant correlation between the strength of the sense of purpose and the level of dynamic capacity. As one executive in the agriculture sector described it:

> A couple of years ago [the top management team] embarked on a quest to find a defining question that we could adopt, that answering it would become our mission as an organization, something that would unite and inspire us. It took us about 18 months but then we decided to focus on addressing the impending global challenge of a world that cannot feed itself, simply won't be able to produce enough food for the projected population with the land and water resources that are available within current farming practices. Now this is something important, meaningful and relevant for our business. It's inspiring and motivating and leads us to try harder in everything we do. As we succeed in addressing this we, of course, are moving the company forward and creating greater shareholder value.

The purpose of the organization aligns the efforts of managers who are facing very different market contexts and conditions. As the senior executive at an alcoholic drinks company said:

> By definition, a total global strategy will fail, because [management] tools in Nigeria don't work in New York, by definition, but a common purpose, well that's different; business is won separately in each market but we need to be aligned – flexibly!

For several organizations, the purpose is derived from the origins of the corporation and the values of the founders. For others, the defining purpose has been adopted more recently, in part in response to discovering the weakness of orienting around short-term financial results when the market is experiencing fundamental changes.

Peer into the ambiguous, uncertain future

The accelerating speed of business and increasing acceptance of unstable, dynamic business contexts are also placing a premium on the skills and aptitude for executives to manage well in ambiguous situations. Ambiguity and uncertainty are the opposite conditions to the environment that the 'principles of scientific management' were intended for. How then are leaders able to be decisive, to make clear strategic choices, when the future is unknown and the context increasingly ambiguous and uncertain?

A key part of the answer to this question is that firms with a high level of dynamic capacity, whose leaders also acknowledge they operate in an environment of high ambiguity and uncertainty, pay great attention to the meta-capability to Sense & Make Sense. Executives often refer to thinking about alternative scenarios that could arise.

Scenario planning

Scenario planning is a tool in strategic planning that starts from the premise that the future is unknown yet we have to make good strategic choices. Importantly, scenario planning focuses on the possibility, not probability, of forecasts. It has proven to be a very robust process, as it is not linear, whereby the merits of favoured solutions are argued about, nor is it conducted in isolation by the 'strategy team'. Rather it is an interactive workshop process that engages the executive team directly. For these reasons, it is particularly valuable in corporations with a forward-leaning orientation toward the uncertain, unfolding future.

Many traditional approaches to strategic planning are 'linear' – ie there is a statement of problem or of objective and then a solution is derived and a plan of action created. The process progresses through a number of steps; we try to solve them as we might for a mathematical equation. We gather data, conduct analyses, map relationships, recognize patterns from prior experiences, estimate probabilities, compare estimates of potential risks and benefits of different options, and make recommendations and take decisions.

The weakness of this type of approach is that we don't have data on the future, so we make assumptions, and the patterns that we recognize are from past experiences that may not have relevance in the dynamics of the future. As an alternative, the use of non-linear planning and decision-making processes is increasing.

Non-linear processes have a number of stages, each combining an initial expansion of the options or aspects that are being considered (divergence), before then a choice (convergence) of one or a very few options that will be taken on further:

- Each exercise to diverge identifies multiple possible options for the future, which requires pushing the thinking further and benefits from including in the team individuals with different perspectives; it provides the opportunity to challenge existing dominant group thinking and assumptions.

- Each exercise to converge, to make a choice, requires debate and discussion as to why; this makes explicit underlying assumptions, providing the opportunity for these to be challenged for relevance in the unfolding future.

An advantage of a non-linear process is that it has to proceed from one stage of diverge-converge to the next, sequentially, as the outputs from one stage (ie the choices made during convergence) are the inputs for the next step of divergence. Similarly, the convergence choice cannot be done until the options from the preceding divergence step have been created. This can reduce the influence of biases and implicit assumptions (eg about the future or what has worked before) that often dominate a linear process, wherein possible solutions or what might be deemed to be unacceptable may be in mind from the outset.

The scenario-planning process diverges in the consideration of all the trends and forces of change before converging down to select what are considered the most impactful and least certain. From these selected forces, there is a divergence in identifying multiple different potential futures that could result if the selected forces were to play out in different ways (typically four or five potential futures are described). A critical part of the process is the discussion that ensues between the executives as they collectively build up descriptions of distinctly different, potential future scenarios. No probability is placed on one or other of these scenarios. No one scenario is designated the best case or most probable; they are all regarded as simply being possible, each representing distinctly different competitive environments for the corporation.

When confident in the description of each scenario, the executives collectively consider each scenario in turn and determine the set of strategic initiatives that would best position the corporation in that scenario. The key is to move from the discussion of the scenario per se to instead focus on the strategic moves that would be relevant in a scenario. Once again this is a divergent step as the number of strategic options generated across the multiple different scenarios could be quite extensive.

The next step is therefore to converge. The executives step back and look across the list of strategic choices identified across all the different scenarios, and typically some similarities emerge. Some strategic choices may have been noted in three or four of the scenarios, some may appear in only one or two, and some may be noted as a positive move in one and instead be seen as negative in another scenario. Consider these two examples:

- For a telecoms operator, building out further infrastructure was deemed to be very attractive if the regulatory environment remained unchanged, but if greater competition was allowed in, they did not want to build out further but instead wished to wait until the next generation 5G infrastructure was ready.

- A consumer goods client used scenario planning to decide whether, when and how to enter the Myanmar market. A high early investment in building up manufacturing and related infrastructure would enable them to influence the evolution of the sector and secure attractive tracts of land. However, it could be a liability financially and to corporate reputation if the political or social conditions in the country deteriorated.

The scenario-planning process

The array of strategic choices can then be integrated into a single coherent strategic plan by assigning each strategic choice into one of the categories shown in step 4 of Figure 5.6 and described below:

- **Do it:** This category is for those strategic choices that appear in most of the scenarios as game-changing in a positive way; or they could positively influence the evolution of the market to a 'preferred' scenario.

- **Create an option:** This is for those positive moves that may only be relevant in one scenario but for which it is important to act early (before knowing if the future is unfolding in the direction of that scenario). An 'option' is a lower-cost initial move that provides the foundation that can quickly be scaled up if appropriate:

  o The consumer goods company contemplating Myanmar identified buying several plots of land for manufacturing and warehousing activities but held off from building on them until there was greater clarity on the evolution of the situation. This signalled their commitment to the country and secured the locations they desired but did not overly commit to them immediately.

- **Back-up insurance:** This category is to protect against competitive weaknesses that might happen in one or other scenario, especially if choices in the 'Do it' category proved to be the wrong move as the actual future emerges:

  o A traditional retail bank was identified to acquire shares in three different crypto-currency start-ups, so that if the traditional banking activities are significantly disrupted then they will themselves also be partial owners of some of the disrupting players.

- **Fast-follower:** Some of the strategic choices may be relevant only if one or other scenario actually plays out, and if it does, then the company can move quickly to implement the identified initiative. To be able to move as quickly as possible, the executives should note the leading indications that will be monitored so that they will not be caught 'flat-footed'.

FIGURE 5.6   Scenario-planning process

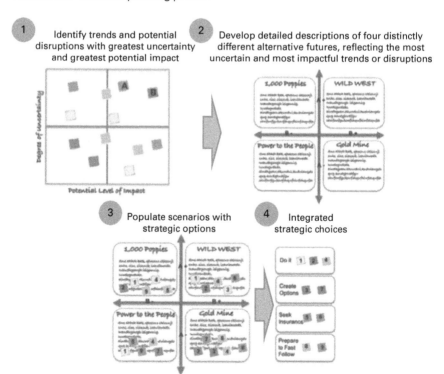

The scenario-planning process is highly relevant for companies that adopt a more leaning-forward strategic posture, as they need to be peering into the ambiguous, uncertain future and yet make good strategic decisions.

Adaptive strategic planning

As long ago as 1994, Henry Mintzberg noted significant flaws in the way that many companies were conducting strategic planning. The flaws were due to the way strategic planning was managed as a process and the implicit beliefs regarding the certainty of forecasts that predicted the future. He correctly argued that when strategic planning is done well it is an art that combines logical reasoning and leveraging data with the acknowledgement of assumptions and recognition of uncertainty. Good strategic plans define and make clear choices against which resources are deployed, and yet also ensure flexibility for adaptability as the future unfolds. The speed of business has only accelerated since then; the faster the evolution, the more critical it is that strategic plans establish clear choices of where and how to compete and also provide the ability to adapt. The unknown future arrives faster and waves of disruption remodel markets and businesses. The three flaws that Mintzberg pointed to are:

1 **Formalization:** The strategy is set through a periodic formal process, and once set, the strategy remains in place until the next planning cycle.

2 **Detachment:** Detachment occurs when the response is that we cannot predict the future nor adhere only to periodic planning cycles, so therefore we should be reactive to the events as they unfold.

3 **Prediction:** Forecasts for the future market, competitor actions or sales volumes, etc, are expected to be precise and are therefore rigidly held onto, despite the oft-quoted recognition that 'the only thing we know for certain about a forecast is that it is wrong, unless we manipulate the future'.

The flaw of *formalization* is a typical approach for many leaders. It can take the form of complying with a planned budget norm of behaviour. An amusing anecdote was shared by an executive at a manufacturer of construction and mining equipment:

> One year the annual strategy planning meeting was held in Hong Kong, so the global president came out here. We had prepared all the data on market share by competitors and predictions of growth rates and presented what we thought were well-argued, fact-based analysis and forecasts for the next year. Midway

through the presentation the president interrupted us and told us that he didn't believe us and that we were 'sand-bagging' and could do much better. We argued our case, but it was clear that we were not being listened to. We dutifully adjusted our forecasts. A couple of days later, at the end of the trip, on the way back to the airport I rode with his private secretary and asked why he had doubted our market analyses and forecasts. The answer was simple – on the ride in from the airport on the very first day, looking out of the window of the limousine, the president had made a mental note of all the equipment he had seen in use on the multiple building sites along the road. His conclusion was that we were vastly over-stating our market share as he hadn't seen much of our equipment. Back at the office the next day I called this the 'windshield survey'. Being in Asia there are many infrastructure projects, many that are not near the main highways, not visible to a passing luxury limousine. Our action plan became clear; the following year we asked all our clients to place our equipment within sight of the road and we told the limousine driver to take a long way to the office, making detours past project sites. Sure enough we were complimented for the growth in market share we had achieved, even though our sales had been a little lower than the forecast (the number that had been revised upwards the prior year).

Falling foul of the flaw of formalization is perhaps particularly easy to understand as corporate processes demand responses. Leaders often feel that they do not have the time, energy or influence to change the corporate policies. Some regional leaders cited that they themselves hope to be promoted back to HQ at some point in the future, and once there they might have the ability to influence change. Until then they would be unwilling to challenge corporate norms.

Others cited that across the portfolio of the countries that they managed, they would expect some 'winners' and some 'losers' in any given period. Crucially, they do not know which will be which, so the regional numbers will hopefully balance out. The formal budget and planning processes provide transparency and ensure accountability, which are positive attributes that should not be lost. However, increasing instability in markets could be met with an approach of 'and what else?' This would mean that when budget plans in some markets are achieved quickly, there is still the expectation to achieve more, whilst continuing to pursue targets for other markets that might be experiencing difficulties.

The second flaw is of *detachment*; it occurs when the management doesn't try to forecast or predict the future. This mindset is often found in start-up situations where the leaders are focused internally on delivery and externally

on demand generation. They may do this because they have limited histori-
cal track records on which to base their projections.

However, a form of detachment is observed in some long-established,
domestically dominant firms. These entities have protected or even monopo-
listic positions in their home markets. Although such corporations sometimes venture abroad, their primary source of value capture is little impacted
by open-market forces. Regulated businesses such as banking, telecommunications, media and utilities often enjoy privileged positions in their home
market. They are impacted by longer-term cycles and technological disruptions but as incumbents are protected from the turbulent dynamics that can
make and break companies elsewhere.

For years (prior to the Royal Commission investigation[13]) Australian
banks reaped supernormal profits while financial institutions in other markets
struggled through financial crises, increasing deregulation, sector consolidation and the rise of FinTech. Such corporations reap the advantages of their
positions and seek to shore up the regulatory defences that protect them. The
main priorities of such companies are to defend their advantageous incum-
bent position and manage relationships with regulators, government stakeholders and the media, rather than direct much attention to predicting market
dynamics and the impact that will have on their business.

To quote one executive at an Asian regional bank with its HQ in
Singapore:

> We know that major change is going to happen, but it won't happen that fast,
> probably 20 years or so, we are very protected by the regulator. So 'yes' we have
> to be aware, watching and thinking and making a few adjustments, but the
> structure of the industry is good for us here.

In exceptional cases, a leader (typically from outside the entity) is appointed
into such organizations to drive a major turnaround, reversing long periods
of stagnation or decline.

A stand-out example of such a leader is Eddie Teh, who led the turnaround
and subsequent substantial growth of PSA Corporation (the port terminal
operator based in Singapore but with global presence). The actions of such
leaders provide insight into how major corporations can be refreshed, and
even sluggish entities can become more agile. However, such leaders tend to
be short-lived; they are quickly dismissed once it is deemed the emergency has
passed and more conventional leadership is once more preferred at the helm.

Prediction, the third flaw that Mintzberg warned about, is adhering to
the belief that the future can be foretold. Business executives recognize this

behaviour, especially when seeking approval from HQ for investments or other new initiatives. The following anecdote from a global consumer goods company executive describes it well:

> The Myanmar market will be very important for us, but it's very unpredictable right now. In order to make the investment case pass through the internal hurdles we have had to create a very positive picture. If we miss the opportunity to be operating on the ground, in country early and building relations with the military, then we will set back our business significantly and [major global competitor] will secure a dominant position. No one at HQ or in Finance wants to hear the truth, so we just told them what they wanted to hear in order to get the investment approved. Sooner or later I will no doubt be dragged before the powers that be to explain why we have missed the numbers – but by then we will have got our foothold established, and anyway, who knows? Perhaps the forecast numbers will work out – it's a wild frontier of a market.

A similar example from Brazil:

> I recently signed on to represent [a leading UK-based clothing brand] in Brazil. The brand is quite well known but they have never had anyone appointed to represent them here before. After going through all the vetting about my knowledge of their products and validating my existing business they then asked if I would guarantee them [$X,000,000] of business in the first year. How would I know? They have never sold here before, I don't know if they will be difficult or easy to work with, what their internal prioritization of support will be, if they will provide suitable product support or training, etc. I could see it was a deal-breaker for them, so I just said 'yes'. I'll try to figure it out of course, but we are off to a bad start when they are showing such a naïve attitude. Somewhere, someone in their administration department has probably now filled in a box in an Excel table and thinks that has somehow locked it in as a forecast.

What Mintzberg labelled as the 'fallacy of detachment' is the failure to make and adhere to clear strategic choices. Many clients with whom I have worked have held onto the excuse of reactive flexibility (ie making the choice to not decide) rather than commit to clear choices. If leaders don't sufficiently commit to key initiatives, they don't sufficiently create new or reinforce existing sources of competitive advantage for the corporation. They develop too many options and have too many initiatives ongoing. This dilutes management attention and dissipates resources. By contrast, corporations that achieve superior performance do so by achieving an artful blend of being adaptive whilst also remaining firmly anchored on a consistent long-

FIGURE 5.7   Avoid the three fallacies of strategic planning[14]

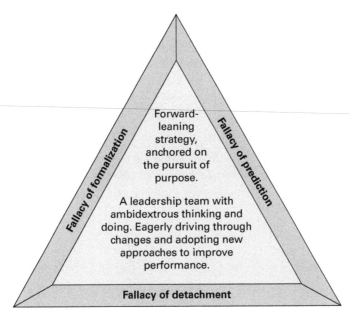

term strategic plan. They build and leverage dynamic capacity. These firms operate within the zone bounded by the dangers of the three fallacies of strategic planning.

Adaptive strategic planning – strategic plans and choices are still required to be made in contexts that are fast changing and uncertain. On the basis of those choices, investments are made and resources deployed, in order to make competitively winning moves. However, strategic analysis and choices cannot be made in absence of recognition of the inherent uncertainty and ambiguity. Leaders need to create a balance between formal (eg periodic) and informal (eg episodic) planning processes and between developing a point of view about the future but not holding rigidly to forecasts.

Leadership traits: purpose-led, forward-leaning

Purposeful leadership

A purpose is aspirational. It explains how the people involved with an organization make a difference, giving them a sense of meaning. Leaders need to be able to point to the greater good of the purpose, inspiring others and themselves. For the organization to be purpose-led requires that everyone is engaged with the purpose, especially the leadership and executive cadre, who are most visible. Actions and decisions must be aligned with the purpose; words and actions must be consistently reinforced. Each executive must authentically connect personally with the purpose, being able to tell their personal story to others. They must role-model appropriate behaviours, demonstrating how their personal outcomes are united with the pursuit of the collective good. They must be effective at energizing each individual and the teams that they manage in the pursuit of the purpose, able both to celebrate successes and to address misalignments. They must also be adept at holding peers to account, focusing on primary importance of the collective good.

Strategic thinking in complexity and ambiguity

In 4IR businesses there is heightened complexity in how to think strategically, not only for the choices of today based on the analysis of market and competitive data and trends, but also with forethought to the different possible futures that could emerge and the different paths that the organization could follow. Strategy remains the art of deciding clearly what to do and, equally importantly, what not to do – then to commit sufficient resources to the choices made so as to be able to achieve differentiating outcomes. However, in 4IR there is added complexity as technologies are enabling non-traditional competitors to enter markets, leveraging scale advantages from other business domains and thus the boundaries of industries and sectors are blurring and being redrawn. The corporation of 4IR is focused not only on achieving economic returns but also on the pursuit of its purpose and increased commitment to and scrutiny of its social responsibilities. Within this matrix of objectives and constraints the speed of evolution of the marketspaces is increasing, necessitating strategic planning for multiple steps, further compounding the complexity of each choice.

Decision making in uncertainty

Executives in 4IR businesses must be able to take carefully weighted and thoughtful decisions whilst recognizing inherent ambiguity and uncertainty. They must avoid projecting assumptions from the past (or today) to try to make sense of the emergent future, instead being open to the emergence of a different reality with alternative customer and competitor dynamics.

They must also avoid the temptation to delay making decisions until more data is accumulated. Not committing sufficiently to the choices made or spreading resources across a broad series of options will undermine performance. Similarly, executives cannot seek unrealistic assurances and guarantees about forecast accuracy from team members; the executives must themselves carry the burden of decision making in ambiguity and uncertainty. Approaches such as choice structuring can help focus attention on decision-critical assumptions, which can then be explored through the design of specific tests and experiments. Similarly, a 'real options' approach explicitly includes consideration of probabilities of path development. Mastery of these and other techniques can help executives develop competence in making good decisions in full recognition of uncertainty and ambiguity.

Mindset: Courageous

Executives need to be courageous. They must have the courage to set ambitious goals, to pursue purpose and share their personal story of their connection to the purpose. They must be willing and able to share and discuss their logic for decisions and choices and to have their interpretations and perspectives challenged by others. They need to take decisions responsibly whilst conscious of the inherent uncertainty.

KEY CONCEPTS: CHAPTER 5

A key factor determining the corporation's ability to achieve competitively superior performance, whilst being buffeted by the dynamics of 4IR, is being able to leverage its dynamic capacity in the consistent pursuit of a long-term vision. For the leadership team to be forward-leaning there are three important components.

- Purpose-led:
  - Determine the purpose for the corporation. Where the distinctive capabilities of the organization can be combined with the heart-felt passions of the employees and stakeholders to address a meaningful societal need.
  - Activate pursuit of the corporate purpose. Aligning strategic and operational choices, establishing and reporting in key metrics, and establishing a culture of holding each other accountable and reinforcing the pursuit of the purpose.

- Possibility not probability:
  - o Peer into the ambiguous uncertain future. Connect the pursuit of the corporate purpose with insights for how the future may unfold, establish period-specific mission and objectives.
  - o Use techniques such as scenario planning to embrace divergent perspectives, explore options for action and establish an integrated, coherent plan.
- Adopt adaptive strategic planning:
  - o Avoid the three fallacies of corporate strategic planning: over-reliance on formal plans and processes; conviction that forecasts are correct; and avoiding responsibility for developing a point of view on the future.
  - o Create a balance between formal (eg periodic) and informal (eg episodic) planning processes and between developing a point of view about the future but not holding rigidly to forecasts.

Leadership traits that support being purpose-led, pursuing a forward-leaning strategy:

- purposeful leadership;
- strategic thinking in complexity and ambiguity;
- decision making in uncertainty;
- mindset: courageous.

Endnotes

1 Mackey, J and Sisodia, R (2014) *Conscious Capitalism*, Harvard Business Review Publishing

2 www.bridge-institute.org (archived at https://perma.cc/DC7D-68AY)

3 https://cvshealth.com (archived at https://perma.cc/38HF-C65K)

4 CVS Health (2014) CVS Caremark to stop selling tobacco at all CVS/pharmacy locations, https://cvshealth.com/newsroom/press-releases/cvs-caremark-stop-selling-tobacco-all-cvspharmacy-locations (archived at https://perma.cc/38HF-C65K)

5 https://nikoi.com (archived at https://perma.cc/FR3S-99N7)

6 https://cempedak.com (archived at https://perma.cc/XKL9-4W77)

7 Inkrot, E (2015) Coca-Cola today vs. 1998, Seeking Alpha, https://seekingalpha.com/article/3218856-coca-cola-today-vs-1998 (archived at https://perma.cc/R82Z-PQ3L)

8 Coca-Cola annual report, 1999. Chairman's statement

9 https://www.coca-colacompany.com/our-company/mission-vision-values (archived at https://perma.cc/5HWV-VHUW)

10 https://www.coca-cola.com.sg/stories/world-without-waste (archived at https://perma.cc/JX3S-672P)

11 Business Wire (2018) The Coca-Cola Company announces new global vision to help create a world without waste, https://www.businesswire.com/news/home/20180119005104/en/Coca-Cola-Company-Announces-New-Global-Vision-Create (archived at https://perma.cc/4FZ3-W682)

12 Borderless (2017) How to successfully transition into a new leadership role, https://www.borderless.net/news/borderless-leadership/how-to-successfully-transition-into-a-new-leadership-role/ (archived at https://perma.cc/EAP9-VZF3)

13 https://treasury.gov.au/publication/p2019-fsrc-final-report (archived at https://perma.cc/LCC2-R9VB)

14 Adapted from Mintzberg, H (1994) The fall and rise of strategic planning, *Harvard Business Review*

06

Ambidextrous: 'Both AND' mindset

IN BRIEF

Ambidextrous leaders are able to simultaneously pursue seemingly conflicting goals, for example optimizing business results today whilst also investing in new research and development and other activities that will help improve performance in the future. The greater the proportion of executives who are required to manage the tensions of seemingly paradoxical options, the better the competitive performance of that organization. Conversely, corporations that seek to organizationally divide by reference to the tensions (eg a future business team vs core business team) struggle to adapt as the future unfolds. For example, a traditional retailer may think it simpler to initially establish and operate an online business completely separately, but over time it will need to integrate the customer insights and supply chain solutions from the online business to adapt the traditional business in order to remain competitive. If the retailer had established two separate organizations then the crossover of insight will be slowed, individually the business units will pursue actions that optimize their part of the whole, and an eventual merger of the two will be resisted or more complex to achieve, which undermines overall performance. Ambidextrous leaders manage across the tensions of competing objectives and they thrive when in positions that span organizational boundaries:

1 **Ambidextrous leaders** pursue two (or more) seemingly conflicting goals at the same time, such as achieving the results this period whilst investing for better performance tomorrow. Conversely, leaders who are unable to operate ambidextrously may swing between alternative positions, thereby enhancing short-term results but undermining overall performance. For example, if the company is ahead of revenue (or profit) forecasts they may deploy excess income into investments with longer-term benefits (such as

upgrading equipment). Conversely, if the company is underperforming the forecasts, they may withhold such investments, even if budgeted for, as they seek to match the forecast performance for the period. Ambidextrous leaders seek to consistently invest in the improvements for tomorrow whilst also delivering on the present period results, irrespective of the conditions they face in the market.

2 **Winning together** is when colleagues consciously make choices that they believe will improve collective performance whilst recognizing that their decision may have negative implications for themselves. This may be with regards to loaning key talent, disproportionately funding a corporate project, or other ways. Additionally, winning together means a sharing of information and insight, acting with the recognition that information shared heightens collective performance, whereas information withheld may give a fleeting sense of greater power for an individual.

3 **Productive reasoning** is the choice to engage with others with whom you might disagree in order to understand why they hold their point of view or have reached a particular conclusion that you disagree with. It is the willingness to explore and test your own and another person's logic, interpretation and data set in order to enhance understanding, with the goal of learning, to uncover biases or blind spots and to find new ways forward.

Executives who thrive in ambiguity and are able to simultaneously pursue seemingly conflicting goals increase the dynamic capacity of the corporation. The greater the proportion of the executive cadre that is expected to think and act ambidextrously, the greater the dynamic capacity. Ambidextrous leaders:

- optimize results today, whilst investing for better performance tomorrow;
- thrive in ambiguity and uncertainty, able to take and pursue clear strategic choices.

Ambidextrous thinking and doing

Since the earliest days of management theory, the dominant model of organization has been to separate individuals into groups that focus on specific tasks and have metrics of performance that maximize transparency, leaving minimal space for ambiguity or discretion. This model was first put forward by Frederick Winslow Taylor in his 1911 book *The Principles of Scientific Management*[1] (to which I referred in Chapter 3). It is why most corporations today are organized by function and not, for example, by multifunctional teams. It is also why hierarchical decision making and authority are preferred over self-governing teams. In most corporations today there is the preference to separate out who or which parts of the organization focus on the future and which focus on delivering the results today; there are new product development teams or new venture groups which are ring-fenced and managed separately to core business units. The dominant belief is that the greater the focus of the team, the greater their ability to optimize performance and the easier to measure.

As the speed of business accelerates and instability is the 'new normal', the separation of goals to different teams or individuals is an impediment to adaptability and flexibility, requiring top-down adjustments of organization structure, performance metrics and incentives. Instead the complexity and paradox being created by the changes in the marketspace must be confronted and managed by the individuals and teams closest to the issue, achieving performance results today whilst adapting for tomorrow in order to consistently pursue the longer-term purpose. As discussed at the beginning of this book, in contrast to previous eras, in 4IR greater value is created by the ability to navigate to the future than in the results produced today.

All customers want the best solution for their needs and expect their needs to be understood and innovatively serviced by the vendors, irrespective of which internal business unit they may be assigned to. Executives that are exposed to, expected to and supported in being able to optimize conflicting goals proactively test and probe constraints and seek new ways forward. They seek solutions for their customers (internal or external) that combine the best of what's new and what's existing.

Since the mid-1990s, management literature has increasingly reflected the realization that value creation and business performance innovations are often the result of executives being required to hold and manage with two or more seemingly conflicting goals. The tension caused them to solve the conundrum by understanding complexity, testing constraints and challenging assumptions, rather than simply being focused on one or the other or allowed to seek a compromise outcome. Now, with the speed of evolution of 4IR, we see clear evidence that the greater proportion of executives expected to think and act ambidextrously, the better the performance of the corporation.

> The greater the proportion of the organization engaged in managing the tension between the conflicting goals on a day-to-day basis, the greater the dynamic capacity of the firm.

In 4IR the rapidly changing circumstances create more rapid swings in performance, and as such it is increasingly not viable to structure the organization around the pursuit of different objectives. It is increasingly important to develop the ambidextrous thinking (and doing) of managers at all levels, echoing the conclusion of Professor Derek Abell, former President of the European School of Management and Technology:

> All managers must be able to wear both hats. Solutions at the very top, however, are only a part of the story. Duality is also needed further down the line. Companies must be aware of the trap of believing that today-for-today is primarily the task of middle management, while today-for-tomorrow is the preserve of top management…
>
> … Many employees […] closer to customers and supply-chain partners are confused by what they interpret as contradictory signals about today and tomorrow. The two agendas can be integrated only if those who need to implement today and change for tomorrow understand the reasons.[2]

The ability of executives to operate effectively whilst holding in tension the need to optimize performance results 'today' and prepare for a 'tomorrow' that is uncertain is referred to as being ambidextrous, which Tushman and O'Reilly describe as 'establishing a balance between optimizing current firm performance (refining routines) and seeking new configurations of activities and assets for future competitive advantage'.[3] Those firms that have a high proportion of executives who routinely think ambidextrously (eg Unilever, Tata Communications) have higher dynamic capacity. An executive at a global heavy equipment manufacturer noted:

> I think this is a big challenge because we are becoming more mobile, more multinational, there are big implications for how we develop leadership teams, how to build global understanding, and yes that concept of simultaneously managing short- and long-term needs.

Professor Roger Martin, the former Dean at Rotman School of Management, published his work on integrative thinking in 2007. He highlighted the differentiating impact of integrative thinking (managing with the tension of opposing objectives) for the performance of corporations and exceptional leaders:

> Successful CEO(s) […] have the predisposition and the capacity to hold in their heads two opposing ideas at once. And then, without panicking or simply settling for one alternative or the other, they're able to creatively resolve the

tension between those two ideas by generating a new one that contains elements of the others but is superior to both. This process of consideration and synthesis can be termed 'integrative thinking' [dual leadership].[4]

He emphasized that 'it is this discipline – not superior strategy or faultless execution – that is a defining characteristic of most exceptional businesses and the people who run them'.[5]

Whilst ambidextrous thinking (adopting the 'both AND' mindset) is increasingly recognized as being essential for firm performance, it is also hard to achieve. The prevalence of traditional organization models (whereby functions and responsibilities are divided into specialized units) mitigates against the expectation and opportunity for managers to develop or demonstrate ambidextrous thinking. An executive at Syngenta believed that conflicting priorities should only be addressed at the senior-most level; however, he also pointed out that they have worked on increasing the awareness of competing goals and pressures through training of the top 300–500 executives.

An executive from a major beverage company reflected on the period of transformation that the company had journeyed through, a transition that he estimated to have taken over 10 years. The businesses were being disrupted and, slowly, the culture of the firm, not only its portfolio of beverages, was changed:

> Looking back, there has been a fair amount of turnover in the senior
> management team during transition. Different models have been implemented,
> you have a reorganization, which means that in our case definitely you have
> less units, and because of that, you need fewer senior managers. There's greater
> ambiguity and complexity now. Sometimes it's more driven by capabilities that
> need to change. Results today are crucial, but the ability to decide, commit to
> and consistently pursue longer-term priorities is also essential. Now, there are a
> lot more deliberate choices on what is important for the long term. Balancing
> the short- and long-term objectives still sits largely with senior management as
> not everyone has been able to make that transition.

Developing mastery at ambidextrous thinking and doing is not easy, requiring awareness, developing the right techniques, support from the leadership, performance metrics that require management of conflicting goals – and lots of practice.

Like most executive skills, ambidextrous thinking, and doing, can be developed:

- An essential first step is to see the need and the opportunities to apply the duality of thought. Be aware when tempted to jump into making trade-offs or 'judgement calls'; perhaps it is better to pause and reflect and to explore the apparent tension between the seemingly opposing outcomes.

- Explore the assumptions and the constraints that have led to the apparent tension between desirable outcomes. A second important ingredient is a sense of curiosity and desire for continuous learning.

- A third ingredient is the sense of ownership for the overall resulting performance, optimized through addressing the tension, rather than only making trade-off decisions.

- Practice and feedback – training oneself to pause, reflect and look more broadly is difficult, especially in the face of time or cultural pressures to act decisively. A mentor can help, or if none is available, asking a confidant in the team to help keep you on track can provide the signals to remind you to make space to reflect.

Like all muscles, this management muscle will need training, so don't expect to be an expert immediately. Keeping in mind the three foundations of behaviour change – motivation, opportunity and ability – ask for feedback, consider the impact of your attempts to be effective and seek to inculcate the behaviour with others in the wider group, so you can support one another.

An executive at a global beverage company noted:

> Historically we were a company that rewarded somebody who had a great idea and implemented it. Then somebody else would say, 'I want the same success. I too need to come up with my brilliant idea.' We had a bit of that 'lone hero' culture. Nobody really was interested in taking somebody else's idea and then making it more successful, because that was not really rewarded on a personal level. Now our emphasis is on bringing in new ideas, things we may have seen work somewhere else, sharing them for the benefit of everyone and also to build on each other's ideas and initiatives – we get smarter together.

Professor Derek Abell noted, 'Managing with dual strategies [ambidextrously] is a state of mind, not just another management tool.' Roger Martin develops this line of thinking when he contrasts integrative thinking with conventional or binary, 'black and white' thinking:

> The consequences of integrative thinking and conventional thinking couldn't be more distinct. Integrative thinking generates options and new solutions. It creates a sense of limitless possibility. Conventional thinking glosses over

potential solutions and fosters the illusion that creative solutions don't actually exist [...] Fundamentally, the conventional thinker prefers to accept the world just as it is, whereas the integrative thinker welcomes the challenge of shaping the world for the better. [6]

Winning together

A unified sense of being on the same team, winning or losing together, stands out as the 'secret sauce' of firms that evolve executives who act ambidextrously. Two specific practices enable and underlie the sentiment of winning together:

- There is an understanding that sharing, rather than withholding, information enables greater collective performance. Several of the companies stressed how they have to make significant concerted efforts to create open access to information internally:

  o An executive at Syngenta noted: 'Sharing knowledge and resources is so very important, requiring that there is both the willingness to give the knowledge as well as the willingness to receive it and use it. We have worked on this extensively.'

- There is flexible allocation or sharing of resources whilst recognizing that collectively there is a resource-constrained environment. By supporting one another, trapped or under-leveraged resources can be better deployed for the collective good:

  o An executive at a leading ceramics company shared: 'New perspectives must be embraced as "no one is as smart as everyone together"'; also, 'The best new ideas and opportunities are often at the boundaries between departments, or even through our collaborations with external parties... for example research universities, or our suppliers.'

  o A global leader in household goods and FMCG noted: 'I've seen more of a shift away from the vertical, and silo, and very linear thinking to a lot more of the partnership thinking. A lot more of the senior executives, even if it's not clearly stated in their KPIs, realize the culture is to support the whole company.'

A further example of these behaviours can be seen at Google, where the discipline and culture ensure everyone stores and accesses all their documents on the shared cloud drive that anyone can interrogate to find documents and initiatives across the globe. Plus, everyone is encouraged to work on projects that inspire them within the firm but that may be outside of their area of responsibility. There is an in-house platform where individuals can post the initiatives they wish to create and seek volunteers from across the firm to lend support.

In contrast, a transportation company had been struggling to transform to become more customer focused and competitively agile despite a 'burning platform' of accumulating losses and a new direction being clearly communi- cated by the senior leadership. A stumbling block was the lack of a strong sense of 'winning together'. The culture throughout the corporation was said to reflect the national culture of being very respectful of one another. Upon examination, 'very respectful' meant not commenting on each other's activi- ties, initiatives or reports. It meant not collaborating across boundaries (for fear of being seen to be interfering) and not holding each other to account. To move forward, they had to broaden their understanding of the term 'very respectful', to recognize that everyone has a responsibility to everyone else to support the collective success – and that requires collaborating and challeng- ing across boundaries. Providing high challenge, coupled with overt high support for one another, and working on joint initiatives proved to be essen- tial ingredients in order to build momentum in their transformation.

Productive reasoning

Tasked with realizing significant adaptation of the scope of activities, lead- ers must be effective at communicating their case and equally at listening to and understanding the perspective of others. Productive reasoning leads to greater mutual understanding and results in mutual commitment to a path- way forward. The concept and techniques were pioneered by Chris Argyris and Donald Schön, published in 1974.[7]

They coined the expression 'double-loop learning'. The first 'loop' is to apply established decision-making rules and processes to achieve the desired goals. However, when the outcomes are not as intended or agreement cannot be reached, then a second 'loop' is undertaken, which is to explore each other's assumptions and those assumptions that are embedded in the way the problem has been defined, the desired outcome defined or that have shaped the established decision- making process. This second loop is intended for mutual learning; it can lead to creativity and innovation and reframe what seemed to be paradoxical situations. Double-loop learning can also resolve tensions between colleagues, providing a common language and approach to explore differences and work together to find better solutions. The approach moves understanding from narrow to broader,

TABLE 6.1 Common (Model 1) behaviour compared to productive reasoning (Model 2) behaviour[8]

	Model 1		Productive Reasoning
Governing variables	Action Strategies	Governing variables	Action strategies
Define goals and try to achieve them	Design and manage the environment unilaterally (be persuasive, appeal to larger goals).	Valid information	Design situations where participants can originate actions (experience high personal causation).
Maximize winning and minimize losing	Own and control the task (claim ownership, be guardian of definition and execution).	Free and informed choice	Task is jointly controlled.
Minimize generating or expressing negative feelings	Unilaterally protect yourself (use inferred categories, little or no directly observable behaviour, be blind to impact on others).	Internal commitment to the choice and constant monitoring of its implementation	Protection of self is a joint enterprise and oriented toward growth (speak in directly observable categories, seek to reduce blindness about own inconsistency and incongruity).
Social virtue: help and support	Give approval and praise. Tell others what you think will make them feel good about themselves.	Social virtue: help and support	Increase others' capacity to confront their own ideas and to face unsurfaced assumptions, biases and fears.
Social virtue: respect for others	Defer to other people; do not confront their reasoning or actions.	Social virtue: respect for others	Attribute to others a high capacity for self-reflection and self-examination.
Be rational	Unilaterally protect others from being hurt (withhold information, create rules to censor information, hold private meetings/conversations).	Be relational	Personal investment in understanding and promoting the learning and development of others. Bi-directional protection and support whilst also challenging.

from static to dynamic. Beyond its application to a single issue, the double-loop learning approach can be adopted organization-wide and may result in positive changes in the culture-as-lived of the firm, supporting being a learning organization with stronger collegiality. Argyris described 'Model 2' behaviour, required of the executives if double-loop learning is to be successful (whereas he contends that most people default to Model 1 behaviours).

Leadership traits: ambidextrous leaders

Own the dilemma

Executives are ambidextrous leaders when they simultaneously pursue goals that seem to be in tension with each other – there is a paradox or dilemma. They need to hold themselves to address the tension, pursuing both objectives, not allowing themselves to drop down into either-or or trade-off and compromise, eg optimizing results today whilst also investing to improve performance tomorrow. This is hard to do and requires that they have a high sense of ownership responsibility to achieve the seemingly impossible. Ownership is the anchor that prevents them dropping down into quick fixes, or only owning one side of the paradox and giving the other over to someone else or delegating both sides of the paradox to separate teams with the hope that the separate solutions will somehow be complementary (eg a futures division and the business-as-usual team). A strong sense of ownership empowers them to explore the construct of the paradox and to probe and test constraints and embedded assumptions. Given a task of reducing customer support costs and manufacturing costs they might return with a solution to streamline the product range. Compelled by the strong sense of ownership, they will take the time they require. This may infuriate those seeking resolution and instruction, but they will not be rushed into compromise – the status quo may continue until they own the answer.

Embrace new perspectives

To resolve the two (or more) sided dilemma, the ambidextrous leader needs a new way of thinking about the situation. To do so they will explore alternative perspectives that others may bring. Unless someone else has the exact answer to the paradox, through enquiry the ambidextrous leader will seek to understand how experiences elsewhere could be relevant. They listen attentively to the explanations of the situational context, the underpinning logic and the insights from elsewhere. They then seek to adapt the 'key' that worked elsewhere to unlock their current dilemma. The executive needs to develop their ability to look outside of their context, identifying situations and people whose perspective may be relevant. They must be able to engage those people with an open, enquiring mind, to distil key insights. This requires not being dismissive or judgemental about what they are hearing as they precisely need a new way of thinking about the dilemma; it would no longer be a dilemma if their existing approaches were adequate.

Creative, systems thinking

Creative thinking is essential for managing paradox. The very definition of the paradox is a result of the beliefs and assumptions and the systems by which the corporation operates. A corporation operates with a nested set of policies and practices that have evolved over time by incremental choices and conscious design. Planning cycles, financial controls, organization structure, HR policies – maintaining these as they are will result in the continuation of the paradox as is. Resolving a paradox requires understanding the system, identifying which practices, if changed, would remove the dilemma. It also requires identifying what adjustments would be required throughout the rest of the system in order to support the proposed change, considering if these would create negative complications elsewhere. For example, if managers are required to maximize results today whilst also preparing for better performance tomorrow, how should they be incentivized? Should it be only on the results delivered today? The 4IR is increasing the speed of evolution of both the external context and the internal structures and operations. The consequence is that more managers must be ambidextrous, managing paradox and dilemma; managing both results today and heightening performance today. This necessitates that executives must acquire greater competence in developing creative solutions and an alignment of the measures and rewards of individual contributions.

Mindset: Problem solver

Ambidextrous leaders must own the paradox, investing time and energy to understand the systems and to explore new perspectives that can lead to them developing creative solutions. The key mindset is that of a problem solver; whilst they are working day-to-day they keep turning over the dilemma in their mind, seeking to resolve the enigma.

KEY CONCEPTS: CHAPTER 6

As the speed of business accelerates, executives increasingly have to confront ambiguity and uncertainty. The greater the proportion of executives who are able to resolve paradox, to think and act ambidextrously, the greater the capacity of the firm to respond to the changes, challenges and opportunities of 4IR:

- Ambidextrous leaders recognize paradoxes and instead of opting for trade-off decisions they explore the assumptions and constraints that define the tensions of the dilemma. They embrace new perspectives and the application of new technologies and techniques as they seek ways forward that enable overall performance to improve.

- There is a strong sense of winning together, whereby the objectives and metrics of performance for an individual are accepted as being subordinate to the collective objectives of the team, or corporation. In the spirit of winning together colleagues share information and enable key resources to be deployed across boundaries. Colleagues hold each other to account whilst also supporting each other's performance.

- Ambidextrous leaders pursue collective and individual learning and collaboration. Techniques such as productive reasoning help to mitigate conflicts and misunderstandings whilst facilitating engagement with one another, especially on important issues where there may be impassioned debate.

Traits supporting leadership ambidexterity:

- own the dilemma;
- embrace new perspectives;
- creative, systems thinking;
- mindset: problem solver.

Endnotes

1   Taylor, F W (1911) *The Principles of Scientific Management*, Harper and Brothers
2   Abell, D (1999) Competing today while preparing for tomorrow, *Sloan Management Review*, 16 April
3   Tushman, M L and O'Reilly, C A III (2006) Ambidextrous organizations: managing evolutionary and revolutionary change, *Managing Innovation and Change*, 1 July

4 Martin, R (2007) *The Opposable Mind: How successful leaders win through integrative thinking*, Harvard Business School Press

5 Ibid

6 Martin, R (2007) How successful leaders think, *Harvard Business Review*, https://hbr.org/2007/06/how-successful-leaders-think (archived at https://perma.cc/HBR7-GFJ7)

7 Argyris, C and Schön, D (1974) *Theory in Practice: Increasing professional effectiveness*, Jossey-Bass

8 Adapted from Argyris, C and Schön, D (1996) *Organizational Learning II*, pp 93, 118, 120, Addison-Wesley Publishing

07

Continuous evolution

IN BRIEF

The speed of business is accelerating; for a firm to maintain and build success it must act nimbly, creating and seizing opportunities as well as responding and adapting to changes in their environment. The firm will be in continual flux and movement; just like a professional athlete, they will not be 'rooted to the spot' but always adjusting. This challenges the traditional perspective of change which expected a sequence of 'unfreeze – move – refreeze' phases to be navigated. In 4IR, change is constant. People are not expected to be trapped in functional or business unit silos, but to be working in cross-functional teams or to have boundary-spanning roles. Individuals and firms must be comfortable in flux and change; the performance of the organization not slowing down during disruption caused by change but rather being invigorated and energized as new skills, roles, tools and processes are adopted.

Continuous evolution relies on three key mechanisms:

1 **Acceleration officer**

   A person in charge of pushing the adoption of new technologies and management techniques in order to enhance corporate performance in 4IR. Knowledgeable about the technologies being developed and adopted globally and the possibilities for restructuring business models and processes. Firms establish such a point of coordination in different ways but increasingly a new permanent position is being included in the C-Suite. The person acts on the mandate to change and transform the corporation, making it future-ready, now. They set the tempo of change, they act as clearing house for transformation issues arising, and they have the ability to redirect resources.

2 **Doctrine of change**

The approach to managing change and transformation in 4IR is different. There must be a doctrine that is understood by everybody, that acts to unite efforts whilst allowing autonomy of movement and empowerment of individual teams. The doctrine must encompass the values of the firm with regards to treatment of employees and other stakeholders and it must help to align team efforts towards the pursuit of the corporate purpose. The doctrine of change, consistently applied, builds trust, confidence and understanding, which support faster implementation of future and ongoing transformation initiatives.

3 **Evolution roadmap**

Creating and updating a transformation roadmap brings alignment and commitment as it enables dialogue between individuals who may have competing priorities. The roadmap shows how seemingly disparate initiatives will come together and how each move contributes towards the objectives, thereby enabling each individual affected to understand their contribution.

Change has changed in 4IR

Beyond the focus on the technologies that are fundamental to the 4th Industrial Revolution there is an equally significant shift occurring in how leaders lead and managers manage. The adoption of technologies, or more precisely accessing the benefits that technologies such as AI, machine learning, IoT and robotics bring, is a key dimension of the transition of an organization to thrive in the 4th Industrial Revolution. However, another equally important dimension is empowering and enabling 4IR talent. One of the most stark examples of the interplay between these two dimensions is the dramatic change in how leaders lead and managers manage transformation. Indeed, the term 'transformation' is decreasingly used by leaders operating in 4IR. Rather, there is an increased expectation of, and hunger for, continuous evolution, both incremental and transformational, and for that to be driven by managers and teams within the organization, not by top-down edict.

The mere mention of an impending 'transformation programme' may once have been enough to send managers and employees into a state of heightened anxiety. It may have been decided at the top of the firm that a great leap forward was necessary, perhaps changing the way it participated in the market, adopting a new technology or platform (such as SAP), digitally transforming, becoming more agile, or drastically changing the cost base or organization structure, etc. A transformation office may have been established to drive a wave of change through the organization, possibly with the support of external consultants, the hierarchy of actions being first to embrace a vision of the anticipated outcome state, then to design and execute a process for orchestrating change, and once achieved to then embed the new procedures and practices through retraining and aligning performance metrics.

FIGURE 7.1 Prior to 4IR: programmatic transformation; step-changes in technology advancement; transformation programmes to adapt and align talent and processes to leverage technology advances, resulting in transient superior performance of the organization

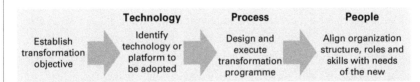

In the 4th Industrial Revolution change and adaptation are as pervasive as technology adoption; episodic transformation is supplanted by constant acceleration and agility. Our research shows that to achieve such dynamism an organization must nurture and celebrate a growth culture in which managers and staff are catalysts of change. In such organizations, the hierarchy of actions is the reverse of that of traditional approaches to transformation. Managers and staff throughout the organization are engaged in the pursuit of the purposeful mission. They are equipped, empowered and expected to see and pursue opportunities for improving the organization's performance. In the process of evolution they may identify, adopt or adapt new technologies. Of course, such organic growth also needs to be coordinated across the organization and insights, learnings and discoveries of processes, behaviours and technology applications.

FIGURE 7.2 4IR: continuous evolution; in 4IR technology is pervasive and continually evolving; talent that can enable speed and agility through the successful adoption and adaption of technologies is a critical (limited) resource that differentiates performance

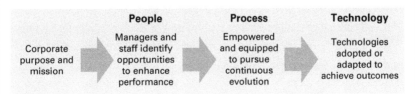

Competing and succeeding in 4IR requires firms to transform, to embrace new technologies, reformat processes and reimagine the roles of humans and machines. Before the speed of business accelerated to current levels transformation was often regarded as the process of moving from 'State A' to 'State B'. Indeed, one of the most influential early scholars of change management, Kurt Lewin, in the 1940s defined a three-step model as being 'unfreeze – move – refreeze', with the language clearly communicating the expectation to end up in a fixed, though new, configuration.

The speed of business in 4IR is accelerating and will continue to do so, which places a premium on the ability to continuously transform, absorbing the new and leveraging the strengths so created for dynamic advantage.

Let's return for a moment to the analogy of the tennis player introduced earlier in this book. When we are a beginner player we may be 'rooted' to the spot and stand square towards the net. We react to the balls that come at us. Highly proficient players, however, are constantly moving around the court to position themselves optimally. To update Lewin's model of 'unfreeze – move – refreeze': the real challenge is to stay in the 'move' phase. Beyond this is also the appreciation that the speed of response, the speed at which the corporation can adapt, can also be a source of competitive advantage. As with a tennis player, speed, agility and fitness may sometimes overcome strength and strategy.

Acceleration Officer

The Acceleration Officer ensures that the organization is continuously adapting, evolving through leveraging the new technologies, techniques and business models that are reshaping the dynamics of the marketspaces. The role of the Acceleration Officer is to look outwards in order to orchestrate internal change, in line with the pursuit of the overall purpose of the organization. The role may be incorporated within the position of the Chief Operating Officer or Chief Innovation Officer or similar, or may be a dedicated person. However, it should not be positioned as a singular programme of change or transformation, but rather an ongoing requirement, to be continuously evolving and accelerating.

- The Acceleration Officer plays an important role in navigating evolution. They peer intently into the fog of the unknown future, providing insights and assessments for the executive team. They are like a navigator on a boat that is approaching a rocky shore on a dark night, in thick fog facing strong winds and tides. This person is intently reading the instruments at hand, guiding the captain on how to adjust course and speed to avoid dangers, to find the clear passage that takes them safely and quickly towards their destination.

- The Acceleration Officer acts as a catalyst for change, being knowledgeable about the new technology and management practice options. They are responsible for helping to formulate the evolution roadmap. They also provide governance of the evolution journey, coordinating across all the different initiatives that are being pursued at any one time. As new technologies and practices are often novel to the executives of the organization, the Acceleration Officer also seeks to increase awareness and understanding of external developments and possibilities and their potential implications.

- The Acceleration Officer also establishes the mechanisms for coordination between teams working on different aspects of the transformation, ensuring that learnings from one team are shared with others and, if required, resources from one team can be redeployed to support another.

What's next?

In 4IR the firm is continually evolving, reflecting the 'new normal' of unstable, dynamic business contexts and the rapidly advancing technologies that can be adopted by the business. Change processes do not paralyse the organization with anxiety and confusion; rather, they breed enthusiasm, an appetite for more change, and the questioning of 'what's next' or '...and what else'? Stakeholders (including employees) come to expect change and are energized by the new possibilities that open up for them, which itself fuels the expectation to move even faster. A recent study by Harvard Business School professor Joseph Fuller[1] discovered that employees are anxious for change and to update their skills as they understand that this is needed to ensure that the firm survives and that they have jobs in the workforce of the future.

A key enabler is a strong sense of belonging that permeates the firm and, guided by a clearly articulated doctrine for change, enables a broad population across the firm to be empowered to drive implementation and alignment of change initiatives. The following examples illustrate the importance of mastering change in this way.

CASE STUDY
IBM

IBM has spent five years undertaking a continuous series of organization changes as it pursues the transition to a new set of business lines. The latest restructuring moves away from the divisions of Hardware, Software and Services to create new business units for Research, Sales & Delivery, Systems, Global Technology Services, Cloud, Watson, Security, Commerce and Analytics. 'Our choice is clear,' said then-CEO Ginni Rometty. 'We pursue a model of high-value innovation, rather than commodity technology, products and services. Our commitment to this model compels us to reinvent businesses continually; grow new ones organically and through acquisitions; and occasionally divest businesses that do not fit our profile.'[2]

A senior global executive at a European beer company shared the observation that:

> There is no one organizational model that works all the time; rather you think about a pendulum that is in continual motion, swinging at times more towards localization and other times more towards central control. It is important that the pendulum keeps swinging so that we remain fluid and adjusting.

As well as playing critically important hands-on roles (scouting the horizon for new technologies and techniques, custodian of the evolution roadmap, coordinating across change initiatives), the Acceleration Officer is a symbolic appointment. The Acceleration Officer promotes the culture that change is constant, that it is everyone's responsibility to create new possibilities. The mindset should be of 'never settling' but rather to always be seeking new ways to adjust and to improve.

Doctrine of change

The approach for managing change and transformation in 4IR is different than previously. Firstly, as mentioned, transformation is no longer considered to be episodic (from 'A' to 'B') but is a continual process (continuous evolution).

Secondly, the process is not to be endured, causing fatigue and anxiety that undermine well-being and performance, but is positive, bringing new opportunities and possibilities. Another key difference is the need to move from a 'top down' authority-driven programme to instead being embraced and driven by leaders distributed throughout the organization. The Acceleration Officer will need to coordinate the energies and initiatives across the organization, redirecting and redeploying resources as required. However, a key role is to connect the distributed leaders with the purpose, with enabling technologies and resources, and with each other. All transformations have some kind of model but in 4IR, where change and transformation are expected to be constants, it is important to establish an approach to the change process that is consistent and transparent such that managers and staff become confident, trusting in the process, able to involve others and coordinate between initiatives.

In 1996, Harvard Business School Professor John Kotter published the seminal work *Leading Change*,[3] in which he described an eight-step process to manage the transformation from State A to State B. However, in reflection of the acceleration of change in the contexts of business, he updated this model in his 2014 book *Accelerate!*,[4] wherein he describes an iterative process that, instead of being linear, cycles through an adjusted eight-step process.

An effective model for managing change that is readily understood and can therefore be broadly adopted is known by the acronym CLEAR. It is expected that the activities included in the CLEAR approach will be cycled through repeatedly and often conducted in parallel as cadence and dynamism build.

C – Connect: with the purpose of the organization and to the external drivers of change.

L – Leadership: personal leadership, effectively engaging stakeholders and distributed leadership of change initiatives throughout the organization.

E – Enablers: resources, tactics and actions to build momentum and overcome obstacles.

A – Align: strategic, operational, organizational and cultural alignment throughout the organization and at the external interfaces.

R – Reinforce: sustain achievements, refine the changes, extract key lessons for improving future management of change. Identify 'what's next' so that the cycle of evolution can be repeated.

FIGURE 7.3 John Kotter's models of managing change 1996[5] vs. 2014[6]

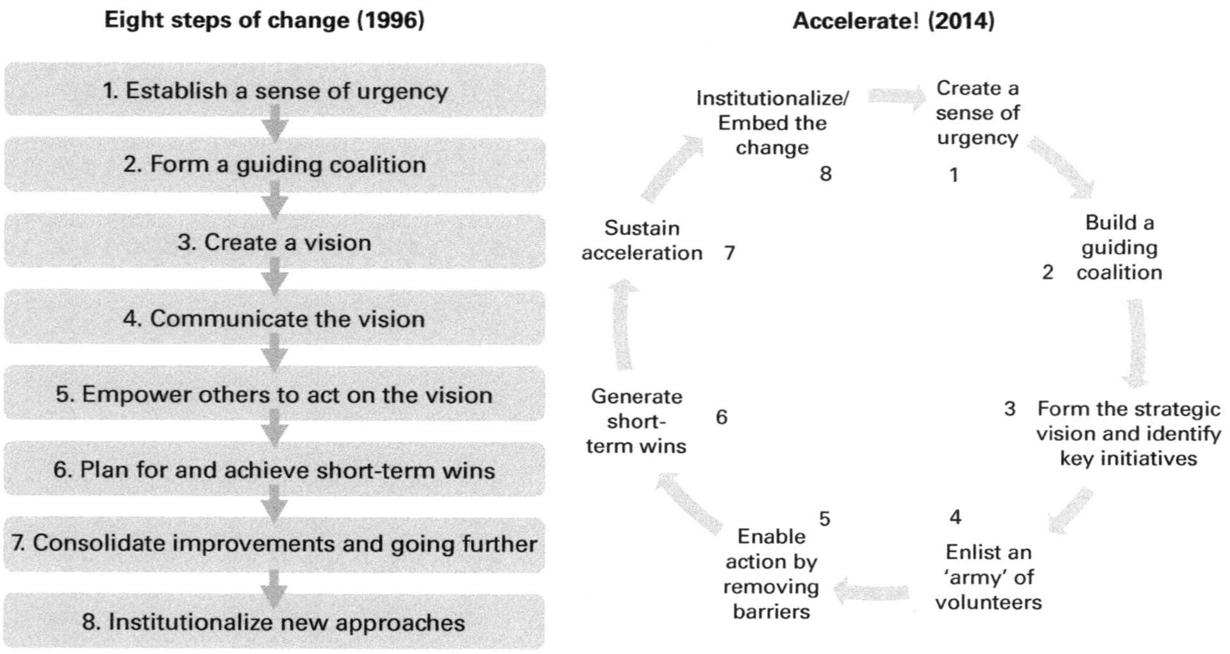

Eight steps of change (1996)

1. Establish a sense of urgency

2. Form a guiding coalition

3. Create a vision

4. Communicate the vision

5. Empower others to act on the vision

6. Plan for and achieve short-term wins

7. Consolidate improvements and going further

8. Institutionalize new approaches

Accelerate! (2014)

Create a sense of urgency 1

Build a guiding coalition 2

Form the strategic vision and identify key initiatives 3

Enlist an 'army' of volunteers 4

Enable action by removing barriers 5

Generate short-term wins 6

Sustain acceleration 7

Institutionalize/ Embed the change 8

C – Connect

Two types of connection are essential for effective evolution in the fast-paced context of 4IR, anchored on the pursuit of the purpose and aligned with the forces of change and evolution in the competitive marketspace.

There should be a strong connection with the purpose of the organization; answering the questions, How can we further improve our performance with respect to achieving the purpose? Is this change initiative that we are considering in line with our values and will it help us accelerate towards our purpose? The importance of having a clear motivating purpose that engages and mobilizes stakeholders is discussed in Chapter 5. The connection to the purpose provides teams and individuals with motivation and also supports alignment between initiatives.

There must be a strong connection to the forces of change and evolution in the market-competitive space in which the organization operates, the 'winds and tides' that are reshaping the context of the organization. The workforce and other stakeholders need to have the confidence that change initiatives will be setting the organization up for success in the unfolding future – 'skating to where the puck is going to be'. This requires heightened abilities both to Sense what is changing in the context of the firm and to be able to Make Sense of the changes. These themes are explored in Chapter 2.

- Sensing what is happening externally and internally whilst avoiding either being overloaded with noise or over-filtering what is happening.
- Making Sense is the ability to distinguish what matters most, what the implications could be and to decide, in a timely manner, what to do about it.

These connections must be constantly communicated, celebrating successes and reinforcing why the status quo is insufficient. Communications should be multi-channel and consistent, reinforcing key messages whilst tailored to the specific audience. The communications should foster the sense of winning together, belonging to the same overall team, celebrating each other's achievements and fuelling the desire to be included in the next acceleration initiative. Leaders who have achieved significant changes in their organizations, such as Jeff Immelt, Paul Polson, Elon Musk and Ginni Rometty, are widely recognized for their constant attention to effective and consistent communication.

L – Leadership

Achieving effective timely evolution in 4IR requires integrating three areas of leadership: personal, stakeholder and distributed.

- Personal leadership in driving continuous evolution necessitates having curiosity, a passion for learning and discovery, and the ability to ask questions and make observations that lead to breakthroughs. The standout leaders of 4IR organizations are part dreamers, chasing visions, and are equally able to accumulate and combine a wide spectrum of idea fragments. A skill that Moss-Kanter describes as Kaleidoscope Thinking.[7]

- Stakeholder leadership is particularly critical to successful ongoing evolution in 4IR, for several reasons. The speed of evolution requires the leadership team to be peering into the complex, unknown future; more insight and perspectives integrated together better inform visioning, decision making and planning. The 4IR organization is adaptive, adjusting as the future unfolds – maintaining the flow of insight/intelligence is critical, as is maintaining stakeholder support for the overall journey, not just a particular individual step or transient outcome. It is therefore essential to regularly map stakeholder groups and engage each group in a different tailored manner, building and maintaining support.

- Distributed leadership: as described in the introduction of this chapter, continuous change necessitates that it is driven from within the organization rather than being episodic transformations driven top-down. Continuous change is participative and adaptive as it responds to discovery and learnings. This requires that leaders and teams throughout the organization are expected, equipped and empowered to not only implement but also initiate change. Nitin Nohria and Michael Beer of Harvard Business School described a similar approach as Theory O, noting, 'Theory O change strategies are geared toward building up the corporate culture: employee behaviours, attitudes, capabilities and commitment. The organisation's ability to learn from its experiences is a legitimate yardstick of corporate success.'[8] Initiatives that empower multiple teams often reveal hitherto unrecognized talent – embracing such individuals can further energize the organization.

Balancing the elements of change leadership as the organization accelerates is one of the roles supported by the Acceleration Officer, ensuring that stakeholders are constructively engaged, change agents are multiplied through the organization and the corporation is steered along in approximate alignment with the intended roadmap.

E – Enablers

Enablers are the resources, tactics and actions that build momentum and also overcome obstacles. An example of such an enabler is the tactic to 'tackle the hardest issues first', which is a part of the doctrine at Google. Rather than being busy making progress on easier or less impactful issues, it is important to address the most challenging obstacles first. Overcoming them leads to new insights that influence the approaches to the ancillary issues, and builds confidence and commitment to the acceleration initiative. If they can't be overcome, then that saves the time and expense that would have otherwise been invested on the smaller ancillary issues.

> A full-service airline had slipped into losses and announced a major restructuring plan. Front-line cabin crew were dismissed (with an impact on customer service), and behind-the-scenes operations staff were required to improve efficiency and reduce head count. These moves were difficult for the staff, but what particularly undermined morale was that the management appeared to be failing to gain productivity improvements from the pilots, who collectively represented the majority of the personnel costs. The pilots were heavily unionized and had beaten off proposed management reforms previously. It seemed to some that the rest of the workforce was being asked to take the pain of management's inability to achieve reforms.

Quick wins are commonly used, important enablers. To have momentum-building impact, 'quick wins' must be (a) quickly achieved, (b) visible to the wider organization, (c) unambiguous, ie convincing, and (d) relevant.

Quick wins are sometimes positioned as experiments (such as the launch of new beer formulations in developing markets and pop-up concept stores), using the Agile[9] approach to learn as much as possible from the market or prototype as quickly as possible in order to be able to iterate and improve. However, planning for, achieving and celebrating quick wins can have far greater impact than an experiment if it is designed to resolve a contentious point or build confidence to move towards a new approach abandoning prior practices.

Another type of enabler is the use of expert agents from outside the firm, such as consultants and board advisers. Such agents can create a way forward to resolve important complex issues upon which opinion within the leadership team is divided. Their expertise both in subject matter and in the process of coming to agreement on a clear, choiceful way forward can be invaluable, enabling the organization to accelerate rather than stagnate. Consultants also can facilitate a step-change in the cadence of the organization, bringing a high work rate that the organization and leadership respond to.

CASE STUDY
Government department

A media-related national agency viewed their mandate as fulfilling a key social mandate whilst also demonstrating themselves to be fiscally prudent. Upon appointment, the new head realized that over the many years, complacency had gradually set in – a dominant culture of 'this is how we do things here' that blocked innovation. He recognized that if the organization were much more energized and growth focused, they would better fulfil their societal objectives and be more attentive to understanding, serving and shaping the needs of the consumers. The challenge was, how to bring about change when there was no fiscal 'burning platform' and their survival was guaranteed by the national charter? The first step was to create a new vision of the emergent future and, given that context, what the organization could be and could achieve. Whilst this inspired a few executives, most remained comfortable doing what they had been doing for years and showed little enthusiasm. The CEO decided that he could afford to take some time to achieve the transformation and that his priority was to take as many of the executives along with him as possible. The roadmap was designed to begin with leadership development to inspire changes in mindset, and to equip with new skills such that managers could start to behave in new ways (collective responsibility, individual accountability, data-driven decision making).

The second stage embraced new content delivery opportunities, being created through online and mobile channels. The executives in charge of pursuit of these initiatives quickly saw the opportunity to move beyond adapting existing content to new channels. They started to experiment with new interactive content and enrichment to traditional content, working exhaustively to understand and to get closer to the consumers. The initiatives enabled the hiring of some new senior executives, selected for both their technical expertise and their mindset and behaviours for leaning forward into the new. All the while the CEO kept on repeating the messaging of the vision. He also identified younger talent within the organization that could join teams in the newer areas of operation. He required all areas of the business, new and old, to share regularly what progress and changes had been achieved (in particular celebrating 'quick wins'). With external support he changed the form and functioning of the leadership team meetings, encouraging discussion and debate where previously they had predominantly felt like one-way briefing sessions.

The third phase of the transformation involved changes to the organization structure. Executives who had shown themselves effective at managing change or energizing their teams were given bigger areas of responsibility whilst others had their scope of influence reduced; some opted for early retirement or to make a career elsewhere. The impact on the performance of the organization was profound. The culture inside the organization and the behaviours of the executives reflected renewed energy, with positivity for what more could still be achieved. There is a new level of pride and a greater sense of purpose.

Explicit management of the nature of the process of change is also an important enabler. Choices need to be made, managed, monitored and adjusted on the rate and the nature of the evolution journey; explicit management of the cadence of the 'heart rate' at which the change journey beats and the balance that is struck at any one period between competing goals for the nature of the change journey itself.

- The cadence of the change journey is regulated by the frequency of the review meetings and the ambitiousness of the targets to be achieved between those reviews. For some firms that have adopted Agile[10] approaches, this is set by the choice of the intervals between Scrum-style[11] coordination meetings and the scope to be achieved in the intervening Sprints.[12]

- At each stage of the journey of evolution there is a choice between whether to prioritise speed of progress or to prioritise taking everyone along with the change at the same rate (or to let a small group push ahead whilst others may be brought along later), and to what extent operational risk needs to be avoided or to some extent can be tolerated.

FIGURE 7.4 Adaptive change: actively manage the competing priorities during the journey to enable the process

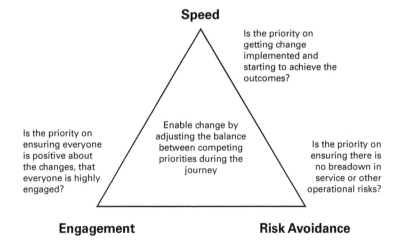

Speed

Is the priority on getting change implemented and starting to achieve the outcomes?

Enable change by adjusting the balance between competing priorities during the journey

Is the priority on ensuring everyone is positive about the changes, that everyone is highly engaged?

Is the priority on ensuring there is no breadown in service or other operational risks?

Engagement   **Risk Avoidance**

A – Alignment

Organizations are themselves complex, but they are also a part of wider, more complex eco-systems. No change manager can model all the complexities and provide a perfect solution, nor the pathway to get there. Equally, during the change initiative itself the wider organization and the eco-system are evolving. As such the process of change is adaptive, responding to discoveries and to evolutions. To achieve or exceed the intended performance benefits, the changes made must interface effectively with other processes and practices – as well as, where appropriate, influencing those components to also evolve. Attention is required to steer alignment in four areas – strategic, operational, organizational and cultural – both within the organization itself and at external interfaces.

- Strategic alignment may be achieved by reference to and repeated cycling through the choices of the strategic choice cascade, an approach developed at the Monitor Group and the focus of the book *Playing to Win*[13] by Roger Martin.

- Operational alignment necessitates ensuring the smooth hand-off between parties and processes, internal and external, in particular ensuring that enhanced capabilities in one area (e.g. AI-enabled data analysis) are not lost at the hand-off (eg to the decision-making process). Gains in one area may be lost in an adjacent downstream area if there is mistrust of the new procedures or a preference to retain activity levels (and resources). This can be particularly problematic when the 'hand-off' is at the boundary of the organization, necessitating effective collaboration across boundaries to create solutions that are mutually beneficial.

- Organizational alignment requires that the structure, decision rights, performance metrics, talent development and other elements of organization are all aligned with the intended outcomes, new performance outcomes. An executive from an industrial products company noted, 'Decreasingly we think about structure, increasingly we just think how to deploy the most relevant people, whether inside the firm or outside, to solve this challenge. No one taught us this at business school, I feel that I am making it up as I go along, but the energy is unlike anything I have experienced anywhere else before.' Also, as explored in Chapter 3, communication technologies are diminishing the difficulties of distance and time zone; firms are often organizing around customer groupings or clustering together territories with similar dynamic conditions.

- Talent alignment. As Marshall Goldsmith noted, 'What got you here won't get you there.'[14] Although he was speaking about the behaviours and mindsets of the individual executives, the same statement is often true of management cadres, infused with existing culture, both overt and unstated values sets and rules of interacting that have enabled past success but stand in the way of continuous learning, adaptation and future success. 4IR organizations are always questioning whether they have the right talent for the new organization, operations and culture. Disproportionately high investment (approximately 20 per cent more than their sector peers) is made in mapping talent, providing training, feedback and coaching in 4IR organizations. 4IR organizations acknowledge that data-based insight on individual and team performance is critical. Investing significantly (as Google does) in monitoring team and individual performance, including engagement with and rate of learning of team-based skills, is a key enabler of success in 4IR.

R – Reinforce

In all change initiatives the gains or changes made must be sustained. In 4IR continuous evolution, the new state is the platform on which to build new changes, to reach higher. Moving on dynamically from stepping-stone to stepping-stone, each position providing only transient, fleeting superior performance, but mastery of change management being itself an enduring source of competitive advantage. Across the inputs from the executives who supported the research there emerge four distinct yet interrelated capabilities:

1 **Reinforce:** the emphasis is on sustaining the gains that have been made. Specific actions that were highlighted included the importance of communicating and celebrating progress made and milestones achieved, yet equally important to acknowledge and discuss failures and setbacks. With recognition of the importance that leaders role model by their actions and decisions, the changes and the expectations they have for the functioning and the values of the organization.

2 **Refine:** the 'new' is not perfect on 'Day 1', adjustments will be required. An executive at a major construction equipment manufacturer noted, 'It is said that it takes 10,000 hours of practice until mastery of something is achieved; it is therefore essential to expect and to support the learning curve.' The mindset of continuous improvement and learning should be embedded and nurtured throughout the management cadre. In their article 'Is yours a learning organization?', David A Garvin, Amy C Edmondson and Francesca Gino identified three capabilities:[15]

   – a supportive learning environment, where employees feel safe challenging one another and asking potentially naïve questions;

- overt structured learning processes, where experimentation is encouraged, knowledge and data formally gathered, synthesized and distributed;
- leadership that reinforces and role models learning for themselves and investing time and effort in supporting the learning of others.

Every change initiative requires ongoing refinement and adjustment, particularly so in the context of 4IR, which is rapidly evolving. Such reviews and refinements also spark reflection on what has worked well and less so, of the changes adopted, and of the change process. Distilling and sharing these learnings increases the change ability of the organization in the future.

3 **Repeat:** as mentioned throughout this chapter, the notion of change has changed. In 4IR leaders do not think of change as episodic but rather as continual. The cycle of seeing and pursuing opportunities for performance improvement and to adapt to the unfolding future not only repeats but is described by several executives as accelerating.

- Building change management as a source of competitive advantage requires nurturing the mindset and skills of change agility. The best time and place to do this is through direct involvement of managers in change initiatives, whilst ensuring that they are supported and that lessons learned are distilled and shared.

One of the ways that Unilever reinforces the changes made in pursuit of the goals of its Sustainable Living Plan is by highlighting and reporting on progress against targets and milestones, whether pulling ahead or falling behind. For several years the company did this by including the Sustainable Living performance metrics both in its annual reports and in a separate dedicated annual report.

CASE STUDY
Unilever

Prior to 2009, the consumer goods giant had experienced a decade of stagnation, and its low share price made it a prime target for takeover. Understanding radical change was required, and the then newly appointed CEO Paul Polman launched the Unilever Sustainable Living Plan (USLP). They adopted the mission to 'Make sustainable living commonplace', setting out ambitious strategic objectives to double revenues whilst halving the environmental footprint of products, to sustainably source 100 per cent of agricultural raw materials, and to help 1 billion people improve their health and well-being. New business and financial models for the corporation were established and an ambitious roadmap explained the journey ahead. The USLP generated excitement and heralded significant transformation in what the company did and how it operated.

The corporation's leadership fostered collaboration, pursued a global mindset and embraced the digital enablement of the 4IR, championing a culture of harvesting and harnessing data for insight and decision making. A major initiative was rolled out to engage the leadership and executives with the USLP and to familiarize them with the required mindsets, behaviours and culture. A new cross-functional team-based organization model was created that increased the capabilities to spot and seize opportunities as well as raise accountability. Polman stated that the Country-Category Business Teams were 'the centre of gravity of the business... mini entrepreneurs, with full responsibility and accountability for delivering the results... It really is a different operational model that affects everybody in the organization. This makes it challenging and makes it one of the biggest change efforts this company has ever done. It fundamentally changes the way we do business'.[16]

Unilever sought to reconfigure its activities, significantly strengthening its ability to acquire and integrate new companies and brands as well as to dispose of others. By 2018, Unilever had acquired completely, or had significant stakes in, over 30 companies and in the same period sold out of 14 others.[17] Over the years after the launch of the USLP, Unilever established itself as a sustainability leader – in other words, they established a strong sense of purpose to guide strategy and unify the culture. By 2019, Unilever reported that its purpose-led Sustainable Living Brands were growing 69 per cent faster than the rest of the business and delivering 75 per cent of the company's growth.[18] The company was also able to increase its attractiveness as an employer and propel itself from being outside of the list of the top 75 most desirable employers to being within the top 10.

In March 2019, CEO Alan Jope (who took over from Paul Polman on 1 January 2019) announced new leadership and organization changes, explaining that 'today's increasingly fragmented consumer, channel and media environment requires us to operate with more speed and agility than ever before'.[19] The company stressed the need to continue to transform into a faster, leaner and more agile company. They illustrate well the shift from 'unfreeze' to 'move' – which is where the corporation will continue to move.

In 4IR change is a constant; the ability to manage change is therefore a source of competitive advantage. The expectation of change and confidence in the ability to manage change become energizing for employees – there is an expectation of 'what's next' and an anticipation of greater acceleration to come. Energy begets energy, momentum builds momentum.

Evolution roadmap: plan future-back

The roadmap not only defines identifiable steps and timeframes but also identifies the processes, governance structures and key roles that will enable the transformation. Getting this right is critical not only to realizing the intended outcomes of the transformation but also for building enduring capabilities in change management. Therefore, both in the establishment and during the transformation journey, there should be the expectation of 'experimentation – learning – adjustment'.

The Acceleration Officer owns the roadmap and has responsibility for updates and adjustments. The map is the equivalent of the training plan for a person preparing to win a tennis tournament. It indicates the transitionary steps and milestones that the person (the corporation) will make over the period before and during the tournament. It details how they will build up the 'muscles' (mindsets, behaviours, capabilities and management practices) and how they will apply these accumulating strengths to overcome each round of challenges that the corporation faces in pursuit of the ultimate goal.

As the firm acts with greater dynamic capacity, it will move more fluidly from one position of competitive advantage to another. There must evolve the recognition that the new position will itself be transient, a stepping-stone facilitating progress to the next. Therefore, the roadmap will evolve and will be extended in ways, as yet unknown, beyond the current one.

Roadmapping is an excellent tool for envisaging and planning the journey into the future. As Clayton Christensen stated, 'We only have data on the past or at best the present, yet we have to take decisions for the future.' As there is no data on the future, everyone can have an opinion and all opinions can be equally wrong – we just don't know the future. The two key principles, discussed above, for moving forward into the unknown as an aligned and committed leadership team are:

- a strong sense of purpose (and a common understanding thereof);
- collective opinion and intelligence integrated.

But there is still the need to have a strategic plan to focus efforts and coordinate resource deployment and investment. As Henry Mintzberg noted, this plan needs to avoid the three fallacies of strategic planning (see Chapter 5): Prediction (we think we know the future); Detachment (we can't know the future so let's just be reactive); and Formalization (every period, we make a plan and we just stick to it, then make a new plan next time).

Roadmapping is a powerful and effective process for senior leaders to develop the overall strategic plan (roadmaps). It is iterative and workshop based. It is a collective, interactive process in which participants discuss their different points of view in order to arrive at an agreement of how to proceed, hence the process builds cohesion, aligns expectations and creates a shared sense of ownership and commitment for the plan that is developed.

The process separates objectives into time blocks, in which the executives both individually and collectively address six core questions in a process that is both divergent (eg individual inputs) and convergent (collectively weighting and prioritizing). The six questions are:

- Planning 'future-back':
  o Where do we want to go?
  o Where are we currently?
  o How will we get there?
- Dimension of strategic choice:
  o Why do we need to act?
  o What should we do?
  o How will we do it?

Then, to create the integrated roadmap, the group connects and sequences the prioritized initiatives, as shown in Figure 7.5.

Note: Answering most of the questions requires being knowledgeable about the technologies and techniques being adopted; it requires staying informed of the leading edge of how business practices are changing in 4IR. It is often advisable therefore to engage the support of external experts in the impact and application of 4IR technologies, to support the internal executives to develop the roadmap. Apart from my team, the Institute for Manufacturing (IfM) at the University of Cambridge is a centre of excellence in the technologies of 4IR and provides support to clients for the process of roadmapping.[20]

FIGURE 7.5   The roadmap process to transform performance

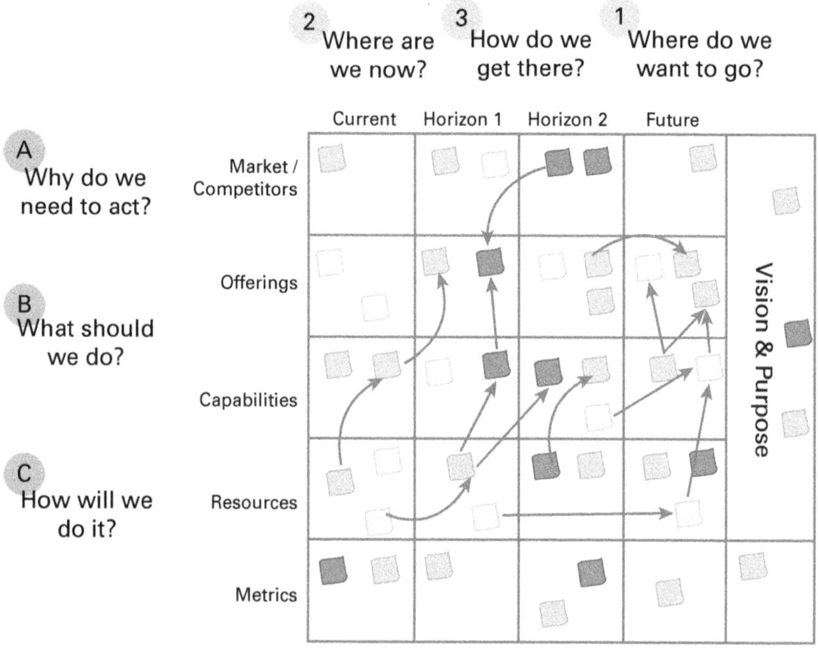

Sometimes companies need to urgently turn around operations with poor, declining performance or loss-making. The urgency of such situations places a priority on speed of outcomes. However, even in such situations there is no reason not to also build up prowess in change management; to establish the role of the Acceleration Officer, the Doctrine of Change and the practice of creating a roadmap for future evolution. It is important to maximize learning during the turnaround process by not only involving executives and staff members in the turnaround activities but also ensuring they are prepared for a future where change and evolution are constants. With greater prowess in managing change, a mindset and the practices that support continuous evolution, the firm can avoid a future where another desperate turnaround is required.

Leadership traits: continuous evolution

Provide meaning/connect to purpose

Change is a constant for companies operating in the 4IR. As such, leaders cannot approach the change process as a transition, a period of disturbance during which anxiety and ambiguity may undermine performance. Change is the new normal. Leaders need to maintain the focus on the higher purpose of the organization, inspiring each individual to regard the fluidity of change processes as creating opportunities to improve themselves and their operations, to seize emergent opportunities and to challenge, redesign and abandon obsolete practices, behaviours and systems. Leaders need to maintain communication and reinforce the messages of 'why' the changes and 'how' new process, practices and behaviours will help to improve performance. The 'what' (eg adoption of new cloud-based systems, productivity tools or office robotics) are specific projects within the journey of continual acceleration and transformation. The change leader needs to set the tempo for the change process, not allowing momentum to be lost in one or other initiative. The change leader needs to be observant and informed, spotting if and when they may need to step in directly or reallocate resources to bolster progress in an initiative that is falling behind schedule.

Organization savviness

Organization savviness is the ability to navigate effectively around the organization in order to bring about positive change. It requires knowing how decisions actually get made and the unwritten rules of the game. Knowing about the informal networks of relationships, how different people take decisions, and what are the hidden as well as the explicit sources of influence. Due to the fluidity of structure and the increasing propensity to engage with external vendors, contract workers and consultants, 4IR companies rely significantly on informal networks of relationships. To be effective, the change manager must know and be a part of these networks and energetically leverage them. Successful leaders of change rarely use positional authority to achieve their objectives, knowing that for the changes being introduced to be effective they will need the good will of those affected to refine the systems, policies and practices. Change initiatives gather momentum when the people involved in the initial steps celebrate and share the positive benefits being achieved and they themselves inculcate the passion and energy for change into the wider network via their own networks of relationships.

Executive presence

Change leaders must inspire trust; they need to give confidence to others to move beyond their existing routines. A change leader may have had little prior relationship with individuals from whom they need followership, and as such their presence, their demeanour and how they carry themselves as well as what they say must all signal competence and trustworthiness. Dr Albert Mehrabian[21] from UCLA, who researched the topic of executive presence, places only 7 per cent importance on the words someone speaks – he places 38 per cent on tone, and the remaining 55 per cent on body language. Executive presence, how the executive carries themselves, is more important than what they actually say! Executives who have high presence are able to adapt to each environment whilst also remaining authentic to themselves. As the famed manager of Manchester United soccer club, Sir Alex Ferguson, noted, you need to 'match the message to the moment'.[22] Be adaptive, know what's appropriate for each environment; this applies to the way you dress, your tone and body language, as well as the words that are used.

Mindset: Never settle

Prior to the 4th Industrial Revolution the expectation was that change would be required periodically or episodically. Transformation processes induced stress and anxiety which often reduced productivity during the change process itself. In 4IR evolution is constant, and change creates new possibilities and opportunities, for growth of the organization and the individual. Managers and staff are empowered to drive change, under the coordination of an Acceleration Officer. The 'Never Settle' mindset celebrates resilience: resilience resulting from adaptability, the capability to flex and to grow rather than fragility that might be the result of intransigence in the face of change or uncertainty. Professor Carol Dweck[23] described this as having a 'growth mindset' rather than a 'fixed mindset' in her influential book *Mindset: The new psychology of success*:

> The passion for stretching yourself and sticking to it, even (or especially) when it's not going well, is the hallmark of the growth mindset. This is the mindset that allows people to thrive during some of the most challenging times in their lives.[24]

KEY CONCEPTS: CHAPTER 7

Prowess at implementing change is essential in 4IR. Change is a constant as the speed of business and the rate of disruption and transformation of businesses are accelerating. This is powered by forces that are increasing in strength – the rate of invention and adoption of new technologies, the rise of non-traditional competitors, and the rapid evolution of customer behaviours and expectations. There are three components to mastering near-continuous change in an organization:

- **Acceleration Officer**

  A senior executive who manages transformations that adopt the technologies and techniques of 4IR with overall responsibility for enhancing the performance of the corporation. Knowledgeable about the technologies and possibilities for restructuring business models and processes created by 4IR. Firms establish such a point of coordination in different ways but increasingly a new permanent position is being included in the C-Suite. A key function of the CAO, in addition to implementing the planned changes, is to be looking further ahead, seeking to understand what could be next and then aligning the results from the current transformations to be platforms for continuing acceleration.

- **Doctrine of Change**

  In 4IR, prowess at managing change is a source of competitive advantage as the organization needs to be continuously evolving. The doctrine is the approach by which change is implemented; it enables consistency across the organization such that managers and staff become confident, trusting in the process, able to involve others and coordinate between initiatives. A suitable change model is CLEAR:

  o **C – Connect**: with the purpose of the organization and to the external drivers of change.

  o **L – Leadership**: personal leadership, effectively engaging stakeholders and distributed leadership of change initiatives throughout the organization.

  o **E – Enablers**: resources, tactics and actions to build momentum and overcome obstacles.

  o **A – Alignment**: strategic, operational, organizational and cultural alignment throughout the organization and at the external interfaces.

  o **R – Reinforce**: sustain achievements, refine the changes, extract key lessons for improving future management of change. Identify 'what's next' so that the cycle of evolution can be repeated.

- **Evolution roadmap**

  The Acceleration Officer owns the roadmap and has responsibility for updates and adjustments. Roadmapping is an effective process for developing a transformational plan as it anchors on the vision for the future and then senior leaders develop the plan back from the future to the situation today. It is anchored on the objective. It does not seek to plan forwards from the situation today. Roadmapping is a collective, interactive process in which participants discuss their different points of view in order to arrive at an agreement of how to proceed.

Leadership traits:

- provide meaning/connect to purpose;
- organization savviness;
- executive presence;
- mindset: never settle.

Endnotes

1 Fuller, J *et al* (2019) Future positive: how companies can tap into employee optimism to navigate tomorrow's workplace, Harvard Business School, https:// www.hbs.edu/managing-the-future-of-work/research/Pages/future-positive.aspx (archived at https://perma.cc/7FGU-WPF9)

2 IBM Annual Report 2014. Letter from the Chairman, https://www.ibm.com/ annualreport/2014/bin/assets/IBM-Annual-Report-Chairmans-Letter.pdf (archived at https://perma.cc/EK77-495C)

3 Kotter, J P (1996) *Leading Change*, Harvard Business School Press, Boston

4 Kotter, J P (2014) *Accelerate!* Harvard Business Review Press

5 Kotter, J P (1996) *Leading Change*, Harvard Business School Press, Boston

6 Kotter, J P (2014) *Accelerate!* Harvard Business Review Press

7 Moss-Kanter, R (2005) *Leadership for Change: Enduring skills for change masters*, Harvard Business School

8 Nohria, N and Beer, M (2000) Cracking the code of change, *Harvard Business Review*, May–June

9 Beck, K *et al* (2001) The Agile Manifesto, Agile Alliance. http://agilemanifesto. org/ (archived at https://perma.cc/F6R2-BWMA)

10 Beck, K *et al* (2001) The Agile Manifesto, Agile Alliance. http://agilemanifesto. org/ (archived at https://perma.cc/F6R2-BWMA)

11 https://www.scrumalliance.org/about-scrum/definition (archived at https:// perma.cc/4QFJ-JEB8)

12 https://www.agilealliance.org/glossary/sprint-planning/ (archived at https:// perma.cc/ND3J-RQ3Q)

13 Lafley, A G and Martin, R L (2013) *Playing to Win: How strategy really works*, Harvard Business Review Press

14 Goldsmith, M and Reiter, M (2007) *What Got You Here Won't Get You There: How successful people become even more successful*, Hyperion

15 Garvin, D A, Edmondson, A C and Gino, F (2008) Is yours a learning organization? *Harvard Business Review*, March

16 Best, D (2016) Unilever on organizational change, outlook for food, spreads' future – 2016 investor day takeaways, https://www.just-food.com/analysis/unilever-on-organizational-change-outlook-for-food-spreads-future-2016-investor-day-takeaways_id135146.aspx (archived at https://perma.cc/7KA3-9G8Z)

17 https://www.unilever.com/investor-relations/understanding-unilever/acquisitions-and-disposals/ (archived at https://perma.cc/E28M-YBMA)

18 https://www.unilever.com/news/press-releases/2019/unilevers-purpose-led-brands-outperform.html (archived at https://perma.cc/768Z-WMGK)

19 https://www.unilever.com/news/press-releases/2019/unilever-announces-leadership-and-organisation-changes.html (archived at https://perma.cc/6Q7V-KZBP)

20 https://www.ifm.eng.cam.ac.uk/ifmecs/business-tools/roadmapping/roadmapping-at-ifm/ (archived at https://perma.cc/C7GG-57AE)

21 Mehrabian, A (1972) *Nonverbal Communication*, Aldine Transaction, New Brunswick

22 Elberse, A (2013) Ferguson's Formula, *Harvard Business Review*, October

23 Carol S Dweck, American psychologist, Professor of Psychology at Stanford University

24 Dweck, C S (2006) *Mindset: The new psychology of success*, Random House, USA

PART FOUR

Win the 4IR talent race

Talent is key to winning in 4IR, being able to interface with technologies and to navigate in ambiguity with an increasing role for creativity. Continuously developing 4IR skills and optimally deploying talent by fluid teaming to match the shifting challenges. Employing Human-Centred Workforce Management practices that enable talent to perform at their best whilst fulfilling the duty of care.

The 'war for talent' is over, nobody won!

The 'war for talent' was predicated on the notion that there was a pool of available talent 'out there', for which companies had to compete. Recognition of the profound changes in the skills and competencies required to win in 4IR has led to the realization that there isn't a large enough pool of existing talent to fight over. The war for talent has been supplanted by the race to develop, deploy and retain 4IR talent. Part Four explores:

- **Race to develop 4IR talent**
  Most executives have skills learned and honed pre-4IR yet to be effective in 4IR they must acquire both new skills and new behaviours, so there is a 'race to develop 4IR talent'. Developing executives for impact on the job, in the flow of business, requires new 'learner-centric' development design.

FIGURE IV.1 Win the talent race: develop & deploy with a duty of care

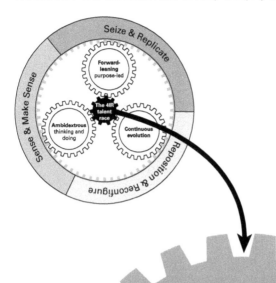

- **Deploy 4IR talent effectively with fluid teaming**

  The often scarce 4IR talent must be deployed highly effectively. This requires the ability to rapidly assemble, adjust and dismantle teams to tackle an ever-changing line-up of challenges. Teams are the 'engines of performance' in 4IR organizations. The people management infrastructure and systems must enable the entire organization to function as a fluid team made up of multiple fluid teams.

- **Duty of care**

  Talent is a critical and scarce resource in 4IR, which places a priority on attracting, retaining, empowering and maintaining the engagement of talent. Human-Centred Workforce Management (HCWM) promotes worker well-being and inclusion, particularly through flexible working arrangements. HCWM results in enhanced productivity, performance and increased tenure, all of which support employer branding – and the ability to attract the desired talent.

08

The race to develop 4IR talent

IN BRIEF

The war for talent is largely over! Nobody won. The 'war for talent' was predicated on the notion that there was a pool of available talent 'out there', for which we must compete. In 4IR it is accepted that there isn't a pool of suitable talent, at least not of a size worth fighting over. It is estimated that due to technological innovation, executives need to be mastering a new skill each year, and that up to 20 per cent of the skills we have already mastered will be obsolete within three years. In higher education, where it takes three years to design, launch and recruit the first intake of students for a new master's programme, this means that by the time the first cohort of students graduates from a new two-year MBA programme, 20 per cent of what they have learned will be out of date! Recognition of the profound changes in the skills and competencies required to win in the 4IR has led to the realization that there isn't a large enough pool of existing talent to fight over. The war for talent has been supplanted by the 'race to develop talent'.

Leaders and executives must master the competencies of operating effectively in the dynamic, ambiguous, technology-enabled, dislocated context of 4IR. Where fluid teaming is more important than standing organization structures; where impact is determined more by a leader's ability to connect and collaborate rather than to command and control; and where the pursuit of a purposeful vision through innovation, insight generation and nurturing talent creates greater economic value than achieving period financial results. The ongoing development and adoption of technologies, social and demographic shifts and the acceleration of business that combine to create the 4th Industrial Revolution – all these forces create the need for significant reskilling of much of the workforce, including leaders.

Corporate and individual spending on executive training and education is booming, estimated to be growing at 7–9 per cent per annum and to have a total value over US $200 billion.[1] No longer do the majority of talent development officers rate shortage of budgets as their main concern (27 per cent in 2019 vs 49 per cent in 2017)[2] and even so, 43 per cent of talent development officers are expecting their budgets to be increased again in 2020. Despite the increasing spending on training and development, two-thirds of senior executives believe these investments deliver a poor return. Yet those most affected, the workers, are increasingly keen to reskill and upskill, both in their own time and, when possible, with company support.

Executive development: changing behaviour

In 2002, as Managing Partner of the management consultancy Monitor Group, in Southeast Asia, I was leading our support in a major turnaround initiative at PSA Corporation (a port operator with activities globally). Although the new strategy was clear, and the changes in the operating model and the structure of the organization were starting to emerge, it was becoming increasingly obvious that the mindsets and behaviours of the executive cadre would also need to evolve. With the support of global thought leaders in executive development and adult learning (Bernie Jaworski, David Kantor), we successfully established the first foray into the Asia Pacific region for Monitor Executive Development.

Later on, in my role as head of Singapore Management University's business unit for Executive Development, I oversaw the training of up to 3,500 executives each year, coming from many different companies, sectors, nationalities and functional areas. A key common factor was that their organizations were all operating in uncertain and rapidly changing contexts across Asia – conditions similar to 4IR. Another common factor was that they were all busy executives. What became apparent was that how executives develop is very different from how students learn. I was able to blend the principles and practices of Monitor Executive Development with the breadth of subject matter content and scale of the programmes provided bespoke to client corporations. The focus was on achieving on-the-job behaviour change, through engaging with the executives in the most relevant manner, such as employing the most relevant content with the objectives of the corporation. We ran many experimental programmes. We applied and refined our own insights whilst benefiting from client learning and development officer feedback on what techniques and approaches had greatest impact on actual on-the-job performance for their executives. Through these experiences emerged an andragogical (how adults learn) model for executive development.

Adults learn differently from children. However, too often, 'pedagogical' (how children learn) approaches are used for executives – and not surprisingly, the impact and return on the investment of time and money are poor! Since the 1980s, research into achieving behaviour change has embraced the 'M-A-O model', which describes three factors (Motivation-Ability-Opportunity) that need to come together to achieve change.[3] To achieve changes in the behaviour of executives, in order to enhance their performance on the job, all of these three factors must be explicitly managed:

- **Motivation**
  Executives are not immersed in a learning environment like school, and the 'grades' that they obtain for their learning have little, if any, bearing on their performance review and compensation. Learning for many executives is perceived as a distraction from the 'day job', which could have negative consequences. The foundation for executive development needs the individual to be motivated to learn in order to improve their performance in ways that they perceive are relevant to themselves. An executive must first become aware of the need for them to enhance or update their skills in a certain area, and there must be the personal desire to do something about improving.

- **Ability**
  Unlike the linear learning journey of a child, executives have often already proven themselves competent in certain ways of executing tasks and achieving results. They will not abandon those approaches until they gain confidence in new ways of acting – hence the development approach must emphasize the safety of experimentation whilst mastery is developed: support for the executive to acquire the skills and knowledge to be able to operate in new ways; knowing what to do differently and gaining confidence and mastery through experimentation.

- **Opportunity**
  Behaving differently on the job requires developing experience in actually applying the new skills and knowledge. This is dependent upon the roles and tasks to which the individual is assigned or the opportunities they seize and create to apply and further enhance their new skills and knowledge.

Enhancing and empowering each of these three factors requires a supportive environment, where awareness of a skills gap is not pointed to as a weakness but as an opportunity for development; where experimentation with new skills is recognized as a process towards mastery; where learning and development are themselves applauded and encouraged. Supportive feedback and personalized coaching combined with reinforcing mechanisms of review, reward and recognition.

Motivation

Executives develop skills in order to perform better. The benefits that the organization wants to receive from all the investments in development are better operating results and higher ability to navigate the uncertain future. The learning has value when it is applied and produces improved results. A key factor for successful adult learning is the need to be personally motivated to learn. Given the multiple pressures and competing commitments, it is easy for an executive to withdraw or to be distracted away from a learning process. Not seeing the utility of the learning for themselves, irrespective of the level of external encouragement, will undermine the effectiveness of any development initiative. Executives need to be personally motivated to

FIGURE 8.1 Andragogy of executive development

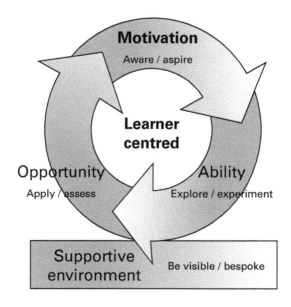

join in a development programme, to persevere through it and to coura-geously apply the newfound knowledge and insight on the job, and in their lives. As such, to be effective, the talent development team needs to build up the executive's personal motivation. Two primary levers are to enable Awareness and encourage Aspiration.

- **Aware**
  Executives need to know the competencies they should be mastering in the 4IR and how well they are performing. This means that in 4IR, Talent Development Officers are more frequently updating their corporate's competency framework and also building up the capabilities of their assessment feedback systems. The executive comes to the recognition that they can improve performance in a particular area. This could be as a result of assessment feedback, personal curiosity or by directly facing a new challenge on the job for which they see they need to master new skills.

- **Aspire**
  The executive must decide for themselves if they want to do anything about the skills gap that has been identified. Some executives take the view that they should play to their strengths and not overly worry about improving each area of comparative weakness, preferring to work with individuals with complementary areas of strength (see Strengths-Based Leadership[4]). Others may not be motivated sufficiently to find the time to address the gap. However, urgency to acquire new skills to apply immediately on the job is often the most powerful motivator for prioritizing personal development. With the speed of evolution of 4IR this is driving the increasing shift to just-in-time learning, which may be in bite-sized short modules or even 'on demand'.

Ability

Value is created only when the executive successfully applies the new learn-ing to a situation on the job and achieves a better outcome. 'Doing' builds understanding, contextualizes the learning and demonstrates results. However, comfort, confidence and expertise are only achieved over time and through repetition, hence it can be difficult to replace existing behaviours with new ones. The best approach is to have an experimenter's mindset. Try out the new behaviour and observe what happens:

- **Explore**

  The individual explores the topic; there are many ways that this can be done, online, in a class, asking others, etc. Exploring the topic can be self-directed or guided (eg by a trainer). They develop an understanding of and familiarity with the tools and techniques of the desired capabilities and mindsets. Each person will absorb learning in their own way and at their own pace, hence it can be very limiting to have only one medium and a programme that proceeds at a predetermined pace, which is a limitation of programmes that are heavily dependent on in-person seminars. I recommend that Explore should include, as a minimum, self-paced discovery and multi-party interactions, plus reflection on online materials, which can be frequently repeated. There should be 'additional texts' beyond the core which some individuals will want to explore and the opportunity to interact with individuals who have developed great prowess and experience with the skill.

- **Experiment**

  Experiment by applying the tools and techniques on the job, with recognition that mastery will not be immediate; the initial practice may be supported by facilitation and may be in designated 'safer' situations of specially ring-fenced projects. Simulations can also be a helpful medium for experimentation, whether online or in person (such as role-play), although they should not be over-used as on-the-job doing provides most meaning for the executive. Experimenting with doing should be accompanied by receiving feedback as quickly as possible, and with a bias for quickly recycling and repeating. Different individuals will want to cycle through these steps in their own manner, at their own speed, moving between Explore and Experiment whilst they gradually build up confidence and mastery in use.

Opportunity

- **Apply**

  The objective of investing in development is to enhance the performance of the executive on the job. As such, the return from the investments (of time, effort and resources) is achieved when the executive applies the new skills and knowledge. To improve the effectiveness of the development investments it is important to minimize any gap between learning and doing. This discipline, in combination with the increased rate of learning driven by the evolution of 4IR, is leading to the concept of learning that is 'just in time', on-demand for when new skills and knowledge are needed to be applied immediately to a workplace challenge.

- **Assess**

    Sharing learnings with others and obtaining feedback on application experience helps consolidate the skills development and improve the on-the-job performance. Short-cycle feedback, if constructively given and managed, can significantly assist the rate of improvement. In addition to the formal processes, I encourage regular informal peer-to-peer feedback within teams, either periodically or after key events. The giving and receiving of short-cycle constructive feedback can significantly help to reinforce a culture of learning and growth as well as enhance the sense of trust within teams.

Supporting environment

As humans are 'socially alert', the community around the executive conditions their behaviour and influences their mindset. Collective learning and development experiences can create a new set of norms, a common language and a set of tools and techniques that enable the members to support each other in adopting and applying the new learnings. Individual development can be greatly helped by the community in the workplace as they support application, encourage even faltering experimentation and celebrate progress. Or it can be greatly hindered, pulling the individual back into established behaviour or mindset norms – which is why explicit attention must be given to create a supportive environment:

- **Be visible**

    Across the executive cadre, from the most senior onwards, there should be an appetite for self-improvement and to stay current. Executives and leaders should seek out feedback and opt in to development programmes. Training should not be seen as remedial (ie 'you need some training to strengthen a current weakness') but rather as a way to strengthen existing prowess and to be future-ready. Leaders should share their stories of their own development activities that they are currently engaging with, in order to reinforce the culture that everyone needs to be investing in self-improvement.

- **Bespoke**

    The talent and learning management systems of the organization should be able to recognize that individuals are developing at different rates, being precise enough to differentially adjust the learning support. Individual performance evaluations should capture and provide timely feedback on changes in the behaviour demonstrated on the job, whether the product of formal or informal training and doing. The workforce in 4IR is increasingly heterogeneous (age, background, culture, nationality, gender), and talent management systems should provide insight on individual performance and tailor the development support to how they learn.

Learner-centred development

Spending globally on executive training and development is estimated to be over US \$250 billion and growing at 7–9 per cent per year. This is not surprising, as the context of business is becoming increasingly dynamic, and the impact of a leader's decisions and performance can make or destroy billions of dollars of firm value in an ever-shrinking timeframe. In a previous study I ran in 2015, corporate leaders were asked to rank their top three human capital priorities, and almost 70 per cent of the respondents identified leadership development as their first or second concern – however, less than 20 per cent reported that their companies were effective at developing leaders. A separate study indicated that almost a third of companies can identify specific situations where they have failed to exploit opportunities because they lack enough leaders with the right capabilities.

Almost three-quarters of the total spending on developing executives is still tied to moving participants up a competency framework or to support studying to obtain qualifications: 'just in case' training. Less than 20 per cent is spent on training to support executives to immediately address challenges that they are facing today, 'just in time'. As such it is hardly surprising that there is little evidence of tangible impact of the investment in training on business performance. As one respondent commented, 'Failure of application of learning in the businesses is the number one problem.' It is therefore predictable that 'this investment doesn't produce an acceptable return on investment (ROI) as the learning doesn't lead to better organizational performance'.[5] Indeed, what we have seen in each chapter is that without managers and leaders adopting new behaviours and the underlying mindset shifts, the ability of the firm to compete successfully in 4IR will be greatly hindered.

The combination of the increasing need to upgrade leadership capabilities (to win the race to develop talent) and frustration with the results achieved from current investments in training is driving CHROs (Chief Human

Resources Officers) and Learning and Development Officers to approach leadership development differently, enabled by the technologies of the 4IR.

With the tightening labour market and the shortening shelf life of skills, creating and maintaining market leadership hinges on talent development's ability to help employees acquire and grow the right skills. Talent developers now have the support and resources that they need to take on the skills gap challenge.[6]

Digital-enabled development

Digital-enabled development has come of age, after more than 20 years of trialling and evolving. Technology enables better assessment of the skill gaps of individuals and matching to the individual a large curated library of specific content. Increasingly the content format is designed to be readily digestible, bite-sized, accessed online and on mobile. By contrast, many previous digital initiatives floundered as they sought to provide an online version of an in-person taught class. It is now increasingly common that each module (or mini-module) not only explores the topic with context-relevant examples but also guides the learner to apply the content. The interactivity of the digital platform also facilitates learner reflection and sharing of experiences and impact achieved from the application. Learners are encouraged to self-navigate to achieve higher skill levels in topics and techniques that they themselves prioritize. Machine learning can monitor individual engagement, areas of interest and rate and stage of progression, being able to prompt and adapt the content format and themes to accelerate learning application. Learners within or across organizations (on the same platform) can be paired or grouped appropriately to support each other's development, collaborating or competing with each other. Other technologies such as virtual reality and gamification are also transforming the learning experience. Both technologies often support simulations both of hard skills, such as a line clearance from breakdowns on a manufacturing plant, and of soft skills, such as giving an employee difficult performance feedback.

All these factors mean that digital-enabled development is increasingly effective and taking over the duty of supporting executives to acquire core competencies: more targeted content, more flexibility (time, location, rate, depth), supporting on-the-job application, and, for corporations with large populations of executives, cheaper and easier to scale than traditional instructor-led programmes. According to the 2019 Workplace Learning Report[7] on trends in corporate learning conducted by LinkedIn, 59 per cent of corporations have increased their spending on online learning since 2017, whilst 39 per cent report spending less on instructor-led learning.

From 'just in case' to 'just in time' development

In 4IR, executives are increasingly pressed for time and yet also needing to learn and apply new skills. This trend is transforming executive development, increasing the demand for focused content, delivered in short interventions (bite-sized), conducted just in time to be applied on the job. The intervention is designed for the context and effectiveness of the experience for the learner. Increasingly companies are investing in developing training content that is bespoke to their own context, objectives and challenges; 85 per cent of talent development officers report to be developing bespoke content. The role of talent development managers is evolving, increasingly focusing on curating the content and designing the learning experience. Line managers, with intimate insight on the individuals they lead, and knowledge of the challenges they are addressing, are increasingly influential in guiding and recommending learning content and development opportunities for their team members. Simon Brown, Chief Learning Officer at Novartis, stated it as such:

> ... the next big leap [...] is the concept of embedding learning directly into people's day-to-day work [...] Rather than learning up front, we can instead provide nuggets of learning throughout the flow of work [...] Associates wouldn't have to take time out and go off to a class or log in to a platform; rather, the learning would be seamlessly embedded in the flow of what they do day-to-day. It would also give them the training they need when they need it, rather than frontloading it and hoping associates remember what they learned when they need it.[8]

Leadership competencies in 4IR

The 4IR is impacting how leaders lead and managers manage as profoundly as it is also bringing revolution in the content and medium of conducting work for workers throughout the organization and indeed also in how businesses compete and evolve. This book has presented thematically the changes that are occurring and the forces driving those changes, in order to provide a frame of reference to determine how you and your corporation might select and strengthen the competencies most relevant for your management team. Each chapter has highlighted different leadership skills and management practices that are in ascendancy due to 4IR. I have not discussed perennial attributes of leadership (such as trustworthiness), not because they are not important in 4IR, but because much has been said about them previously. The following section presents the competencies (discussed throughout the book) in three groups, familiar to most Talent Managers:

- leading self;
- leading others;
- leading the enterprise.

Leading self

The *mindsets* that support prowess in each of the nine themes of managing in 4IR are:

- **Curiosity:** supporting the capability to Sense & Make Sense.
- **Sense of urgency:** supporting the capability to Seize & Replicate.
- **Adaptability:** supporting the capability to Reposition & Reconfigure.
- **Courageous:** supporting pursuit of purposeful, forward-leaning strategy.
- **Problem solver:** supporting ambidextrous thinking and doing.
- **Never settle:** supporting constant evolution, striving to improve performance.
- **Empathy:** supporting empowerment and protection of talent.
- **Empower others:** support the organization driven by high-performance teams.
- **Talent catalyst:** in support of winning the race to develop talent.

In addition, the following traits underpin the effectiveness of the leader in 4IR. A key theme is that in the uncertainty and ambiguity of 4IR, the leader needs to inspire trust, being seen to take personal responsibility, to be thoughtful and consistent in their behaviours, not swayed with biases or blinkers, and to be effective in making difficult decisions.

- Seize & Replicate:
  - o Personal accountability: in the fluidity and ambiguity of 4IR, accountability for personal behaviour and team results differentially impacts performance.

- Purpose-led, forward-leaning:
  - o Purposeful leadership: consistently oriented to the pursuit of a meaningful and inspiring mission for the betterment of the collective community.
  - o Possibility not probability: mental capacity to 'connect the dots' and explore multiple different possible outcomes and alternative futures.
  - o Strategic thinking: clear thinking through multiple layers of ambiguous data and insight, to be able to determine and structure choices for alternative pathways.
  - o Decision making in uncertainty: ability to make definitive decisions for action, whilst cognizant of risks, uncertainties and likely need for future adaption.
- Ambidextrous leadership:
  - o Ambidextrous thinking and doing: ability to maintain progress between two or more seemingly competing objectives.
  - o Ownership of paradox and dilemma: exploring new ways to resolve apparent dilemmas, through changing perspective, testing assumptions and constraints.
  - o Creative, systems thinking: understanding causality and interconnections, being able to design and implement interventions with consideration for the interface and interactions with other parts of the processes and systems of the corporation.
- Continuous evolution:
  - o Executive presence: ability to communicate credibility and instil confidence through verbal and non-verbal communications.
- Human-centred workforce management:
  - o Authenticity: ability to connect with people and endear their trust through honesty about personal strengths and weaknesses and consistent behaviour.
- Race to develop 4IR talent:
  - o Hunger for learning: a humility about what they know already and an appetite for learning and self-improvement.

Leading others

Three key themes running through these competencies are: (a) the ability to provide meaning, to connect others with the purpose of the organization; (b) the desire to collaborate, to draw upon everyone's contributions; (c) respecting the differences between individuals and supporting their well-being:

- Sense & Make Sense:
  - Crowd-source: encourage others to contribute ideas, observations and insights with the expectation of unlocking value. Everyone is smarter than anyone.
  - Harvest idea fragments: regularly gather snippets of information, interesting soundbites and ideas; do not be judgemental of their potential value as in the future they may be combined with other idea fragments to create innovations.
  - Ask... and what else? Encourage sharing of thoughts and perceptions, even if partially formed, being non-judgemental, providing psychological safety.
  - Experiment: test & learn: accelerate learning by working together and obtaining rapid feedback from the market and customers.
- Seize & Replicate:
  - Collaborate across boundaries: the expectation that new opportunities and new solutions will be uncovered by working with others who have different skills and perspectives.
- Reposition & Reconfigure:
  - Persuasion and influence: developing a repertoire of skills that assist effective collaboration and interactions, particularly when moving into action.
  - Global vision: ability to see opportunities and challenges in different contexts, unbiased and unblinkered.
- Ambidextrous leadership:
  - Winning together: deepening the possibilities for greater give and take between colleagues through the strong awareness of being on the same side, working to the same overall goal.
  - Productive reasoning: establishing effective collaborations through repositioning disagreements as opportunities for mutual learning and discovery.
  - Embrace new perspectives: sharing, enquiring about and listening to other people's (differing) opinions, seeking to learn and to enrich each other's understanding.

- Continuous evolution:
  - o Provide meaning/connect to purpose: overcoming differences between colleagues by focusing on the common objective of pursuit of a higher purpose. Enhancing motivation, providing meaning to the tasks allocated.
- Human-centred workforce management:
  - o Flexibility in support of others: respecting and acknowledging differences between individuals, seeking to accommodate differences where appropriate.
  - o Promote well-being and resilience: seeking to reduce unhealthy stress and to foster an environment conducive to emotional, mental and physical health.
- Deploy talent with fluid teaming:
  - o Accelerating the business through the formation of teams to address opportunities and challenges as they arise, fluidly allocating individuals to teams and depending on the team to deliver important results.
  - o Team-focused development: technical and leadership skills development, in real time, within the context of a working team, in order to enhance their ability to fulfil their mandate.
  - o Pursue excellence (as a team): establishing the expectation and the habit of each member contributing ideas on how to enhance the performance of the team – and the team quickly acting on the suggestions and measuring impact.
  - o Increase the cadence: increasing the tempo of the team in order to increase the productivity of the team, eg shortening sprint cycles.
  - o Challenge and support one another: maximizing the rate of learning and growth for members by taking responsibility to robustly but constructively challenge each other, whilst ensuring a supportive environment and providing psychological safety.
- Race to develop 4IR talent:
  - o Leader as a coach: personal support for the development of the capabilities and performance of the team members. Providing one-on-one support in a timely manner and in the context of the tasks being undertaken.

o Stretch roles and assignments: allocating step-up roles that take the team member beyond their comfort zone, whilst providing support such that they do not become overloaded but maximize their rate of growth.

Leading the enterprise

The role of the leader is to promote the development and support the application of the capabilities and approaches listed below:

- Sense & Make Sense:
  - o Access unique external insight: obtain independent data and insight on customers and the marketspace, generate new insights, enhance internal beliefs and points of view.
  - o Data driven, digitally enabled: establish and reinforce the gathering and analysis of data. Insist on data-supported discussions and use data to test veracity of assumptions and beliefs.
- Seize & Replicate:
  - o Shape the future: facilitate structured debate on the potential futures, create plausible alternative versions of the future, determine and implement actions to influence the development path of the marketspace towards the preferred future.
  - o Move people to access expertise: mission-critical expertise is rare to find and difficult to replicate. Move people to consult with experts or experts to work on problems when mission-critical.
  - o Clusters not regions: cluster together and coordinate between marketspaces with similar characteristics in order to accelerate acquisition, sharing and reapplication of relevant learning.
  - o Rapid scale-up: rapidly scale up winning propositions, locally and across the network; in 4IR speed is a source of competitive advantage.
- Reposition & Reconfigure:
  - o Define new marketspaces: enjoy monopoly benefits by uniquely serving a uniquely defined marketspace. Competitors will struggle to follow exactly or will have to redefine it for themselves, to match their own unique capabilities.
  - o Glide, don't jump: speed of evolution of marketspaces creates the possibility to reduce risk by moving quickly to explore tentatively the opportunities. Similarly, harvesting a position before complete exit

creates the opportunity to confound competitors or to reverse the withdrawal if the context changes.

- o Choiceful duplication: creating and maintaining competing options (supply chain, product line, sales channels, etc) increases flexibility, reducing risk and vulnerability of rigidly depending on forecast accuracy.

- o Simplify, reduce complexity: establish the discipline to continuously challenge and reduce complexity, eg product range proliferation, levels of hierarchy, hand-offs in processes, sign-offs, review meetings and controls etc.

- Purpose-led, forward-leaning:

- o Purpose-led: ensure the enterprise clearly adopts, articulates and follows a meaningful purpose, identified at the intersection of big and meaningful for society, that the stakeholders of the enterprise care passionately about, and that the enterprise has some unique skills or assets that it can apply towards achieving the purpose.

- o Adaptive strategic planning: obtaining a balance of making definitive informed choices about the strategy and the investments and actions required for success, yet being attentive and able to adapt if required as the future unfolds.

- Continuous evolution:

- o Acceleration Officer: a C-Suite appointment with responsibility to know the array of tools, platforms and approaches being deployed in 4IR and for assessing their relevance for the corporation, ensuring that the corporation embraces tools and practices in a timely manner.

- o Plan future-back: a plan co-created by the executive team for the anticipated evolution of the capabilities and performance of the corporation. A point of reference for all those involved in driving the evolution, enabling alignment and coordination.

- o Doctrine of change: a common understanding of the approach for managing change, unique to each enterprise, reflecting the values and purpose as well as the principles and coordination mechanisms. Accelerate change and transformation initiatives by enabling teams to work semi-autonomously.

- o Organization savviness: the ability to 'get things done' and changes made despite what may otherwise be a slow-moving, complex or otherwise resistant environment.

- Human-centred workforce management:
  - Duty of care (guidelines and enrolling supervisors): promoting the well-being of workers, whether employees or not, through practices such as flexible working. Providing an explicit set of guidelines which establishes the boundaries of the expected behaviours as practised by workers and managers, thus reducing ambiguity, doubt and anxiety in how to act. Enlisting and training supervisors and team leaders in how to listen to and respond flexibly to the needs of workers in a manner that is transparent, supportive and equitable for all workers.
- Deploy talent with fluid teaming:
  - Team of teams: a model for organizing and deploying resources to address both short-term and long-term operational and project needs of the corporation. Individuals are fluidly allocated to teams, and their performance on teams is the primary measure of their contribution to the firm.
- Race to develop 4IR talent:
  - Andragogy: changing behaviour – executive development is conducted with the primary goal of positively impacting the individual's performance on the tasks they are currently working on. Just-in-time learning and development.
  - Individual Human Capital Management (digitally enabled): individually tailored development support generated as a result of timely insight into each individual's performance and engagement provided by integrated Human Capital Management software platforms.

The ideal development provider

Business school vs vendor vs corporate academy

Demand for, and investment in, training and development are booming as winning the race to develop talent is a key source of competitive advantage in 4IR. The process of talent development is also being transformed by the combination of the forces of digital enablement, just-in-time learning to address on-the-job challenges, adoption of an integrated andragogy approach to achieve behaviour change, and bespoke customization to the values, priorities and context of the company.

Whilst some business schools have grasped this evolution and reconfigured their executive development practices, most have not. The strong growth of this market is being captured by commercial enterprises, including consultancies (Deloitte, McKinsey), executive search firms (Korn Ferry, Egon Zehnder), specialist training providers (FranklinCovey, Aspire) and online content curators such as LinkedIn and Udacity. Whilst these vendors are adept at designing and delivering learning experiences, they often lack the necessary intimacy with client context and leading-edge insights into the secrets of success for the corporation's strategy. This has led to a significant expansion in the number and scale of corporate academies (there are estimated to be over 4,000 corporate academies now operating, compared with approximately 500 in the year 2000).

The modern corporate academy curates a range of development experiences aligned with the values and capabilities that the corporation has identified as being critical to their competitive strategy. In addition, they provide access to libraries of more standard content for core skills development, provided by third parties. For example, AXA provides learning experiences to 125,000 staff, leveraging a relationship with Coursera. Allianz supports learning for 140,000 employees around the world, with LinkedIn Learning. Many leading corporations (such as Unilever, CreditSuisse, Novartis and others) operate their corporate academy across multiple sites globally, providing bespoke leadership programmes with faculty from leading business schools as well as partnering with multiple vendors, whilst they simultaneously evolve their own technology-enabled learning suite. The modern corporate academy is sponsored by the business units, which regard winning the race for talent as a key source of competitive advantage. Previously, corporate academies were often considered to be a cost centre that should provide a more cost-efficient solution to training rather than relying on external entities. The business units actively engage in the direction and the actualization of the learning journeys, selecting the participants, contributing internal experts, developmental assignments and mentors – and providing feedback on the effectiveness of the training provided.

In 2015, the consultancy Executive Core[9] produced a report and set of recommendations for how business schools should reimagine their value proposition in order to stay relevant.[10] In commissioning the report, the sponsoring organizations (Executive Education Consortium (UNICON),[11] Association to Advance Collegiate Schools of Business (AACSB)[12] and the Executive MBA

Council (EMBAC)[13]) were acknowledging that whilst the sector was booming and transforming, the vast majority of business schools were being left behind. Several of the themes that emerged from the work have increased in relevance as 4IR continues apace but many business schools fail to adapt. A conclusion from the report:

> The business learning marketspace for customized solutions is continuing to grow, the needs diversify, and the needs vary significantly by prospective client. In response to these needs, many business schools continue to lose competitively to professional services firms. Investment and change will likely be required for many [...] business schools will need a radically different strategy.[14]

The business schools that are succeeding (such as IE[15]) have made a clear strategic choice to support the changing needs of corporates in 4IR. They align investment, recruitment and partnering activities to transform the how and what of their offerings as well as their business and operating models.

Two themes in the report neatly describe the challenges that continue to prevent business schools from adapting their offering:

Theme 8: Align business school content to current initiatives and learning modules already used by corporations.

Business school faculty have few incentives to adapt their preferred mental models and approaches to unique requirements, spend extra time onsite with corporations developing broad relationships, and understand the market challenges.

If business schools decide to compete for this business, they will need to examine all of their systems and processes to see if they drive to required behaviours. Rewarding faculty for publishing research and granting tenure to allow academic independence and freedom appears to be in conflict with the needs to reframe insights and concepts to clients' frameworks, effectively collaborate and align with others, and frequently customize learning offerings with a focus on effectively transferring learning back on the job. Some business schools may find it more efficient to outsource this function, give it to adjunct faculty, or install a parallel consulting organization into the school which knows how to do this.[16]

Theme 9: Develop better customer intimacy across the enterprise.

Many key talent management stakeholders also want advanced consulting and ongoing attention from the authors of the models they are integrating into their development activities. Some larger, global customers would ideally like the flexibility to customize their common development programmes and deliver them through a mixture of learning delivery channels including online, face-to-face (real or virtual) and in-person in regional centralized locations.

To achieve the necessary customer intimacy that would enable the understanding of the emerging needs of the client and allow the orchestration of the right resources at the right time, client relationship managers or account management roles would need to be expanded at the business school or management education provider. Of the people we interviewed, they reported that professional services had larger client management teams and several mentioned that they received more contact and flexibility from these teams. Some talent management professionals believe that the executive education teams from universities and their global delivery presence are too lean to meet their more comprehensive talent management needs.[17]

As discussed in the first few chapters of this book, in the 4IR there is a clear competitive advantage achieved by corporations that develop and leverage knowledge and insight faster than others, in particular the theme of making sense of the unfolding future and being able to rapidly test, learn, apply and scale solutions and implement changes. As highlighted in each previous chapter, specific skills are required of leaders and executives to enable the firm to excel in the context of 4IR. In this chapter we have discussed the importance of applying learning immediately in the workplace. In combination this series of factors means that business schools at universities that are leading research in areas of strategic importance for client corporations could be very powerful partners enabling corporate success. However, despite having this powerful combination of resources and the strong growth in demand for executive development, most business schools are failing to reconfigure for success. The opportunity is there for these institutions to shift focus to corporate and executive development needs.

Leadership traits: the race to develop 4IR talent

Leader as a coach

Leaders should seek to excel at coaching others: guiding, stimulating, encouraging and mentoring their team members. The leader as a coach asks questions instead of providing answers, provides support and guidance for their staff's development. The leader as a coach invests in the success of others; they listen, observe, display empathy, show genuine interest in the context and mindset of the individual, and give them support to accelerate their development. As a coach the leader creates emotional safety for the team members and asks powerful questions that help them to reflect, so that they can find their way forward. *The Coaching Habit*[18] by Michael Bungay Stanier lists seven key questions for a leader-as-coach to master: 1) What's on your mind? 2) And what else? 3) What's the real challenge here for you? 4) What do you want? 5) How can I help? 6) If you're saying yes to this, what are you saying no to? 7) What was most useful for you?

Stretch roles and assignments

To accelerate the development of talent, especially the most able talent, the leader must be willing and competent at defining goals and roles that stretch individuals. People develop at different paces and have different capacities to develop; in 4IR winning the race to develop talent necessitates being able to differentiate between individuals and find for each person the stretch that maximizes their rate of development – neither too little nor too much. Big stretch assignments (deliberately assigning tasks that are beyond the individual's demonstrated capability) create stress for the individuals and expose the leader to risk. The leader must therefore provide active support to the individual, monitoring their energies, stress and progress, providing guidance, imbuing a sense of trust, and instilling confidence, whilst also holding them accountable for the results; supporting them to succeed but if failure occurs then helping them to process and learn from that and adjust future behaviour. The stretch assignment should create positive stress, not negative stress, for the individual – delegate but be involved.

Hunger for learning

Leaders throughout the firm must display a hunger for learning, actively investing their own time and energy in self-improvement and development. Learning will take many forms but should include actively seeking feedback from others, the willingness to experiment with new behaviours as well as ensuring they stay current with the developments in-sector. Executives at several firms noted that when they hire in talent or consider someone for promotion, they seek evidence of self-driven learning (eg self-funded studies, personal time invested in development) and adaptation (including decisions to make lateral career moves motivated by self-development). Executives are expected to participate in and contribute to initiatives and platforms that support continuous learning, such as self-directed learning through a corporate curated learning portal, hosting and participating in activities with thought leaders from business and academia, actively sharing insights and 'idea fragments' with one another. Two excellent books that complement the topic and techniques of personal change are both written by Marshall Goldsmith: *What Got You Here, Won't Get You There*[19] and *Triggers*.[20]

Mindset: Talent catalyst

The mindset of every executive should be to enable and develop others and themselves. The required culture being of continuous learning, frequent feedback and transparency of individual and team performance. Leaders need to evolve the mindset that supports this; to prioritize the success of the team and each member within the team, constantly thinking about the best way to make that happen. The manager's success is based on their success.

KEY CONCEPTS: CHAPTER 8

Spending and investment in developing the skills and capabilities of executives is growing rapidly, driven by the attempt to keep up with the changes in how we work and what we need to do being wrought by 4IR. Winning firms are those that can attract, train and retain the best talent. Development investment is not limited to people designated as being of high potential, but must be inclusive of executives and leaders who are already highly successful but who need to reskill to keep up with 4IR. The objective is to win the race to develop talent for 4IR, not to try to win the war to attract and retain talent from an existing pool.

- The leadership competencies to win in 4IR are different from those of the prior industrial ages. Leadership can no longer be described as 'command and control' – it is now 'connect and collaborate'. Given the speed of business evolution in 4IR, no one can know everything, so we must connect and influence a network of individuals, many of whom will not be 'like us' but rather they have evolved and can contribute very different perspectives and insights.

- Development journeys aim to achieve changes in behaviour on the job in ways that positively impact performance. The andragogical approach explicitly addresses and integrates drivers of motivation (aware and aspire), ability (explore and experiment), opportunity (apply and assess), and actively provides a supportive environment (be visible and bespoke).

- Due to the increased urgency and compressed time available, how executives are supported to learn and develop has changed. AI and predictive analytics, as well as the opportunities for remote learning, have enabled learning to be tailored to the needs of the individual. Other technologies are enriching the learning experience through simulations and gamification. Increasingly, learning and development facilitate flow of work; 'just in time' to equip the executive with the skills and knowledge to tackle a current challenge, in digestible 'bite-sized' interventions that allow the executive to stay engaged in their work.

Leadership traits:

- leader as a coach;
- stretch roles and assignments;
- hunger for learning;
- mindset: talent catalyst.

Endnotes

1 Bersin, J (2019) New research shows explosive growth in corporate learning: our biggest challenge? Time, *LinkedIn*, https://www.linkedin.com/pulse/new-research-shows-explosive-growth-corporate-learning-josh-bersin/ (archived at https://perma.cc/DF8P-MV84)

2 2019 Workplace Learning Report, LinkedIn, https://learning.linkedin.com/content/dam/me/business/en-us/amp/learning-solutions/images/workplace-learning-report-2019/pdf/workplace-learning-report-2019.pdf (archived at https://perma.cc/3JUN-8QJN)

3 Batra, R and Ray, M (1986) The moderating influence of motivation, ability, and opportunity to respond, *Journal of Consumer Research*, 12 (4)

4 Rath, T and Conchie, B (2008) *Strengths Based Leadership*, Gallup Press

5 Beer, M, Finnstrom, M and Schrader, D (2016) Why leadership training fails and what to do about it, *Harvard Business Review*, October

6 2019 Workplace Learning Report, LinkedIn, https://learning.linkedin.com/content/dam/me/business/en-us/amp/learning-solutions/images/workplace-learning-report-2019/pdf/workplace-learning-report-2019.pdf (archived at https://perma.cc/3JUN-8QJN)

7 Ibid

8 Brown, S (2019) Enabling 130,000 employees to grow in an organization committed to continuous learning, *Novartis*, https://www.novartis.com/stories/people-and-culture/enabling-130000-employees-grow-organization-committed-continuous-learning (archived at https://perma.cc/UTD4-8ZLW)

9   https://www.executive-core.com/ (archived at https://perma.cc/SU2Z-MDY4)

10   Future trends of Leadership Development: A Research Project Sponsored by AACSB, EMBA, and UNICON by Executive Core, Summer 2015

11   https://www.uniconexed.org/ (archived at https://perma.cc/32GD-YX7E)

12   https://www.aacsb.edu/ (archived at https://perma.cc/Z467-QDKC)

13   https://embac.org/ (archived at https://perma.cc/3S75-KZF4)

14   Future trends of Leadership Development: A Research Project Sponsored by AACSB, EMBA, and UNICON by Executive Core, Summer 2015

15   https://www.ie.edu/business-school/ (archived at https://perma.cc/7Z8F-75TQ)

16   Future trends of Leadership Development: A Research Project Sponsored by AACSB, EMBA, and UNICON by Executive Core, Summer 2015

17   Ibid

18   Stanier, M B (2016) *The Coaching Habit*, Box of Crayons Press

19   Goldsmith, M (2007) *What Got You Here, Won't Get You There*, Hyperion

20   Goldsmith, M (2015) *Triggers*, Profile Books

09

Deploy talent with fluid teaming

IN BRIEF

To compete successfully in 4IR, the often-scarce talent with the most appropriate skills and mindsets must be deployed highly effectively. This requires the ability to rapidly assemble, adjust and dismantle teams to tackle an ever-changing line-up of challenges. Agile, adaptable corporations need agile, adaptable resource configurations: teams. Teams are the 'engines of performance' in 4IR organizations. Individuals across the whole organization must have a common understanding of teaming, enhancing their ability to come together quickly and collectively perform immediately, whether in person or remotely, whether in the same unit or across organizational boundaries. The People Management infrastructure and systems must enable the entire organization to function as a fluid team made up of multiple fluid teams. Functional or department units may be recognized as the 'home team' associated with deepening and broadening an individual's specializations, whereas multifunctional 'away teams' are the groups that are expected to drive breakthroughs.

Teams: the engines of performance

In 4IR, multi-functional teams are essential engines of performance, addressing an increasing array of initiatives, as individuals may simultaneously be members of several teams. Teams may also be short-lived or almost permanent fixtures within the company. Team performance is so important that it cannot be left to chance. How a team comes together, how the individuals of a team interact with each other, how they themselves behave and how they interact with stakeholders outside the team should be made explicit; a codification of behaviours and expectations of each other. The rules and practice for teaming are unique to an organization, reflecting its culture and values as much as perceived best practice. As such, newer employees need to be told exactly what those practices are and all team members need to be held to account, by each other, for abiding by those rules.

Quickly establishing effective teams is particularly important in dynamic organizations where the forming and disbanding of teams smoothly can be a source of competitive advantage. As each team comes together there should be an onboarding of all members which brings into alignment, for this team, all the members' understanding of five key issues:

1   What exactly is the mandate of this team? Why is this mandate important for the wider organization and how is it different from every other team or part of the organization? What exactly is this team accountable for, and what is outside of its remit?

2   What is the role of this team, ie what kind of team does it need to be to fulfil the mandate? Is it a working team or a coordinating team or for governing etc? What is the limit of what this team is responsible for doing, where do others take over, who are they and what is the interface with them?

3   Who should be in the core team, in order to enable the team to fulfil its duties? Which skills and what level of seniority are required to enable the core team to function well? What size should the team be in order to be effective and efficient? The principle should be that everyone on the team is contributing equally. Guests may sometimes be invited into the team if required, rather than being included in the core.

4   What behaviours are expected from everyone in the core team? Everyone should be held accountable by everyone else in the team for behaving in the manner that has been agreed. Everyone should be contributing to the success of the team in approximately equal proportions.

5   How does this team learn and improve? How do team members or stakeholders share feedback, and how does the team renew itself if required? What are the metrics of performance and how are all team members held to account for the success of the team?

Team-focused development

Even with the fundamentals of teaming established as described above, not all teams perform well. Google's performance depends on team performance and so it has invested significantly in understanding what differentiates high- from low-performing teams, concluding that the mix of specific personality types or skills or backgrounds makes little difference. What matters are the group norms, ie the traditions, behaviours with one another and unwritten rules that govern interactions. Norms can be unspoken or openly acknowledged, but their influence is often profound.[1] The psychological bias of most individuals is to want to fit in with the group; as such, group norms usually override individual behaviour preferences. The right norms raise a group's collective performance, whereas the wrong norms can undermine performance, irrespective of the brilliance and dedication of each individual in the team. Some teams energize the members whereas others can drain the energy, leaving individuals feeling exhausted. Google identified that what distinguishes high- from low-performing teams is how teammates treat one another, in particular with regards to what Google researchers labelled 'psychological safety'. This creates the opportunity for individuals to be honest and vulnerable with one another; to share thoughts and fears, successes and mistakes, likes and dislikes with confidence that these will be met with empathy, support and confidentiality.

Google emphasizes the importance of nurturing a culture of dependability and trust between team members, with each person noticing when someone on the team is feeling excluded or down, and acting to include or encourage that person. For the team to perform at its best, each person must contribute; Google concluded that each member should speak for approximately an equal share of the time. Google's analysis of team performance also identified the importance of ensuring that the team has clear goals, that the role of the team is clearly understood, as well as clearly understanding how the output from the team is aligned with and will have an impact on achieving the wider mission of the corporation.

Teams, not individuals, are increasingly recognized as the engines that drive or inhibit corporate performance – as such, team development is increasing in importance as a vehicle for leadership development. Team-centred development requires clearly delineating otherwise often implicit assumptions about what the team does and how its individuals should behave. For a team to excel, every member needs to be aware and aligned in their mindset and understanding of the team's unique mandate and operating model. This shift will require a significant rebalancing of the executive development spending in many corporations, which talent officers confirm is indeed taking place. Most notably, a greater emphasis is being placed on supporting intact teams as they work to address workplace challenges in real time.

Team role types

Professor Meredith Belbin noted that a high-functioning team consists of individuals who take on different types of role within the team.[2] Belbin identified nine different roles (as shown in Table 9.1) that should be present in any team.

TABLE 9.1 Team role types[3]

Team Role Type	Contribution	Allowable Weakness
Resource Investigator	Outgoing, enthusiastic. Explores opportunities and develops contacts.	Might be over-optimistic, and can lose interest once the initial enthusiasm has passed.
Teamworker	Co-operative, perceptive and diplomatic. Listens and averts friction.	Can be indecisive in crunch situations and tends to avoid confrontation.
Coordinator	Mature, confident, identifies talent. Clarifies goals. Delegates effectively.	Can be seen as manipulative and might offload their own share of the work.
Plant	Creative, imaginative, free-thinking. Generates ideas.	Might ignore incidentals, and may be too pre-occupied to communicate effectively.
Monitor Evaluator	Sober, strategic and discerning. Sees all options and judges accurately.	Sometimes lacks the drive and ability to inspire others and can be overly critical.
Specialist	Single-minded, self-starting and dedicated.	Can only contribute on a narrow front and tends to dwell on the technicalities.
Shaper	Provides specialist knowledge and skills.	Can be prone to provocation, and may sometimes offend people's feelings.
Implementer	Practical, reliable, efficient. Turns ideas into actions and organizes work that needs to be done.	Can be a bit inflexible and slow to respond to new possibilities.
Completer-Finisher	Painstaking, conscientious, anxious. Searches out errors. Polishes and perfects.	Can be inclined to worry unduly, and reluctant to delegate.

Whilst every person has a preferred role type, team members should be adept at observing the dynamics of the team to identify which roles are being over- or underplayed and to then be able to adjust their behaviours accordingly. A key insight of Professor Belbin is that 'there may not be a perfectly balanced individual, but there can be a perfectly balanced team', when all role types are appropriately performed. In high-performing teams, all the roles are covered, each person contributes, and there is constructive support and challenge of one another. This is achieved only if there is explicit discussion and agreement on such behaviours when the team is initially formed; during the life of the team, members must also hold each other to account.

Tracking individual performance in teams

One of the most often-cited challenges for firms adopting a team-focused approach is the HR department, or more accurately the HR systems. Traditional HR systems that track performance on annual (or semi-annual) cycles through line managers may work against fluid teaming, as the individual's contribution to the team may not be fully captured. Similarly, highly effective team members, those who repeatedly demonstrate the ability to help enable teams to deliver exceptional performance, may not be the most senior hierarchically and so the HR systems or department may not be willing or able to reward them appropriately.

The HR systems to support team-focused performance need to (a) be able to match the right person for the right team, (b) reward the person appropriately for their contribution to team performance, and (c) provide feedback and support for development. In a fluid, team-based environment this requires capturing and accessing data at the rhythm of team formation and disbandment, not periodically. HR systems are required to be populated with intimate knowledge of the team roles that the individual is most adept at taking on and their track record as seen through the eyes of peers and leaders of previous teams. Additionally, this intimate insight needs to be combined with knowledge of the individual's formal skills and competencies as well as an objective assessment of how effective the previous teams have actually been in achieving their mission goals. An outstanding team member may have been on a dysfunctional team that failed to achieve its goals, or a dysfunctional team that did achieve its goals, due in large part to the efforts of the individual. The HR system needs to know and differentially provide feedback and support for and to reward the individual.

In cross-cultural settings the challenges for HR systems of managing teaming and the team-of-teams approach can be heightened. For example, a few years ago a famous Danish firm established a regional HQ in Singapore and based there several leaders with global remits. They imported a team-based approach that worked at their global HQ, setting accountabilities for teams, including the senior leadership team. However, infighting and mistrust became rife and results fell far below the anticipated growth. They realized that in this multicultural setting, where many new executives had been brought in from the outside upon establishment of the new regional HQ, there was little cohesion and no consistent sense of belonging to the parent company and culture. The team-based performance metrics were creating a situation where few felt any need as individuals to actually take ownership as 'everyone' on the team was supposed to be equally responsible.

As the famous basketball player Michael Jordan noted, 'There's no "I" in team – but there is in "WINNING".' For a team to deliver winning performance, every person needs to commit fully. HR systems need to track, reward, give feedback, and develop each individual's ability and willingness to drive collective team performance. Google sets individual OKRs (Objectives and Key Results) which are tracked for each employee, whilst also recognizing the importance of team performance. In a high-mobility team-of-teams environment, tracking individual and team performance (including feedback from team members on each other) can further enable the HR managers to spot high-performing talent that might have been hidden in more traditional organizations and ensure initiatives are put in place to nurture and retain such individuals.

Team of teams

The concept of 'team of teams' extends the principle of teams being the engines of performance to drive the majority of a firm's activities and performance. Individuals with appropriate technical or functional skills are assigned to one or several teams that are accountable for operating performance, such assignments being of flexible and various durations. The 'team of teams' approach creates high levels of organizational flexibility and reconfigurability. Members need to come together as a team with minimal time for establishing team-specific dynamics. The teams also need to disperse smoothly whilst capturing effectively the learnings and providing one another with feedback. Four mechanisms can help this, all of which should be widely understood by individuals across the organization in expectation that they may be involved directly or indirectly in providing support to a team:

- There should be a standard approach to onboarding and briefing the team on its mandate, objectives and scope.

- Everyone knows what behaviour norms are expected of the team leader and the team members. These norms include how to manage their involvement if they are simultaneously on several different teams, how decisions are taken, and how the team should respond to unanticipated events or circumstances.

- There is open, wide sharing of information across the company such that everyone can be up to speed on the topics and background relevant to the achievement of the mandate of the team. Knowledge sharing through its availability on accessible, searchable databases and the ability to identify and speak freely with relevant individuals is a source of power for the organization with fluid teams.

- The procedures for capturing knowledge and learning from each team initiative are widely understood and practised, ensuring that knowledge is available to future teams. Feedback is provided by all team members to each individual such that they know how to continuously improve their contribution and performance.

Pooling resources

Teams are increasingly perceived as the engines that drive the performance of the corporation. Teams drawing in talent from across the organization are deployed with a specific mission, usually with a specific time frame. The best teams work collaboratively and productively together whilst celebrating diversity of skills, perspectives and contributions between team members. Across all the companies in the research there is an increasing expectation that teaming will increase.

The 'team of teams' concept describes an environment with high mobility of individuals between teams – people coming together for projects and tasks, quickly performing well as a team, and then disbanding from that team to join another. Whilst a team of teams can be empowering for individuals and provides the opportunity for great visibility on their performance, several themes of caution emerged from the research, requiring pro-active management:

- For some managers and functional heads, the assignment of 'their' staff to join teams can be perceived as a distraction from the 'real' jobs that depletes the resources available for achieving the department's goals. As a consequence, the team member may feel unsupported in their team role and concerned that their performance evaluation, which depends primarily on their 'line manager', will suffer.

- This toxic environment must be directly addressed. Approaches cited by executives in the research included providing direct 'top cover' by the CEO for team members or seconding the team members full-time such that it is clear that their reporting lines have changed.

- However, the bigger issue is to garner the support of the 'department head' to accept that fluid resourcing and constant teaming are the new normal. These senior executives can also benefit from the support of temporary teams that are drawn together to support priority tasks relevant to their set of responsibilities and objectives. It is essential to build widespread recognition of the primacy of teams as the engines driving the overall performance of the organization; that participation in teams provides the opportunity to be spotted as talent and rewarded for contribution to team success.

- For people familiar with more traditional organizational approaches, the team-of-teams operating model can feel like 'organized chaos'. From a staff member's perspective, there may be no clear visibility on who exactly is doing what, making finding relevant resources (people or reports) appear daunting. However, firms such as Google use cloud-based shared document databases and search algorithms such that with key words and a few clicks the right people and resources can be quickly identified and contacted. A mid-career executive who moved to just such an organization said the best approach for her was to 'take the plunge and jump in – once you have learned to "swim" you discover that it actually works, you don't drown, it's actually quite empowering!'

- As teams are increasingly being formed and disbanded and the expectation is that they will drive performance, there must be an explicit and commonly embraced model for teaming at this corporation. Teams need to 'hit the ground running', not suffer a protracted period of time 'forming and norming' with one another. Undoubtedly, interpersonal relationships and trust will grow over time; however, from the outset there should be an immediate, common understanding of how teams work here, what good team behaviours look like, and how each member is expected to keep each other and themselves to the highest standards. Everyone on the team is expected to hold each other accountable to that code of behaviour.

Pooling information

When a team forms, it needs to access all information that is relevant to its success, as when it disbands much knowledge and insight could be lost if it has not already been documented and shared. Thus, fundamental for the success of the 'team-of-teams' approach is the continuous open sharing of insight and information. What Unilever calls the 'data lake', and what Google is demonstrating mastery at, is document sharing, storing and accessing – using their outstanding search capabilities. An executive at a major technology company that thrives with the team-of-teams approach described it as follows:

> In my previous company, information was held in the databases and heads of the department heads. There were lots of versions and only really the secretaries knew their way around to find the latest version or recall where something had been tucked away. Knowledge was certainly a form of power, mainly in protecting people from being fired rather than overtly manipulating, but certainly you secured your seat at the table with your access to information and institutional knowledge. Here everyone can access everything, but you have little idea of where it is or who might have put it there, or when, or even if they are still with the company – but it doesn't matter. We are the leaders in search and it's all in the cloud. We are trusted to have access. So [at this firm] knowledge is power too, except here knowledge is widely available; the question is only whether you have bothered to find it, been able to assimilate it and then are able to do and say something useful with it.

In his book *Team of Teams*,[4] retired US Army General Stanley McChrystal described the teaming model that he instigated to make a step change in the performance of the joint forces, special operations command during the war in Iraq. He did this by dramatically increasing the rate of operational deployments and integrating the efforts of a wide range of special units from multiple different armies. In particular, he describes the need to create a 'shared consciousness' with open sharing of intelligence information between units. This represented a significant departure from traditional mindsets and practices of 'need to know' only for the preservation of operational security. If the special operations command of a multi-nation force can share operationally sensitive (and no doubt some covert) information in order to succeed with the team-of-teams approach, then I'm sure every corporate organization can too!

Culture and sense of belonging

As resources are mobile and structures fluid, the sense of position or belonging to a particular department or unit may diminish. Whilst this is a positive for breaking out from silos, it can be bewildering for some individuals. As such there should be deliberate initiatives to inculcate a strong sense of identity and belonging to the whole. What Google aptly calls being a 'Googler', they reinforce through the all-firm meetings (or video calls), 'TGIF', as well as the multiple initiatives that they run internally, and the facilities provided to support each individual to connect with others and to feel part of the Google family. The sense of inclusion, including having access to information and to senior leaders, is critical to reinforce the sense of belonging and to share in the 'shared consciousness' of the organization.

Leadership traits: deploy talent with fluid teaming

Pursue excellence (as a team)

A team that is not improving is breaking down. The team should seek to continuously improve its performance, adjusting roles and processes to increase efficiency and effectiveness. A CEO who was driving the transformation of a hitherto rather complacent government agency noted how he had adopted the language of Olympic Gold medallist Ben Hunt-Davis – 'Will it make the boat go faster?'[5] – to help create a high-performance culture in the senior leadership team. With this simple phrase, executives were expected to challenge one another whilst also reminding themselves that the goal was to transform the agency for heightened productivity and agility through adopting the technologies and behaviours of the 4IR. He expected everyone to come up with ideas for driving the performance of the agency and would not conclude any leadership team meeting until everyone present had contributed a new idea, reminding them that they were all in the 'boat' together. As philosopher Will Durant noted whilst interpreting Aristotle,[6] 'We are what we repeatedly do. Excellence, then, is not an act, but a habit.' Excellence in team performance is achieved by every day reinforcing the habit of pursuing excellence, making small adjustments in the hope of improving performance.

Increase the cadence

As the speed of business accelerates and resources are more fluidly deployed, there is also the need to increase the work rate. An effective way to achieve this is by adopting Sprints. Companies evolve their own version of Sprints: common elements are: (1) clarity on one or two goals and why they matter, that everyone on the team understands and acknowledges; (2) the team defines the action steps to be undertaken to achieve the goals and results expected by the time of the next governance review; (3) fast act-assess cycles (Sprints) by the team, keeping track of progress on actions and results achieved; and (4) review and adjust governance sessions approximately every four Sprint cycles, between the team and the stakeholders.

Challenge and support[7]

Individual accountability and collective responsibility require that team members provide each other with constructive feedback and engage appropriately in difficult conversations. There must be a culture of challenge combined with support, appropriately calling out and discussing observed or perceived underperformance whilst providing positive support, and challenging contributions and suggestions to uncover weaknesses or biases in order to stimulate greater thought and robustness. The team will come together and reach new heights of performance when there is a strong sense of mutual trust; this requires investing in knowing what drives each other, knowing each other's vulnerabilities as well as strengths, and being able to be honest with each other.

Mindset: Empower others

Teams perform best when they know how their mandate aligns with the overall purpose of the organization and that what they are doing is important. The team sponsor, who commissions the team, must therefore ensure these fundamentals are in place. The sponsor should then empower the team leader and the team to achieve the mandate, creating a balance between allowing enough space for the team to find its rhythm and to self-navigate whilst building the cadence. The stronger the team's understanding and connection with purpose and the greater their sense of empowerment and their ability to self-direct, the better its overall performance. Difficulties between individuals can be set aside due to a sense of mutual dependency in the pursuit of a meaningful objective.

KEY CONCEPTS: CHAPTER 9

Teams, particularly multi-functional teams, are the engines of performance in 4IR. Teams can be nimble (quickly deployed), they can be task-focused (achieving high impact) and they can eschew the comfort and complacency that can undermine longstanding groups (eg departments) within an organization:

- The corporation should adopt a code of practices for teaming across the organization, such that everyone understands how teams perform here. High team performance is achieved when everyone understands the objective and knows how they are expected to act as a member of the team and how to interact with others. It requires a high sense of individual accountability for collective performance.

- High team performance requires that there is a high level of trust between individual members, so much so that they are prepared to forego or jeopardize success with their own area of contribution in order to support someone else within the team if their required contribution is more important for overall performance. It also requires that each individual is aware of the type of contribution they are making to the team processes and that they are able to consciously adjust their role if the contributions from others are unbalanced.

- The operating model known as 'team of teams' can very powerfully drive overall performance, particularly in highly dynamic situations. In this model the entire organization is considered as a large overall team made up of smaller individual teams that form and are disbanded as circumstances require. For this approach to work there must be a common understanding of how a team forms and the roles of individuals, as well as there being a high level of trust and information sharing between members.

Leadership traits:

- pursue excellence (as a team);
- increase the cadence;
- challenge and support one another;
- mindset: empower others.

Endnotes

1 Duhigg, C (2016) What Google learned from its quest to build the perfect team, *New York Times Magazine*, 25 February, https://www.nytimes.com/2016/02/28/magazine/what-google-learned-from-its-quest-to-build-the-perfect-team.html (archived at https://perma.cc/D7AC-4QEY)

2 Belbin, R (2010) *Management Teams*, Routledge

3 Adapted from Belbin.com

4 McChrystal, S *et al* (2015) *Team of Teams*, Penguin Books

5 Hunt-Davis, B (2011) *Will It Make the Boat Go Faster? Olympic-winning strategies for everyday success*, Troubadour Publishing

6 Durant, W (1991) *The Story of Philosophy*, Simon & Schuster

7 Nevitt Sanford (1909–1995) was professor of psychology at the University of California at Berkeley, and postulated that maximum rate of growth and development is achieved through a combination of high challenge and high support

10

Human-centred workforce management: Duty of care

IN BRIEF

At the beginning of this book I quoted Klaus Schwab from the World Economic Forum,[1] who described the 4th Industrial Revolution as being 'more than just technology-driven change; it is an opportunity... to harness converging technologies in order to create an inclusive, human-centred future'. There is growing acceptance that firm performance depends on worker well-being rather than worker exploitation and the responsibility for such is falling to the employers, rather than to the state:

- The World Health Organization names an 'epidemic of stress'[2] that is spreading across populations of workers in developed countries.

- In February 2019 the United Nations issued a report on the unsustainability of income inequality,[3] a primary cause of the stress that erodes the mental and physical well-being of workers.

Talent is a critical and scarce resource in 4IR, which places a priority on attracting, retaining, empowering and maintaining the engagement of talent. Human-centred workforce management (HCWM) promotes worker well-being and inclusion, particularly through flexible working arrangements, accommodating differences between individuals in how they manage the work-family life boundary and supporting individual tailoring of job scope. HCWM results in enhanced productivity, performance and increased tenure, all of which support employer branding – and the ability to attract the desired talent.

The essence of this theme was neatly captured by Jack Ma when he said, 'If you want to win in the 21st century, you have to empower others, making sure other people are better than you. Then you will be successful.'

Each person is unique – a unique set of skills and unique set of circumstances. 4IR corporations need to curate networks and communities of people in ways that heighten collective performance whilst engaging each individual person. The content of work, the relationship between individuals and employers and the modes and models of working are all changing significantly. If indeed the 4IR is to be human-centred, then corporate leaders and policymakers need to take action to equip workers to navigate the changes and to be engaged effectively in the economic and social context being created. Some of the most important changes are highlighted below:

- The content of work is changing. The 4th Industrial Revolution is embracing digital automation, machine learning and genomics, which will increasingly dislocate jobs and workers. It will also open up new requirements for interacting with the digitally and bionically enabled capabilities, necessitating learning new skills. Simultaneously, ageing populations globally are increasing the need for healthcare practitioners, as well as the growth of services providing lifestyle support and opportunities for employment that extend beyond the age previously expected for retirement.

- Relationships between employers and employees are becoming increasingly transient, the average tenure of employment having already fallen to below two years in several developed countries. This trend is matched by the increasing preference to engage contract workers rather than offer full employment. The resulting instability in employment is reflected in the attitudes and behaviours of individuals, fostering a portfolio of different income streams rather than depending on one.

- Declining social cohesion between employees. Not only are colleagues increasingly transient but also increasingly co-workers may not have physical proximity to one another. Team members may work remotely, from home or overseas, or may work at different times to one another, whether by preference, scheduling or as a consequence of time-zone differences. The range of ages in a workforce is increasing, many organizations employing individuals from four different generations. Multi-generational workforces also experience less social cohesion as colleagues are at very different life stages with different priorities and constraints.

Duty of care

Apart from the ethical argument that employers should support worker well-being, individuals perform better when they are well. Supporting employees' physical and mental wellness translates into benefits for the employer, for example lower error rates, greater reliability, fewer days of absence and lower staff turnover. However, although the rise in the use of contracted labour provides the corporation with flexibilities for how and when people are engaged to perform work, such contracts may also lead to the corporation not providing the social protections and well-being benefits that full employees would enjoy. Increasingly there is recognition of the importance of actively supporting workers' well-being, whether they are employees or contracted labour. In 2015, the United Nations (UN) adopted 17 goals for sustainable development,[4] with the aspiration that they are all achieved by 2030. Goal 3 is to ensure healthy lives and promote well-being for all at all ages. The human-centred future envisioned by 4IR aligns with the UN sustainable development goal. Providing well-being support also positively impacts the reputation of the corporation as an employer, which can strengthen the network of workers (employees and contractors) that they can engage.

Supporting workers for the changing content of work

As the 4th Industrial Revolution embraces technologies such as machine learning, the 'Internet of Things' and genomics, workers and their roles are being increasingly dislocated. Although there are some concerns about the number of jobs that will be required in the future, the most widely held conviction is that there will be a very significant redefinition of the jobs required to be done by humans. Forecasts of the proportion of jobs at risk to automation vary significantly (from 20 to 40 per cent) in large part due to differences in projections for the evolution of automated capabilities supported by machine learning. As some jobs are replaced by automation, new jobs are also being created that require interfacing with AI and automation.

As the mix of required jobs shifts substantially, people have to learn new skills and transition into new occupations, working alongside increasingly capable machines. Demand for some occupations less suited for automation and AI is growing due to demographic changes, for example care work or teachers. People are living longer, and ageing populations increase the need for healthcare practitioners, as well as the growth of services providing lifestyle support.

The old saying of there being a 'war for talent' has been modified by the 4IR to be a 'race to develop talent', ie to reskill and upskill talent. Forty per cent of Millennials and Gen Z feel unprepared for the changes being introduced,[5] as do a similar proportion of those of older generations who aspire to remain active in the workforce. Businesses will not be able to adopt innovations in automation and big data without the technicians, data scientists and programmers to support their implementation and use. However, a recent survey by Tech Nation UK[6] found that 55 per cent of firms cite difficulties in finding people with the required skills.

4IR is new for everyone, creating a huge need and opportunity for reskilling and upskilling. A recent study by Harvard Business School of the organizational challenges for companies to transform through the 4th Industrial Revolution concluded:

> As companies refine their strategies for managing – and shaping – the future of work [...] employers will need to be more discerning and active in their choices, especially when it comes to preparing the workforce of the future...

> ... a significant, but overlooked, new force for change: the keen sense of optimism that middle-skills workers exhibit about their ability and willingness to prepare for a better future. As companies navigate these unprecedented changes, they have an unexpected ally in that task – their employees.[7]

In 4IR, with an active social media, it is critical to manage the reputation of the corporation as an employer – the employer branding. Employers who recognize and fulfil their duty of care attract and retain better talent. Some of the aspects of the duty of care that extend beyond contractual obligations include:

- flexible working arrangements that are adjusted as the worker transitions between life stages, juggling work-health-family commitments;

- providing foresight of anticipated future workforce restructuring;

- career advisory support for workers who remain with the company, supporting their transition to new roles and upskilling;

- support for the worker to manage their well-being: physical, emotional, spiritual, etc;

- support such as counselling, placement and retraining for those who are not retained in their existing roles.

Supporting workers with flexible working arrangements

Flexible working is a broad term encompassing any form of relationship between an employee and employer that does not require the employee to work a standard day (eg 'nine to five') in a fixed location (eg at an office or factory). In 4IR, flexible work relationships take on a broad definition referring both to arrangements which allow the employee some discretion around where they work (eg working from home some days of the week) and also to flexibility for the employer in how they allocate work (eg changing the required hours, and corresponding pay, from one period to the next). In several occupations flexible working arrangements have been in effect for many years (airline crews, shift working at factories or hospitals, etc); however, these relationships have usually been within a structure that gave both parties some stability from the boundaries of mutual commitment. In 4IR these commitments are of decreasing relevance, which can create greater uncertainty both for the employee and for the employer. 'Zero hour' contracts provide employers with total flexibility as they do not need to give any hours of work to a contractor in a given period. As a consequence, employees may take several such contracts with different potential employers, knowing that they need to have the choice of how to manage their time as they cannot depend on any one employer for any income. The importance individuals attach to flexible working typically varies during their lives, for example being important for those with young children, looking after elderly parents, or managing their own health concerns. However, due to the enforced requirements for many to 'work from home' as part of company or national initiatives to manage the COVID-19 pandemic of 2020, many individuals and employers have become much more positive towards expanding flexible working. Individuals have discovered the efficiency benefits of reducing travel to work locations, with corporations noting the staff productivity benefits as well as seeing the opportunity to significantly reduce office space. A recent CIPD report notes:

> Flexible working isn't equally important for everyone. At any time, evidence suggests the majority of employees are prepared to go along with existing norms for how work is organized – or, generally improvements to this aspect of their working lives is not a high priority. But for some employees, at various points in their working lives, flexible working becomes of much greater importance and value, perhaps essential to them participating in paid employment at all.[8]

As life expectancies increase, so too does the expectation of many to remain employed, staying in the workforce longer albeit in roles and at levels of intensity that are age compatible. This trend is reflected in and reinforced by reforms in state pensions, delaying until later in life when such benefits might be received. This is facilitated in part by flexible working arrangements such as job sharing, whereas an increasing proportion of the workforce are engaged by contracts with flexible hours, some of which guarantee zero hours!

Relationships between employers and employees are becoming increasingly transient. A 2018 report survey of millennials[9] by Deloitte noted:

> Loyalty levels have retreated [...] Among millennials, 43 per cent envision leaving their jobs within two years, and only 28 per cent are looking to stay beyond five years. Among millennials who would willingly leave their employers within the next two years, 62 per cent regard the gig economy as a viable alternative to full-time employment. Loyalty is even lower among the emerging Gen Z employees, with 61 per cent saying they would leave their current jobs within two years if given the choice.[10]

In human-centred 4IR, employers should be concerned for the well-being and development of all workers, whether they are on contracts, partially or fully employed, or with long or short anticipated tenure. Employers should also create opportunities for workers to work flexibly, especially so that they can balance obligations or accommodate constraints due to age, family or health.

The boundary between work and family life

The boundary between work life and personal life is increasingly blurred, whether or not compounded by flexible working arrangements. Each person has their own preferred manner in which they perceive the interplay of their personal and their work domains. At one extreme are individuals (segmenters) who prefer to maintain a separation between work and family domains, whilst at the other extreme are individuals (integrators) who prefer to integrate the two domains. This difference in outlook determines much of how an individual experiences the benefits and negatives of increased blurring of the boundary. For individuals preferring a high degree of separation, increased work-related activities in their personal time contribute to anxiety and stress, as would also interruptions to their working time caused by personal life or family members. However, for people who prefer to integrate work-related and personal activities, such porosity between domains mitigates feelings of anxiety that they may otherwise experience from a sense of being disconnected from important activities or people. If the boundary management preference of the person differs from the requirements of the context in which they operate then they experience anxiety and stress.

People struggling to achieve a living wage experience high anxiety and stress, which may be amplified by income insecurity through low contract hours and flexible working arrangements. However, employees also seek supplementary income through taking on additional jobs with flexible working arrangements. With high work intensity and income insecurity the individual may struggle to fulfil their roles with the family, which may fuel their need to increasingly blur the boundary between work and family activities.

Employers should adopt policies and practices that reflect awareness of different individuals' preferences for boundary management. For example, one executive may wish to be always connected and aware of developments at work and may be inclined to check and respond to emails and messages seemingly 24/7. Another may prefer to be able to focus exclusively on family and personal activities at weekends. The policies and culture of the company should allow both types of behaviour.

Mobile device usage

Mobile devices (eg smartphones) greatly facilitate the porosity of the boundary between work and personal life. Mobile devices enable users to conduct multiple functions and activities from almost any location and at any time of day – or night. These functions can be work related or family and personal life related. As such, there is a significant opportunity for blurring of the boundary between personal and work-related activities, times and locations. As mobile devices are used for an ever-increasing range of personal life-related activities, they are increasingly being regarded as almost an extension of ourselves: accessing our photos, managing our bank accounts, staying in contact with friends and family, learning new skills and languages.

The advantages and disadvantages of mobile device use for work-life balance have been discussed widely.[11] A major advantage is that they can help a person to fulfil their work and family responsibilities simultaneously and from multiple locations.[12] This can both help productivity and have a positive impact by reducing work-family conflict.[13] However, negative effects include being distracted from concentrating on a task due to competing notifications and activities through one interface. The blurring of the boundary between work and personal time is itself a major concern for many employees and employers alike.[14]

There is concern about negative impacts on emotional well-being due to stress, anxiety and intrusion of work into personal time. There is also concern about loss of productivity and efficiency due to distractions and incursion of personal activities into work time. The ability to work late at home that is facilitated by mobile devices is described as a 'double-edged sword'. On the one hand, it enables the flexibility to accommodate both work and family demands; on the other hand, increased availability for work can encroach upon family time[15] and be perceived as increasing workload and stress. The porosity of the boundary between work and personal activities can cause distractions that undermine productivity, behaviours that create work-family conflict, and undermine an individual's perception of their ability to fulfil their role in the family.

Employees can have very strong emotional reactions to the use of mobile devices at the workplace or for work-related activities, which thereby impacts their performance and their emotional well-being:

- On one hand, mobile devices enable the possibility to work from anywhere at any time, allowing employees to feel more competent as professionals and to be more in control of work,[16] which can enable a heightened sense of commitment. Mobile devices are sometimes considered as an extension of the self, being described as 'attached at the hip' or a 'security blanket', which although providing comfort or reassurance can also create disturbances.

- On the other hand, they can induce a greater sense of dependency, compulsive behaviours (eg repeatedly checking messages) and a sense of stress or work overload.[17] Such negative emotions (anxiety, annoyance, anger) can be generated both in the workplace and when mobile.

- However, the 2020 global pandemic caused by COVID-19 forced a rapid switch to online and remote meetings and working, changing habits and for many, evoking more positive attitudes towards online collaboration.

The negative emotions that mobile devices can trigger can be very severe. In research conducted by the University of Bath,[18] employees describe their intense anger in the form of 'hate' in relation to the physical interruptions caused by mobile devices when their own or a colleague's device is respon-sible for interrupting workflow. Others experience negative emotions when in an open plan office; mobile devices can interrupt work by buzzing, flash-ing or ringing. Employees describe how they feel compelled to act, for example by enabling the 'do not disturb' function to hinder the awareness of incoming notifications on their own devices. However, this feeds another negative emotion, anxiety, from being aware of incoming calls, messages and emails on their mobile devices but unable to respond to these commu-nications (because, for example, they are in a meeting). Employees also speak of resentment towards colleagues who do not prevent their devices from disrupting their concentration or discussion. This sense of resentment can lead to assignment of negative characteristics (eg self-centred, exhibi-tionist) towards the colleague, which contaminates the relationship between the two individuals.

Additionally, when users are unwillingly forced to disengage with their mobile devices (eg through a ban on mobile devices being brought into a meeting or through loss), the sense of missing a part of self becomes rele-vant. This can also elicit negative emotions of annoyance and frustration. For the employee this can make it harder to concentrate in the meeting as they remain wondering what is happening elsewhere (eg if their have chil-dren arrived home safely, or if the report that their colleagues are working on is progressing). Such emotions can also carry over into assignment of negative characteristics to the leader of the meeting, such as feeling that they are being deliberately isolated (eg Travis believes he is being targeted by his line manager when forced to switch off his smartphone during the weekly department meetings).

Non-positive emotional responses to the interaction of employees and mobile devices are also linked to less productive action responses, such as delaying responding to notifications or noticing but ignoring the content of the information materializing through the mobile device. These responses to the negative emotions can also lead to, *a posteriori*, the feeling that they should have acted differently, suggesting a degree of regret.

Employers have a duty of care towards their employees. This should include providing guidelines and support to help employees avoid or miti-gate the negative emotions that can be generated in association with mobile device usage. Apart from concern for the emotional well-being of the employees, the emotional reactions described also undermine organizational processes such as decision making.[19]

Personal data or company data

The technologies of the 4th Industrial Revolution are impacting the data capture, analytical insight and interactions of people management in similar ways to other operations within and at the boundary to the firm. This book is not a compendium of the new technologies and tools and how to adopt them but is focused on the implications for management. As followers of comic-book super heroes know, 'with great power comes great responsibility'; data capture and analytics can be misused as easily as they can be used to support positive outcomes such as better recruitment, targeted development, feedback, remuneration, etc. An area of great concern is the monitoring of personal activities and communications that employees conduct using firm-supported hardware, whether or not the firm or the individual have purchased and own the hardware, eg smartphone or laptop. There are vastly differing points of view around the legitimacy of such monitoring and also the subsequent use of the data collected. At one extreme is the view that the company has the right to know where and when the employee is working and what they are doing, and to ensure that confidential company information is not being communicated in unsecured or personal communications. Therefore, it is legitimate for the company to insist that device management software is installed that captures all usage. This view reflects the notion that employees cannot be trusted but should have absolute trust in the intentions and behaviours of the company. The counterbalance view is that companies cannot be trusted either to keep personal data safe or to avoid the temptation to use personal data for profiling. Allowing workers the right to control the privacy of their use of smartphones and computing devices is a powerful signal of trust, yet some firms have established practices and policies that directly oppose this, for example, insisting that Mobile Device Management (MDM) software (spyware) be installed on equipment used for company business, even when that equipment is owned by the worker.

Duty of care: guidelines

From the research discussed above there emerge several clear implications, 'guidelines', for human-centred workforce management.

Individualism: not everyone is the same

Given the breadth and significance of the differences between individuals, a one-size-fits-all approach to human resource policies and practices does not bring out their best performance and may result in increased stress for some. Even well-intentioned initiatives must be rolled out with recognition that individual employees have different competing claims on their energies and different personalities. A morning gym class before work or lunchtime wellness talk or meditation session may be suitable for some, but for others could be added sources of stress. Each person has an individual set of beliefs, values, personality traits, personal circumstances, physical and mental strengths and vulnerabilities, and financial pressures.

I-DEALS

In contrast to standardized human resource practices that apply to everyone, individualization is a strong trend, particularly in developed, western countries. The concept of establishing 'voluntary, personalized agreements of a non-standard nature negotiated between individual employees and their employers regarding terms that benefit each party'[20] is known I-deals. Analysis of such individual arrangements in western Europe indicates that I-deals enhance job satisfaction, reduce the intention to leave the organization and create a sense of organizational support,[21] which is positive for the emotional well-being of the employee. There are four principal types of I-deals, as indicated below:

- **Task:** arrangements that aim to contribute to how employees carry out tasks, for example allowing the use of special (or personal) equipment.
- **Career:** any deals that aim to develop one's career and lead to advancements, for example dispensation to join a specialist taskforce.
- **Flexibility:** individual arrangements that relate to flexibilities in terms of time and location of work.
- **Financial:** arrangements relating to salary negotiations, promotions, perks and other monetary terms.

JOB CRAFTING[22]

This is a form of establishing individual, personalized arrangements for conducting work. Job crafting tends to develop organically, driven by the employee adapting how they do their work or extending beyond the formal boundaries of their role. This is then accommodated by the employer but may well not be formalized, whereas I-deals tend to be formalized arrangements which may have been negotiated. Job crafting mainly occurs in three ways:

- **Task crafting** is mainly through adjusting the scope of the job either by taking on more or relinquishing certain tasks; for example, a maintenance worker who decides to investigate and address the causes of equipment issues (a task normally required of a process engineer) whereas their maintenance job just requires them to fix problems when they occur. Some people task-craft through changing how they accomplish the tasks; for example semi-automating repetitive data entry using their own mobile scanning device (eg smartphone) rather than the expected process of manually entering the data.

- **Relationship crafting** is changing the nature or extent of interactions with other people; for example a production line worker who volunteers to support in training and mentoring new workers, or an office worker who volunteers to join a committee to help organize social events or to be the designated first-aid helper for their department. In each of these examples the objective of the job crafter is to increase their social interaction. Individuals may also craft their jobs to reduce social interaction, such as through minimizing their interactions with team members, focusing instead on their own contributions which they seek to complete and then pass on to colleagues.

- **Cognitive crafting** is the deliberate adjustment of how the employee perceives their task. For example, a creative marketer may loathe the detailed, analytical parts of the role but is able to stay engaged and produce high-quality insights by seeing the analytics as an essential step to revealing insights that inform their creative tasks. Similarly, an insurance claims adjuster may regard their role as helping clients at their most vulnerable moment to recover from setbacks.

Expecting everyone to fit into standard behaviours is unsustainable and can be severely damaging to some individuals' well-being. Equally unhealthy is an environment without any explicit guidelines; in such situations concerns over fairness can trigger significant distress. Also, without guidelines workers may feel compelled to work in ways and for durations that undermine their mental, emotional and physical well-being. Such compulsion may come from peer pressure, financial incentive schemes, a demanding boss, or their own core personality traits (such as competitiveness or insecurity). Boundary conditions and guidelines are required in order to create a safe environment as well as to communicate the positive intent of allowing individualized arrangements.

Remove doubt: clarify the support available

Make it clear through establishing the infrastructure (physical, policies and systems) to promote well-being and overtly establish and promote a supportive culture within the firm. Examples could be family care-giver flexible days off, well-being services/facilities provided in-house or nearby, or external speakers and classes. Establish and clearly communicate policies and expectations on flexible and mobile working, activities that promote well-being, and the ability to manage the work-life/family-life boundary.

Leaders and managers should role-model the range of behaviours that are acceptable by using themselves the services provided to support their own well-being and building a supportive community who encourage one another within the team. Really good examples include:

- ensuring managers and leaders are fluent in and are reinforcing the use of the services and facilities provided;
- being seen to be making appropriate well-being choices for themselves (eg not sending out email requests in the middle of the night);
- clarifying whether or not a message requires an urgent response during employees' personal time.

Allow choice and flexibility

Make it clear that each individual can make their own choices around how they fit within the boundaries of the initiatives, events or activities established by the employer. For example, if an individual has booked into a wellness class during the traditional working day or at lunchtime and is then asked to respond to a request from their manager, is it acceptable to delay responding until after the class?

Mobile devices can evoke very strong emotions in individuals, such as the stress from the sense of being always on, contactable and having to respond to messages and requests 24/7. However, stress, for some, comes from the anxiety they feel if they are prevented from having access to their smartphone 24/7. Equally important, yet positive, emotions are felt when a person feels they have increased autonomy and flexibility which can be derived from mobility facilitated by the smartphone. The same functions lead to both positive and negative effects depending on the context; the user's sense of control over the circumstances is critical to their perception of the outcomes:

- Allowing individuals the option to choose what mobile or computing devices they use as company-issued or mandated devices may be resisted or make employees feel uncomfortable. The device (eg laptop or smartphone) may be used for much more than just the company business and it is perhaps in the interests of the company that the device is always with the person.

- The choice of whether and when to respond to incoming messages or notifications on a smartphone. Notifications may act as a constant reminder of impending work deadlines when the employee should be focused on family life, or can lead to an easy intervention that saves time and anxiety. By taking control over relevant settings, employees can manage the extent to which the device interrupts their flow either in a personal or professional context.

Enrol supervisors

The recognition of the stress epidemic has heightened focus on initiatives to improve employee well-being, in particular in the management of the potential conflict of work and family responsibilities. Managing 4IR places a priority on supporting the emotional and physical well-being of the workforce, irrespective of the contractual obligations. By itself, adopting a set of guidelines does little to change ingrained behaviours and practices; a structured intervention is usually required to move the behaviours of the majority rather than just a few enthusiastic adopters. Even if adopted as an explicit policy it is still essential to establish the culture of the firm through nurturing appropriate behaviours, in particular the role-modelling demonstrated by team leaders and supervisors. Training and monitoring the behaviour of such leaders, particularly with regards to their support for managing the work-life/family-life boundary, positively impacts employee engagement and productivity and has been proven to significantly benefit employee health, job satisfaction and turnover intentions.[23]

A family-supportive supervisor is one who empathizes with the employee's need to balance work and family responsibilities.[24] Supervisors are trained to provide four kinds of support:

- emotional support, by listening and showing empathy;
- instrumental support, such as referrals to child or elder care-givers, allowing increased control and flexibility over work schedules as well as better management of workload (eg part-time work);
- affirmation, through themselves role-modelling behaviour that accommodates work and family demands;
- taking the initiative to define creative ways to restructure work to facilitate employee effectiveness on and off the job.

Trained supervisors better understand the rationale for being family supportive and have a greater understanding of how actually to engage in these behaviours. The running of the supervisor training programme itself also powerfully signals to the employees that the company is concerned for their well-being. Companies that have undertaken such programmes have experienced benefits in employee well-being, commitment and performance within as little as one month after the training. However, fully embedding such practices into the culture of the company requires ongoing monitoring and reinforcement. Reinforcement can be demonstrated by storytelling of the experiences of individual employees, or recognition and reward of the actions of specific supervisors.

The supervisors also play a vital role in creating a supportive environment by enrolling each of the team members, promoting awareness and mutual support, proactively encouraging team member-generated initiatives such as daily step-count champion, or cross-sharing techniques for improving productivity of smartphone usage whilst not allowing the device to be too intrusive into personal time.

Leadership traits: human-centred workforce management

Authenticity

When a leader is being authentic, they inspire trust and followership because it is easier for team members and staff to relate to them as a person. Such leaders explain why something is important to achieve as an organization, using their personal story; why it matters to them and why it should also matter to others. Everyone, leaders included, has flaws and vulnerabilities, each person with their own challenges and their own story. Leaders who acknowledge their vulnerabilities and share their stories of challenges they have, or continue to seek to overcome, are more credible than those who project an image that is 'too good to be true'. The leader should know and be comfortable to tell others what their personal values are, what for them is non-negotiable, and where there is greater flexibility. By so doing they create certainty and clarity for others, but only if their actions are aligned with their words! Leaders should strive to know themselves well, confident in what they have learnt from their life story and recognizing their strengths and weaknesses. They should actively seek feedback, demonstrating a hunger for learning and improvement. By so doing, starting with themselves, they demonstrate the importance of self-awareness and role-model having a growth mindset – important traits for everyone in the organization to emulate.

Flexibility in support of others

A feature of the 4th Industrial Revolution is the extension of the working life of individuals; people are remaining actively engaged in the workforce for longer. This creates a workforce which includes individuals from multiple generations. Each individual, at different times, will experience changes in their circumstances (eg with family obligations or with health or wellbeing) that they will seek to juggle whilst remaining a part of the workforce. A key feature of the human-centred business is to allow flexibility that supports individuals as they adjust to their changed circumstances whilst maintaining equitable treatment for all employees. In particular, the increasing functionality of mobile devices expands the possibilities for flexible working and for many roles reduces the need to be physically present in a given location (eg office) for a set time period. Firm leaders need to take responsibility for putting in place the systems and infrastructure to support flexible working. Leaders themselves need to demonstrate allowing flexibility for others as their circumstances change. Increased flexibility and adaptability are also required as the diversity within the workforce increases. For example, people from different cultures have differing styles of interaction, both spoken and non-verbal. In a multicultural team, members need to be able to work effectively with one another, which may require adjusting norms of interaction that are reflective of only one culture.

Promote well-being and resilience

In the 4IR there is greater awareness of the employer's duty of care towards the members of the workforce (whether defined as employees or contractors). The duty of care exceeds the legally defined contract obligations. The well-being of workers is important ethically as well as economically for the employer, impacting employee productivity and absenteeism and turnover. It is also an important contributor to the reputation of the corporation as an employer, which impacts the quality of talent that applies to work there. 4IR employers proactively provide support for workers to maintain or improve several aspects of their well-being – physical, emotional, social, environmental, spiritual and intellectual. Physical well-being includes both diet and exercise as well as health and safety. Emotional well-being is a particular concern, as lost work days due to workplace stress have increased significantly in the past 10 years, with organizations such as the World Health Organization calling for urgent action by employers. Firm leaders need to curate the culture and put in place the systems and infrastructure to support workers to manage their well-being. Leaders themselves need to role-model through their actions how they are managing their own well-being and demonstrate direct support to others.

Mindset: Empathy

Leaders at all levels of an organization must practise empathy and demonstrate flexibility with regards to those they supervise. Concern for the well-being of team members and allowing individual flexibility within explicit guidelines help to develop commitment and followership.

KEY CONCEPTS: CHAPTER 10

Human-centred workforce management (HCWM) is a key tenet of the 4th Industrial Revolution. As big an evolution is anticipated in how corporations manage their relationships with workers as from the impact from the adoption of new technologies. Managing 4IR requires a workforce whose emotional and physical well-being is positively supported. Whether adopted as an explicit policy or not, establishing the culture of the firm is largely dependent on the behaviours of the leadership and supervisors throughout the organization.

Training and monitoring the behaviour of such leaders, particularly with regards to their support for managing the work-life/family-life boundary, positively impacts employee engagement and productivity and reduces employee turnover and absenteeism. Guidelines that allow individual flexibility and choice in how to manage this boundary and governing the use of mobile devices can help to reduce stress and anxiety:

- Duty of care of employers:
  - support for adjusting to the changing content of work;
  - provision of flexible working arrangements;
  - enabling the worker to make their own choices for how they manage their work-family boundary;
  - clarifying what is personal data vs company data and how either can be used and accessed.
- Provide explicit guidelines for how HCWM will be promoted in the organization. The guidelines should recognize and accommodate without prejudice different attitudes and preferences between individuals. The guidelines are as important for the organization as they are for the individual employee, as they provide the guiderails, clarifying what is and what is not expected.
- The culture-as-lived of the organization is defined by the actions and behaviours of the supervisors. HCWM requires ensuring that supervisors are fully aligned with their mindset, know the guidelines, and have the required empathy such that they fulfil the duty of care for their staff.

Leadership traits:

- authenticity;
- flexibility in support to others;
- promote well-being and resilience;
- mindset: empathy.

Endnotes

1 World Economic Forum (nd) Fourth Industrial Revolution, https://www.weforum.org/focus/fourth-industrial-revolution (archived at https://perma.cc/TPQ2-7Z2B)

2 World Health Organization (nd) Stress at the workplace, https://www.who.int/occupational_health/topics/stressatwp/en/ (archived at https://perma.cc/XG8Y-FXK2)

3 Chancel, L (2018) World Inequality Report, https://www.un.org/esa/socdev/csocd/2019/Chancel2019CSD.pdf (archived at https://perma.cc/REJ3-SLFC)

4 United Nations (2015) Transforming our world: the 2030 Agenda for Sustainable Development, https://sustainabledevelopment.un.org/post2015/transformingourworld (archived at https://perma.cc/U976-EGNB)

5 Deloitte Millennial Survey 2018, https://www2.deloitte.com/tr/en/pages/about-deloitte/articles/millennialsurvey-2018.html (archived at https://perma.cc/SJF8-EQW9)

6 Tech Nation Report 2017, https://technation.io/insights/tech-nation-2017/ (archived at https://perma.cc/5C9N-ABER)

7 Fuller, J et al (2018) Future Positive: How companies can tap into employee optimism to navigate tomorrow's workplace, Harvard Business School

8 CIPD (2019) Flexible working in the UK, https://www.cipd.co.uk/knowledge/work/trends/flexible-working (archived at https://perma.cc/Z8RR-ALBZ)

9 Millennials are defined as being born between January 1983 and December 1994

10 Deloitte (2018) Deloitte finds millennials' confidence in business takes a sharp turn; they feel unprepared for Industry 4.0, https://www2.deloitte.com/global/en/pages/about-deloitte/press-releases/deloitte-finds-millennials-confidence-business-takes-sharp-turn.html (archived at https://perma.cc/C4QK-Z6H4)

11 Valcour, P M and Hunter, L W (2005) Technology, organizations, and work-life integration, in E E Kossek and S J Lambert (Eds) *Work and Life Integration: Organizational, cultural, and individual perspectives,* Lawrence Erlbaum Associates Publishers (pp 61–84)

12 Allen, T and Shockley, K (2009) Flexible work arrangements: help or hype? In R D Crane and J E Hill (Eds) *Handbook of Families and Work: Interdisciplinary perspectives*, University Press of America

13 Chesley, N (2005) Blurring boundaries? Linking technology use, spillover, individual distress, and family satisfaction, *Journal of Marriage and Family*, 67, pp 1237–48, 10.1111/j.1741-3737.2005.00213.x; Golden, A and Geisler, C (2007) Work-life boundary and the personal digital assistant, *Human Relations – HUM RELAT*, 60, pp 519–51, 10.1177/0018726707076698

14 Towers, I *et al* (2006) Time thieves and space invaders: Technology, work and the organization, *Journal of Organizational Change Management*, 19, pp 593–618, 10.1108/09534810610686076

15 Gawronski, B *et al* (2009) Methodological issues in the validation of implicit measures: Comment on De Houwer, Teige-Mocigemba, Spruyt, and Moors (2009), *Psychological Bulletin*, 135 (3), pp 369–72, https://doi.org/10.1037/a0014820 (archived at https://perma.cc/4KUU-YMYV)

16 Mazmanian, M *et al* (2013) The autonomy paradox: The implications of mobile email devices for knowledge professionals, *Organization Science*, 24, pp 1337–57. 10.1287/orsc.1120.0806

17 Jarvenpaa, S and Lang, K (2005) Managing the paradoxes of mobile technology, *IS Management*, 22, pp 7–23, 10.1201/1078.10580530/45520.22. 4.20050901/90026.2; Mazmanian, M *et al* (2013) The autonomy paradox: The implications of mobile email devices for knowledge professionals, *Organization Science*, 24, pp 1337–57, 10.1287/orsc.1120.0806

18 Archer-Brown, C et al (2017) The materiality of emotions: The case of mobile devices at work, University of Bath

19 Clore, G L, Schwarz, N and Conway, M (1994) Affective causes and consequences of social information processing, in R S Wyer, Jr. and T K Srull (Eds) *Handbook of Social Cognition: Basic processes; Applications,* Lawrence Erlbaum Associates, Inc (pp 323–417); Forgas, J P (1995) Mood and judgment: The affect infusion model (AIM), *Psychological Bulletin*, 117 (1), pp 39–66, https://doi.org/10.1037/0033-2909.117.1.39 (archived at https://perma. cc/57A5-7NC6); Schwarz, N (2000) Emotion, cognition, and decision making, *Cognition and Emotion*, 14 (4), 433–440, doi: 10.1080/026999300402745

20 Rousseau, D M, Ho, V T and Greenberg, J (2016) I-Deals: Idiosyncratic terms in employment relationships, *Academy of Management Review*, 31 (4), pp 977–94

21 Liao, C, Wayne, S and Rousseau, D (2014) Idiosyncratic deals in contemporary organizations: A qualitative and meta-analytical review, *Journal of Organizational Behaviour*, 37 (1)

22 Wrzesniewski, A and Dutton, J (2001) Crafting a job: Revisioning employees as active crafters of their work, *The Academy of Management Review*, 26 (2), pp 179–201

23 Hammer, L B *et al* (2009) Development and validation of a multidimensional measure of family supportive supervisor behaviors (FSSB), *Journal of Management*, 35 (4), pp 837–56. doi:10.1177/0149206308328510; Cullen, J C and Hammer, L B (2007) Developing and testing a theoretical model linking work-family conflict to employee safety, *Journal of Occupation Health Psychology*, 12 (3), pp 266–78, doi:10.1037/1076-8998.12.3.266

24 Thomas, L T and Ganster, D C (1995) Impact of family-supportive work variables on work-family conflict and strain: A control perspective, *Journal of Applied Psychology*, 80 (1), pp 6–15, https://doi.org/10.1037/0021-9010.80.1.6 (archived at https://perma.cc/JCF9-8YSY)

PART FIVE

Dynamic advantage

11

Superior performance in 4IR

IN BRIEF

In this 4th Industrial Revolution, as with those that have come before, some firms are the pioneers of new ways of operating and some evolve at slower rates, or not at all. Those that evolve faster generate greater value in large part because they are able to change the nature of competition and influence the future as it unfolds. Management approaches that were adequate in earlier contexts are insufficient in the new. A key choice for the leadership is how soon and how far to take the adoption of new technologies or platforms – as a pioneer, or when widely adopted by others?

A strategic choice for each firm is which of the 4IR capabilities to strengthen. This requires clarity on the choices for how they desire to compete and assessment of the current strength and their ability to improve each of the 4IR capabilities. The difference in performance between those firms that build and leverage 4IR capabilities and those that adhere to traditional management practices is widening as the speed of business continues to accelerate. As such, the imperative to adopt 4IR practices and to know which to excel at is being recognized ever more broadly, whether driven for survival, by stockholders demanding better returns, or by the aspiration of leadership teams.

Assessing the 4IR strengths of the organization and management capabilities can be facilitated by use of an online questionnaire, into which senior executives from across the organization can enter their responses. The response set is anonymously compared with the data set of leadership teams from all firms that have been surveyed, providing a relative evaluation. The executive team should then discuss the implications for their firm, focusing on areas of relative weakness and also areas where their responses differ substantially from one another.

Each marketspace has its own unique dynamics; even within the same industry different countries may be at different stages of evolution, with different levels of competitive intensity and regulatory stability or certainty. As such, a key choice for the leadership team is to decide 'where' to compete, ie in marketspaces with what levels and what causes of uncertainty, dynamism or stability.

A second level of choice for the leadership team is to decide what will be their competitive posture within each of the marketspaces in which they decide to compete. As a firm they may be more cautious or more pioneering. The combination of knowing the relative strength of their 4IR capabilities, their choices of where to compete and their competitive posture will indicate which of the 4IR capabilities they should prioritize for strengthening.

Look ahead: how is 4IR reshaping your marketspace?

A key first step in the journey of deliberate transformation to compete for the 4IR future is to connect with the context external to the firm. Take a fresh look at the dynamics of the marketspaces that the firm is competing in. How are they changing? What are competitors, traditional and non-traditional, doing? How are customers evolving? How predictable and stable, or dynamic, is the future?

- This may entail external speakers coming into the firm and the executives going outside the firm, eg customer visits, invited thought leaders and consultants, or trips to technology leaders or companies in similar sectors or marketspaces that have adopted 4IR practices and technologies.
  - o It is essential that each of the executives makes a personal connection with the external drivers of 4IR. Each person should be able to develop an understanding of the profound changes that are taking place and be energized to help drive the transformation of the corporation.
- In the executive team, discuss the opportunities and challenges being created by 4IR for the effective pursuit of the corporate purpose.
  - o Reflect on the dynamics and changes that are impacting the marketspace in which the company is operating and the confidence with which the corporation is managing through changes and transformations.
    - A question that is helpful for challenging the mindset of executives unused to competing in 4IR is: If your share price has a current P/E of 20, then would you prefer to exceed this period's earnings by 20 per cent or raise investor confidence such that your P/E raises to 24?

Which one will bring you greater financial reward? Which are you more confident of being able to influence? What if you're falling below forecasts this period – do you divert more attention to the present or increase preparation for tomorrow?

o Shape and formalize the call to action. Explore individual views and then draw together a common view that everyone can energetically support.

o Explore the mindset and experience of each member of the leadership team with regards to managing through transformations. What are the individual stories of success or failure?

– A good question to start with is: What did you learn from the last transformation/change initiative you worked through? What would you do differently and what would you build on next time?

o Do the performance metrics and reward incentives encourage stability or agility? Do they track results today (ie the so-called 'tail-pipe' measurements) or leading indicators of tomorrow's performance?

– How do individuals spend their time currently? As a group the executives in the leadership team should spend approximately equal proportions of time influencing current period results (execution) and pushing forward to make the firm more successful in the future (preparation).

o Some issues that can dilute energy include the following:

– *We don't know what we don't know* (ie we don't know what technologies and platforms are available and reliable, so we can't make an assessment). To which a suitable response is to co-create a process of learning through personal exposure and connection.

– *Our biggest gap is talent* – first we need to hire people who know this space and what can be done. To which a suitable response is, this is a race to develop talent; in 4IR we cannot rely on there being a pool of existing talent to draw upon.

Transforming to compete in 4IR must be a collective activity, it cannot be 'driven by the few and inflicted on the many'. It requires changing management behaviours and mindsets, as each individual of the executive team must feel a sense of responsibility and ownership. Once awareness of the importance of competing dynamically has been raised and there has been an insightful review of current capabilities and meaningful debate, then the next step is to decide what to do about it.

Assess the 4IR capabilities of your company

The following pages provide an assessment that an individual would complete whilst considering how they personally experience the performance of the corporation and the management mechanisms and capabilities for success in 4IR.

All members of the executive team should individually (not as a team or collective) complete the assessment of the firm. It should ideally be approximately 20 people, but it is advisable to involve all members of the executive team plus representatives of other stakeholders who have an informed view, eg members of the board of directors.

Note that a seven-point scale is used: '1' equates to 'strongly disagree', '7' equates to 'strongly agree' and '4' equates to the neutral 'neither strongly agree nor strongly disagree'.

A free online assessment questionnaire can be accessed at: http://www.corporaterebirth.com/assess-your-4ir-capabilities.html.

The online questionnaire is shorter and simpler (only 29 questions) than the full assessment included here. It automatically generates and emails out a summary report, reflecting the input answers submitted. The online survey does require entry of personal data, such as email address. Data entered into the online survey is stored, such that average scores across all participants and benchmark information can be calculated and provided in the automatically generated reports. The full questionnaire included in this chapter is most suited for use by the executive leadership team of an organization as a part of a facilitated, workshop-based process, identifying and prioritizing areas for improvement.

Once all the responses are received, the executive team should meet for a workshop facilitated by an expert in 4IR management and leadership practices. The facilitator prepares the workshop by looking at the range and the median scores of the responses to each question (and sub-question), noting areas of common alignment and significant differences in the opinions of the participating executives:

- identify areas of agreed strength and/or weakness;
- identify items where there is a wide spread of differences between the responses.

The workshop enables exploration of individual views, deepening of understanding of each capability (with examples of best practice), identification of options, and the drawing together of a common view that everyone can energetically support.

FIGURE 11.1   4IR management and leadership capabilities assessment

1	Dynamic and competitive nature of the marketspace	Rating (1–7)
		1 = I strongly disagree
		7 = I strongly agree
1.1	Our marketspace is relatively stable, a 3-year planning cycle (with annual updates) is adequate	
1.2	It is becoming less stable (less predictable)	
1.3	Our marketspace is evolving rapidly and is unstable; our planning cycle is annual (or less) and we frequently make updates, adjust plans and redirect resources during the annual cycle	
1.4	It is becoming less stable (less predictable)	
1.5	I believe we out perform in comparison to local competitors in key markets	
1.6	I believe we out perform in comparison to MNC or global competitors in key markets	
1.7	We achieve a valuation premium/discount compared to our most similar competitors	

2	Capability to Sense & Make Sense	Rating (1–7)
		1 = I strongly disagree
		7 = I strongly agree
2.1	We involve everyone in collecting and contributing idea fragments	
2.2	We are expected to access and interrogate the total pool of data collected across the company	
2.3	We collaborate extensively with external parties to source ideas and insight	
2.4	We have detailed understanding of customers' needs and behaviours and know how and why they are changing	
2.5	We conduct multiple experiments, often in parallel in order to accelerate learning and discovery	
2.6	Ready-Fire-Aim: We have a culture of rapid prototyping and testing with customers	
2.7	We encourage and facilitate interconnection between interest groups within and external to the company	
2.8	We are always expected to present our arguments and proposals with strong supporting data	

Rating 1–7 (1 = very weak. 7 = very strong)

Leadership traits	Myself	Across the executive cadre

3	Capability to Seize & Replicate	Rating (1–7)
		1 = I strongly disagree
		7 = I strongly agree
3.1	Fluid Teams, Fire Bucket Brigade and Flying Doctors: We frequently form new cross-boundary teams and rapidly deploy people in order to move insight and expertise around the organization	
3.2	We provide mechanisms and monitor the sharing of ideas between executives	

3.3 We accelerate knowledge exchange across geographies by clustering and administrating by similarity in the customer behaviours

3.4 We accelerate knowledge exchange between business units and between geographies by clustering and administrating by similarity in the dynamics of the markets (ie not only by geographical proximity)

3.5 We actively engage regulators to shape the evolution of key markets

3.6 We undertake bold strategies with the intent to dominate future marketspaces

3.7 We collaborate with partners across the eco-system in order to influence the evolution of the sector

Rating 1–7 (1 = very weak. 7 = very strong)

Leadership traits	Myself	Across the executive cadre

4   Capability to Reposition & Reconfigure   Rating (1–7)
1 = I strongly disagree
7 = I strongly agree

4.1 We have our own unique definition of the marketspaces in which we compete which is reflected in a unique strategy

4.2 We structure major investment and operational decisions as a series of options and choices

4.3 Our abilities to acquire and integrate, as well as to separate and divest operations, is a strength

4.4 We generally seek to harvest positions rather than to cause a rapid divestment or exit

4.5 We deliberately maintain two or more alternative offers/supply chains/channels of distribution

4.6 We are constantly adjusting the range of activities we perform internally and those we source externally – as well as the extent to which we keep the capabilities and capacity in-house

Rating 1–7 (1 = very weak. 7 = very strong)

Leadership traits	Myself	Across the executive cadre

5   Purpose-led, forward-leaning   Rating (1–7)
1 = I strongly disagree
7 = I strongly agree

5.1 We have a clear purpose-led mission, we are making a meaningful difference in society

5.2 We are all aligned with and excited by the purpose-led mission, we hold each other to account

5.3 We regularly think about potential scenarios for the evolution of the marketspace and what actions we could take

5.4   We make clear strategic plans whilst embracing and recognizing the
opportunities and risks of different scenarios that could unfold

5.5   Whilst maintaining clear strategic choices and commitments we are sensitive
to changing market conditions

5.6   We are thinking about the impact we can have on the world/marketspace
in the next 5–10 years

Rating 1–7 (1 = very weak. 7 = very strong)

Leadership traits   Myself   Across the executive cadre

6	**Ambidextrous leaders**	**Rating (1–7)**
		1 = I strongly disagree
		7 = I strongly agree

6.1   We are effective at thinking and acting ambidextrously

6.2   100% of the executive cadre is expected to think and act ambidextrously

6.3   We have a strong sense of being on the same team; we share data, insight,
victories and difficulties with each other

6.4   We always hold each other to account, we challenge each other whilst
also providing support

6.5   We behave in line with our culture to productively engage in understanding
each other's perspective

6.6   We take responsibility to increase each other's understanding and to constructively
challenge one another

Rating 1–7 (1 = very weak. 7 = very strong)

Leadership traits   Myself   Across the executive cadre

7	**Continuous evolution**	**Rating (1–7)**
		1 = I strongly disagree
		7 = I strongly agree

7.1   We have a person/team that is responsible for accelerating the business by
identifying and managing the adoption of 4IR technologies and practices

7.2   I am confident that we know what are and successfully adopt 4IR best
practices/technologies

7.3   Our approach for managing change/evolution is effective

7.4   Our approach to managing change/evolution empowers and energizes
managers and staff

7.5   We have a clear plan for managing 4IR transformation/continuous evolution

7.6   We are successful at driving 4IR transformation/continuous evolution
in a timely manner

Rating 1–7 (1 = very weak. 7 = very strong)

Leadership traits	Myself	Across the executive cadre
Provide meaning/connect to purpose		
Organization savviness		
Executive presence		

8   Human-centred workforce management
Duty of care

Rating (1–7)
1 = I strongly disagree
7 = I strongly agree

8.1   We place a high importance on supporting, protecting and promoting the well-being of all workers (whatever the contractual arrangements with which they are engaged)

8.2   We have key workforce well-being metrics that are tracked and impact the evaluation of my performance

8.3   We promote flexible working and support workers to manage work/family-life boundary

Duty of care: Guidelines

8.4   We allow and support individualism of job boundaries and execution, within guidelines

8.5   Most workers, whether full employees or on contracts, make use of the individual flexibility we offer

Enrol supervisors

8.6   Team leaders and supervisors are motivated and effective in promoting well-being of their team members

Rating 1–7 (1 = very weak. 7 = very strong)

Leadership traits	Myself	Across the executive cadre
Promote well-being and resilience		

9   Teams: The engines of performance

Rating (1–7)
1 = I strongly disagree
7 = I strongly agree

9.1   We have a clear, widely understood and applied doctrine for teaming

9.2   We track the performance of the individuals in each team

9.3   Coaching support to develop the performance of teams is welcomed and widely used

9.4   We place a high priority on ensuring 'psychological safety' and building trust between team members

9.5   I support my best staff to join in important multi-functional teams

9.6   There is a very strong sense of belonging to one firm which overrides department or function identity

Rating 1–7 (1 = very weak. 7 = very strong)

Leadership traits	Myself	Across the executive cadre

10	The race to create talent	Rating (1–7)
	Leadership competencies in 4IR	1 = I strongly disagree
		7 = I strongly agree

10.1 We have updated our leadership competency framework to align with the needs for winning in 4IR

10.2 Most of our leaders and executives have developed prowess in all the 4IR competencies relevant for us

10.3 Our approach to leadership development focuses on changing behaviour on the job

10.4 I readily join in leadership development activities as they enhance my performance

10.5 We have very effective programmes that combine personalized digital content delivery and feedback

10.6 Our executive development support is available on-demand, when you need it

Rating 1–7 (1 = very weak. 7 = very strong)

Leadership traits   Myself   Across the executive cadre

Decide the strategy for competing in 4IR

Where to play

Building the dynamic capacity of the firm is always advantageous, as no marketspace is completely static. However, the faster the evolution of the marketspace (eg driven by the influence of digital technologies), the more important it is to build the management capabilities and practices of 4IR. An important choice for the leadership of the firm to consider is at what level of 4IR capabilities they are comfortable to operate. For example, are they comfortable being the early adopters of new technologies, developing and launching products and services that are intended to be game-changers, seeking to redefine competitive dynamics (chasing a 'winner-takes-all' approach)? Or do they prefer a more measured pace of evolution? When they know themselves, then they can assess in which marketspaces their preferred stance is likely to bring about winning performance – the strategic choice of 'Where to Play'[1] with reference to the level of dynamism of the marketspace as well as the attractiveness and relevance for the corporation. Highly dynamic marketspaces require that the company has high dynamic capacity to succeed competitively. One of the companies that participated in the research is a long-established, founding family-influenced German company. They knew that they were underperforming competitors in supplying into major mobile phone manufacturers in China. Through the lens of understanding the dynamic capacity of the company, they realized that they would be more comfortable harvesting their participation in a highly dynamic marketspace rather than seeking to transform the firm to operate with a much higher level of dynamic capacity.

For each of the marketspaces in which a firm chooses to compete, it should also assess the choice of positioning within that market, particularly reviewing customer segments with the perspective of their rate of evolution. Clients that are 'early adopters', for example, may require greater levels of 'Sensing & Making Sense' compared to other segments. If the capabilities of the firm to 'Sense & Make Sense' are strong then early adopters may be a good set of customers for the firm to target; if not, the firm may do well to focus on others.

In making the choices of 'where to play', it should be remembered that being engaged in relevant marketspaces with a wide diversity of dynamics can help to strengthen the dynamic capacity of the corporation. Participation in a diversity of marketspaces can increase the ability to Sense & Make Sense of emergent signals by enabling comparison across marketspaces.

How to win

Once the 'where to play' strategic choices have been made, then the choices of 'how to win'[2] are considered. In Part Two, we explored the management mechanisms and behaviours that enable the firm to behave dynamically. All three of the meta-capabilities described must co-exist, as it is the product of their working together that amplifies or diminishes the overall performance of the corporation. Determine which management capabilities and practices to prioritize to be able to significantly enhance firm performance, ie where is the biggest gap currently in the performance of strategically important capabilities. Determine what 'good' will look like for the capability being strengthened.

It should be a deliberated choice for the firm to determine whether to disproportionately emphasize one or more 4IR capabilities. For example, Google invests tremendous attention in mining the data that it has access to, particularly through being the most popular search engine in the world (thus strengthening its ability to Sense & Make Sense). By contrast the European beer company mentioned in Chapter 3 has achieved mastery in the capability to Seize & Replicate, a result of ensuring fluid communications and close relationships across the senior leadership team and adopting a global-local organization structure that increases transparency and responsiveness.

The findings from the assessment as well as benchmarking to other companies can help form a view on the size of performance gaps and indicate metrics that could be used to track improvements to a desired level of performance.

Adopt leading indicators and metrics

Whereas executives at all firms are concerned with shareholder value, most also know there is a conflict between optimizing short-term, period-by-period KPI and placing their energies against mid- to long-term objectives that drive greater shareholder value. 'We need to meet the results that the analysts expect today, otherwise I won't be around to steer the company tomorrow,' quipped one executive at a leading equipment manufacturer.

However, another executive noted, 'If we were really only focused on quarterly results, our employment would go up plus or minus 25,000 every quarter. We need to have a longer-term perspective, for the global network and portfolio to have any kind of stability.'

Many executives are measured and rewarded on current period results whilst they recognize that this influences against choices to support initiatives that will equip the firm for higher performance in the future. When asked to rank the relative importance of KPI by which they are measured, most executives ranked the shorter-term financial performance results higher. However, when subsequently asked what measures they themselves thought most important for value creation given the dynamic nature of the industry and markets, most referenced business indicators (eg market share) and a mid-term time horizon. An executive at a major global asset management company noted:

> When I stop and think about us performing against competitors, I think in terms of things like market share, customer satisfaction surveys etc. It's such a professional thing. There are all kinds of analysts and consultants and people that spend all their time gathering information and telling us what they found out. It's wonderfully easy to do that. But when I think about [performance] results, I would say I consider multi-year trends.

An executive at Rolls-Royce noted:

> We also look at our profitability performance versus competitors, our growth in profitability, our growth in sales compared to competitors. We look at how we're investing versus them: What is it? Basic R&D, product related? Is

it machinery and equipment or buildings? That's certainly not a short-term measure, although market share, we have a pretty keen focus on that; it is short term but with longer-term implications.

Firms that both successfully pursue current period results and formally track leading indicators of future performance outperform their competitors. A senior global leader at a leading equipment manufacturer noted:

> We want to keep that market leadership position, and the only way we can do that is to have customers make more money with our products and services than they can with competition. That comes at a cost. We need to invest effectively [...] to do that consistently we want the biggest slice of industry profitability so that we can reinvest in our factories and our product and our distribution organization etc.

An executive at a media conglomerate reflected on the importance of focusing on the immediacy of customer experience metrics in order to be able to attain the longer-term vision of the CEO:

> The CEO wants us to be the most admired company in the world. It is not just pretence or show. We put our customers number one, because he wants to create the best fan experience, the best guest experience in the theme parks. That is number one, we can't slip on that. We look at those metrics first at every quarterly review and at the annual planning meetings.

Having decided to adopt the imperative to compete dynamically and defined the set of metrics against which to track performance, it is crucial to commit publicly, and message clearly both internally and externally. As much attention should be given to tracking, reporting and rewarding performance on the leading indicators as to operating results.

KEY CONCEPTS: CHAPTER 11

The greater the rate of market and industry evolution in which a firm participates, the greater the importance of 4IR management capabilities and practices. However, in the absence of a crisis, executives may prefer to stay with the existing approaches and mindset. The difference in performance between those firms that build and leverage 4IR capabilities and those that adhere to traditional practices increases as the speed of business accelerates.

We will see more firms transforming themselves, adopting the technologies and management practices of 4IR, whether driven to change for survival, by stockholders demanding better returns, or by the aspiration of new leadership teams.

Simply adopting new digital or technology tools and processes will not transform the performance of the corporation and, indeed, could create significant operational complexity. The choice of how and what management processes and capabilities to invest in transforming must be aligned with the strategy to achieve the corporate purpose. This requires knowing the most important capabilities for the firm to excel with, and what is the biggest gap between current performance of those capabilities and that required to have a competitive advantage.

The process of assessment and decision making is of strategic importance, determining 'Where to Play' and 'How to Win':

- Charting the waters ahead: connecting with external context, customers, competitors and consultants to understand the opportunities and challenges for the firm due to 4IR.

- Structured assessment of the strengths and weaknesses of 4IR capabilities.

- Decide where to play: defining marketspaces and customer segments with respect to their rate and nature of evolution.

- Decide how to win: identifying with which 4IR capabilities the firm can outperform competitors.

- Leading indicators and metrics of future performance should be adopted in addition to achieving current period results.

In 4IR, executives need to lean forward into the unknown and uncertain with the aspiration that they will shape the future as it unfolds. There should be a culture of positive optimism and expectation that motivates all stakeholders, both within and external to the firm. As Steve Jobs (founder of Apple) quipped, to 'put a "ding" in the universe'.

Endnotes

1 Lafley, A and Martin, R (2013) *Playing to Win: How strategy really works*, Harvard Business Review Press

2 Ibid

PART SIX

Summary

12

Boosters and key themes

In this book we have explored how firms are adjusting their management and leadership practices to thrive in the accelerated world of business ushered in by the technologies, social and demographic pressures and political uncertainties of the 4th Industrial Revolution. The driving forces of this revolution were making an impact long before the term 4IR was coined. Most organizations have felt the pressure to refine their business models and management practices and to revisit their leadership skills competency frameworks. They have noted the changes in the skills required and have witnessed wider diversity in their workforces and established greater flexibility in the manners in which they engage with them. Many firms have also undertaken major transformations, adopting digitally enabled platforms and approaches, overhauling corporate culture, running campaigns to fan the flames of innovation, flattening organization structures, and significantly refashioning the portfolio of lines of businesses they pursue.

With all these examples of corporate initiatives there is now a sufficient body of evidence to draw upon to see what works as the forces of 4IR exert dominance in shaping the future. We're at the end of the beginning of 4IR. The question is, what are you, at your firm, going to do about it? How will you ensure you thrive, rather than just survive in 4IR? Will you opt to be a follower or a leader? Will you compete in the mainstream or in the backwaters?

Note: Chapter 11 provides you with a methodology and a manner to ask these questions of the leadership team at your organization.

Boosters

People are at the heart of the 4th Industrial Revolution. Chapter 8 explored how to empower and protect talent, with particular emphasis on the importance of an employer fulfilling their duty of care for all their workers, irrespective of contractual arrangements and the benefits of individual flexibilities in work arrangements. In addition, throughout this book, interwoven across the practices of management and leadership in 4IR, are three principles that boost effectiveness: inclusion of diversity, engagement, and empowerment.

The inclusion of diversity

Throughout this book I indicate that inclusion of diversity is a good thing. Inclusivity is also a common theme across several of the UN Sustainable Development goals,[1] for example Goal 4 (ensure inclusive and equitable quality education and promote lifelong learning opportunities for all) and Goal 5 (achieve gender equality and empower all women and girls).

- Being present and actively engaged in a diversity of markets can strengthen the firm's ability to Sense & Make Sense if:
  - the organization culture is inclusive of different opinions and perspectives;
  - the central management is willing and able to identify opportunities to execute multiple marketplace experiments in parallel, in the different markets.
- Including representatives of diverse markets in decision making enhances the ability to Seize & Replicate as well as to Sense & Make Sense:
  - if diverse voices are included in debates and encouraged to productively challenge group thinking;
  - if the corporate protocols and practice for virtual collaboration and communication accommodate diverse voices and cultures.
- Engaging with diverse groups of customers can enhance robustness of overall revenues, through the mechanisms of Reconfiguring & Repositioning that allow sales to be moved from one group to another in response to shifting demand conditions:
  - for example, between customers in different countries or between premium and budget customer groups, unheeded by corporate policies and organization structure.

- In Chapter 5 we explored the importance of bringing together a diverse set of skills and perspectives in the pursuit of an overall, unifying goal. And, how a strong sense of purpose is able to attract and unify the efforts of a highly diverse team, transcending differences.

- Human-centred workforce management (HCWM) is a key tenet of 4IR, reflecting the recognition that inclusion of an increasingly diverse workforce is a strong positive for society and a duty of the firm. Apart from national and cultural diversity, HCWM also responds to the uniqueness of the individual reflective of gender, age, disability, life stage, etc:

  o the provision of flexible working arrangements;

  o empathy and flexibility in treating each person fairly, within transparent guidelines;

  o promoting all-round well-being.

- Chapter 9 highlights the importance of diversity of individuals for the performance of a team:

  o contributing different skills and perspectives, whilst engaging constructively;

  o adopting different roles within the team and adapting to one another to enhance team dynamics.

Employee engagement

This theme runs throughout the book as employees with high (yet sustainable!) levels of engagement are more satisfied with their work and perform better:

- Employees that are engaged with the mission and purpose of the firm are more motivated, are more observant of opportunities for improvement, and are more creative in terms of potential solutions. These characteristics enhance the capability of the firm to Sense & Make Sense.

- The capability to Seize & Replicate is enhanced by higher levels of engagement as there is a greater propensity for the individual to look throughout the firm for resources, experiences or emergent solutions that can be redeployed to address local market issues.

- A strong sense of purpose increases engagement. This is highlighted in Chapter 5, which discusses that a meaningful purpose for the corporation to pursue is to address a major societal need that the stakeholders (including employees) are passionate about and for which the firm has a set of uniquely relevant capabilities and skills to apply.

- Employees who are engaged in the pursuit of the mission of the company develop a greater sense of winning together. This sense of being on the same team, collaborating for the success of the overall firm, means it is particularly important for leaders to be ambidextrous, able to pursue seemingly conflicting goals simultaneously. Such leaders need to be able to explore and understand each other's perspectives, objectives and constraints.

- Workforce management that is human-centred is empathetic with and responsive to the needs and circumstances of the individual. This approach increases employee engagement, reinforcing the sense of being valued and respected.

- Not only is employee engagement important to success in 4IR but also new digitally enabled Human Capital Management (HCM) systems provide greater visibility and therefore possibility for managing engagement. Employee engagement happens at the level of the individual, yet prior to modern HCM systems engagement initiatives were conducted at an aggregated programme level. Analysis of an individual's activities (eg use of learning and development tools, use of corporate social media and discussion forums) and their network within the firm can quickly highlight their level and the trend line of engagement.

Empowerment

In 4IR the speed of business has increased and is continuing to accelerate. In this context teams and individuals throughout the organization need to be empowered to act, expected to take the initiative:

- The development and adoption of digital platforms and application are providing wide accessibility to data and the ability to interrogate that data as well as to communicate broadly. This is empowering broad populations within corporations and across societies. This leadership trait of being data driven and digitally empowered is highlighted in Chapter 2 (Sense & Make Sense).

- However, empowerment can be used for good or bad outcomes, to the benefit of the collective and the individual or to benefit of the individual at the expense of the collective. Therefore, greater empowerment should be paired with greater responsibility and accountability. Personal accountability is highlighted as a core leadership trait in Chapter 3 (Seize & Replicate).

- Personal accountability and collective responsibility are crucial for the performance of teams and the functioning of the fluid-yet-powerful approach of team of teams (explored in Chapter 9). The differentiating mindset that is highlighted in this chapter is Empowerment.

- Individuals and teams that are empowered to act must also know how to act: in which direction to progress, and what decisions, actions and behaviours are appropriate, reflective of the culture and values of the corporation. Chapter 7 discusses the doctrine of change, an approach to empowering and coordinating the activities of multiple teams across a fluid organization.

Axioms of superior performance in the 4th Industrial Revolution

1 Build dynamic capacity: thrive in 4IR

Build the capacity to thrive in the dynamics of the 4th Industrial Revolution. The dynamic capacity of the firm is the product of the interaction between three sets of capabilities – Sense & Make Sense, Seize & Replicate, Reposition & Reconfigure – enabling the organization to adapt and pivot in a timely manner, moving from one position of transient competitive advantage to another.

2 Drive audacious growth: be purpose-led

Drive audacious growth in pursuit of a purposeful vision. This requires commitment to a meaningful and motivating purpose, developing a cadre of managers who are able to think and act ambidextrously, resolving dilemmas and overcoming seemingly conflicting goals. It requires establishing the expectation and the mechanisms that facilitate continuous evolution.

3 Win the 4IR talent race: develop, deploy, duty of care

Talent is key to winning in 4IR, able to interface with technologies and to navigate in ambiguity with an increasing role for creativity; continuously developing 4IR skills and optimally deploying talent by fluid teaming to match the shifting challenges; employing human-centred workforce management practices that enable talent to perform at their best whilst fulfilling the duty of care.

The greater the capability of the corporation to Sense & Make Sense of the unfolding future, the greater the opportunity for making correct and timely decisions on how to act. In 4IR, digital technologies are enabling corporations with broad networks to capture and interrogate vast amounts of data, creating the possibility for advantage in the ability to Sense & Make Sense over firms with more limited networks. However, to be effective, appropriate management practices must also be adopted:

- Activate people across the network to contribute data and idea fragments; crowd-source, as everyone is smarter than anyone. Then use technology and good practice to filter the high-value ideas and insights from the 'noise'. In particular focus on understanding customers and the changes in their needs and behaviours.

- Adopt an approach of test and learn, running rapid experiments, often in parallel, with the objective of accelerating knowledge acquisition that can lead to more deliberate actions and choices.

- Look below the surface of ideas, insights and news that are shared to understand the drivers for which the resulting data (symptoms) has been reported. Challenge and interrogate colleagues to learn about their thoughts, hopes and fears with regards to the data presented. A technique that can help to avoid the development of debilitating 'group thinking' is to disperse team members across different locations, encouraging them to interrogate and challenge one another from their own perspective.

The greater the capability to Seize & Replicate, the faster the firm can scale new approaches to market, seizing opportunities and bringing effective defence against competitive threats.

In 4IR, global platforms and communications solutions enable news, insights and experience to be shared rapidly; however, to be most effective, appropriate management practices must also be adopted:

- Whilst global platforms and virtual communications greatly improve efficiency of regular activities, each market invariably requires some adaptation and experiences local exceptions. The fastest and most effective manner in which to apply new knowledge and leading-edge expertise is often to temporarily move people across the network.

- To accelerate knowledge flow requires minimizing the number of handoffs between people and across organization boundaries. When markets with similar dynamics are clustered together (in the same organizational grouping), it can significantly increase the transfer of market-relevant knowledge, accelerating roll-out and scale-up.

- 4IR is driving an increase in the speed of evolution of competitive dynamics in many marketspaces. In such fluidity, timely actions can significantly shape the subsequent evolution of the marketspace. Combining and applying learnings from other markets across the network of the firm can be a source of competitive advantage, acting before regulators or competitors have determined their positions.

The greater the capability to Reposition & Reconfigure, the greater the ability of the firm to exploit advantages of arbitrage (eg out- vs in-sourcing), scale (eg consolidating activities in different parts of the supply chain) and to enhance the robustness of overall revenues (eg moving revenue recognition between alternative product ranges or operating companies). In 4IR, analytics and digital modelling can accelerate and improve such decision making but for complex decisions to be efficiently implemented also requires belief about the unfolding future, collaboration and mutual adjustment between executives. Examples include:

- Defining a new marketspace, as yet non-existent, by combining insight and intuition. Creating demand by designing and launching a new type of service/product. Market research struggles to support a non-existent (not yet existing) market.

- Morphing into new marketspaces and out of existing marketspaces in response to perception of potential opportunities, eg for growing sales, or the benefits of denying a competitor a position in a market, or to extract profits by harvesting a non-strategic position.

- The decision not to optimize for efficiency in the supply chain or not to consolidate all learnings into an integrated customer experience can seem to be illogical until the possibilities of disruption and uncertainty of demand are considered. Deliberately creating or maintaining operational inefficiencies in order to increase strategic flexibility is a key mechanism to enhance the dynamic capacity of the firm.

The ability of the corporation to achieve its purpose (its future objective) is dependent on its ability to navigate the turbulence of the present. This requires the ability to adapt the plan of action, to be strategically agile whilst remaining anchored on achieving the long-term objective:

- The greater the sense of purpose, the greater the motivation of the workforce to pursue it, and the greater also the ability to be resilient when encountering setbacks and disappointments. The consistent pursuit of a meaningful purpose is a pre-requisite for high performance in the uncertain and fast-changing context of 4IR.

- Stakeholders' confidence in the ability of the management to navigate the uncertain future is the primary driver of corporate value. Such confidence is often low for traditional firms that successfully deliver on quarter-by-quarter profit forecasts (eg General Motors P/E ratio = 7) yet high for firms that have clear vision for the future (eg Tesla, which has barely ever produced a profit, has a P/E ratio of 80).

- Whilst being future-anchored, 4IR leadership teams need to display sound judgement and decision making whilst developing and implementing strategic plans. They need to be able to blend approaches that make clear decisions based on the best information available whilst recognizing that any forecast is flawed. They need to provide stability and clarity so that the organization can follow, whilst recognizing that updates and changes to the plans will be necessary.

Leaders in 4IR need to be able to manage in ambiguous situations, maintaining a balance between pursuit of the long-term vision and strategic plan whilst also being responsive to the unfolding current situation. Being able to compete for tomorrow, whilst delivering results today:

- Leaders able to simultaneously pursue seemingly conflicting objectives are said to be 'ambidextrous'. Such leaders redefine the problem of an apparent paradox in order to find a new solution; they often do this by exploring and testing the assumptions that define current actions and decision making and that have led to current dilemmas.

  o Such mental dexterity differentiates leaders in 4IR where businesses and leaders are seeking to break with paradigms and assumptions that have previously defined management thinking and practice.

- Conflicting objectives often arise due to organization structure design, which separates functions and creates incentives for maximizing performance within each silo (eg marketing being separate from warehouse operations for an online retailer). A strong sense of being in the same team, to win together, may bring the warehouse manager and the head of marketing together to find a solution that benefits the overall firm.

- When the executives in one or another department enquire with an authentic ear to understand the constraints, objectives and assumptions of other executives, genuine learning can occur. This leads to discovery of ways to resolve apparent dilemmas.

o An executive seeking to improve warehouse efficiency vs marketing effectiveness may discover that investing in quicker and more accurate order fulfilment leads to greater customer satisfaction which in turn results in an opportunity for more effective social media marketing, which raises the volume throughput of the warehouse, which increases operational efficiency.

An impact of 4IR is to accelerate the speed of business, the rate of evolution and adoption of business practices and new technologies. The ability to continuously evolve is a source of advantage; progressing smoothly from one position of transient advantage to the next, from one 'stepping stone to the next in the journey across the river'. Key practices that support such prowess are:

- Appointment of a senior executive who is focused on identifying and understanding new technologies and applications that are being developed and deployed globally and can determine their relevance for adoption. This Acceleration Officer not only focuses on the technologies and their potential for impact but also understands the adjustments that are required by the organization in order to realize the anticipated benefits.

- A doctrine for implementing changes that drive the evolution of the business. If the doctrine is widely understood it can enable individuals and teams throughout the organization to implement change initiatives and to make refinements semi-autonomously, which can both speed up the rate of evolution and ensure greater refinement.

- The collective development of a roadmap for the anticipated evolution of the firm enhances understanding and ownership across the executive cadre. The roadmap is anchored on the vision for the future and then developed back from the future to the situation today. The roadmap indicates how individual initiatives are aligned with pursuit of the overall purpose of the corporation.

In 4IR, the 'race to develop talent' has replaced the 'war for talent'. As in 4IR, the changes in the required content of work, work practices and work environment are so widespread and happening so fast that traditional approaches have been incapable of developing or retraining people in sufficient numbers.

- In 4IR the required leadership traits and management skills emphasize connecting with and collaborating with others, rather than traditional approaches of command and control. Knowledge acquisition and creation by co-creation, working together and experimenting quickly to test and learn – these are replacing research-based proposals and experience-based approval.

- The race to develop talent focuses on developing the requisite skills and knowledge in real time, as needed, for addressing actual issues on the job, the goal being to support behaviour changes that positively impact performance. This reduces the time and uncertainty from investment in training (both by the individual and by the corporation) to achieving a tangible return on that investment.

- 4IR technologies are significantly changing how human capital is managed, enabling the migration from cohort to individual insight, and from periodic to real-time support. For example, tracking individual performance and engagement, the provision of comprehensive, precise and timely feedback, and individually tailored development support. 4IR technologies are helping individuals to discover and achieve greater potential within themselves and to face the retraining required for the future with greater confidence.

In 4IR, teams, be they formal or informal, short-term or standing, are recognized as the engines driving the performance of the enterprise. Agile, adaptable corporations need fluid teaming, ie agile, adaptable resource configurations:

- Team performance is so important that it cannot be left to chance. How a team comes together, how the individuals of a team interact with each other, how they themselves behave and how they interact with stakeholders outside the team should be made explicit – a codification of the behaviours and expectations of each other and to which all team members need to be held to account by each other.

- For a team to perform well there must be a high level of trust and a high level of psychological safety between all team members. Additionally, every high-functioning team consists of individuals who take on different types of role within the team, and who are ideally skilled enough to recognize the role types and to adopt others for the benefit of overall team performance. Team-centred development strengthens these characteristics whilst the team continues to address the workplace challenges for which it has been assembled.

- The 'team of teams' approach to organization design seeks to deploy teams to address an increasing array of issues, including both 'standing' teams for ongoing business-as-usual performance and 'sprint' teams that assemble quickly to address an immediate issue and then are quickly dissolved once it is solved. The 'team of teams' approach creates a highly fluid, performance-focused environment. This environment also accentuates the ability to discover talent and provide opportunities for them to quickly rise up.

Human-centred workforce management (HCWM) is a key tenet of the 4th Industrial Revolution. As big an evolution is anticipated in how corporations manage their relationships with workers as from the impact of adopting new technologies. Apart from the ethical considerations, promoting the emotional and physical well-being of workers helps to increase productivity and attract and retain talent:

- Duty of care: providing support for adjusting to the changing content of work by providing training for reskilling and upskilling, as well as flexible working arrangements without prejudice, in order to support a worker to manage their potentially conflicting obligations between work and family.

- Individual agreements: much of human resource practice has been underscored by policies creating uniformity in the treatment and progression of workers (for example, job grades, feedback and promotion cycles). However, there is growing evidence that allowing individual arrangements enhances engagement and empowerment that can result in greater productivity and higher retention. Approaches such as flexible working, job crafting and 'I-deals' allow a degree of personalization whilst retaining perceived fairness between colleagues and sufficient management coordination.

- Explicit guidelines: the guidelines are as important for the organization as they are for the individual employee, as they provide the guiderails, clarifying what is and what is not expected. The guidelines address causes of potential anxiety and stress for the individual, eg how to manage the work-life/family-life boundary, the use of mobile devices, the usage of personal data, etc. The guidelines should recognize and accommodate without prejudice different attitudes and preferences between individuals.

- Provide training for supervisors and leaders to equip them to fulfil the duty of care and to themselves. Role-model a healthy lifestyle, particularly with regards to their management of the work-life/family-life boundary. HCWM requires that supervisors fulfil the duty of care, demonstrating empathy for their staff.

FIGURE 12.1 Leadership traits for thriving in 4IR

Build 4IR dynamic capacity

Sense & Make Sense	Curiosity
	• Harvest idea fragments
	• Data driven, digitally enabled
	• Experiment: test and learn

Seize & Replicate	Sense of urgency
	• Rapid scale-up
	• Personal accountability
	• Collaborate across boundaries

Reposition & Reconfigure	Adaptability
	• Simplify: reduce complexity
	• Persuasion and influence
	• Global vision

Drive audacious growth

Forward leaning	Courageous
	• Purpose-led
	• Strategic thinking
	• Decision making in uncertainty

Ambidextrous leaders	Problem solver
	• Own the paradox
	• Embrace new perspectives
	• Creative, systems thinking

Continuous evolution	Never settle
	• Provide meaning/connect to purpose
	• Organizational savviness
	• Executive presence

Win the 4IR talent race

Human-centred	Empathy
	• Authentic
	• Flexible in support of others
	• Promote well-being

Team-driven performance	Empower others
	• Pursue excellence (as team)
	• Increase the cadence
	• Challenge and support

Race to develop talent	Talent catalyst
	• Leader as a coach
	• Stretch and support
	• Hunger for learning

Leadership traits summary

Leadership in 4IR requires mindsets and competencies that drive the organization to absorb and adapt to the new; to be both pre-emptive and responsive; to connect with, be influenced by and influence stakeholders within and beyond the boundaries of the firm.

The leadership competencies, mindsets and paradigms for success in 4IR are summarized in Figure 12.1.

Conclusion

Technology developments, in combination with the rising expectation that corporates will be increasingly proactive and responsible with regards to the needs of workers and society, have created the 4th Industrial Revolution (4IR). The result is significant turmoil both for workers and for companies. Business models are changing, industry structures collapsing; as change accelerates, there is greater uncertainty, greater risks and greater opportunities. The revolution is impacting management practices and leadership skills as much as it is dislocating workers, changing what needs to be done, how it is done and where. To make sense of the apparent turmoil caused by the revolution this book has looked at three core themes that are reshaping management practice. Each of the three main sections, Parts Two to Four, consists of three chapters:

- **Part Two – build dynamic capacity: thrive in 4IR**
  Build the capacity to thrive in the dynamics of the 4th Industrial Revolution. The dynamic capacity of the firm is the product of the interaction between three sets of capabilities – Sense & Make Sense, Seize & Replicate, Reposition & Reconfigure – enabling the organization to adapt and pivot in a timely manner, moving from one position of transient competitive advantage to another.

- **Part Three – drive audacious growth: be purpose-led**
  Drive audacious growth in pursuit of a purposeful vision. This requires commitment to a meaningful and motivating purpose, developing a cadre of managers who are able to think and act ambidextrously, resolving dilemmas and overcoming seemingly conflicting goals. It requires establishing the expectation and the mechanisms that facilitate continuous evolution.

- **Part Four – win the 4IR talent race: develop, deploy, duty of care**
  Talent is key to winning in 4IR, able to interface with technologies and to navigate in ambiguity with an increasing role for creativity. Continuously developing 4IR skills and optimally deploying talent by fluid teaming to match the shifting challenges. Employing Human-Centred Workforce Management practices that enable talent to perform at their best whilst fulfilling the duty of care.

In this final chapter I have brought together, in order to focus on them, just the management practices and leadership traits that are in ascendancy in the 4IR, bereft of the perspective of why they are in ascendancy and how to apply them. The task for any firm wishing to thrive in 4IR is to select which leadership skills and management practices to strengthen to become sources of competitive advantage; this is discussed in Chapter 11. The good news is

FIGURE 12.2 Management and leadership in 4IR: achieve and sustain superior performance

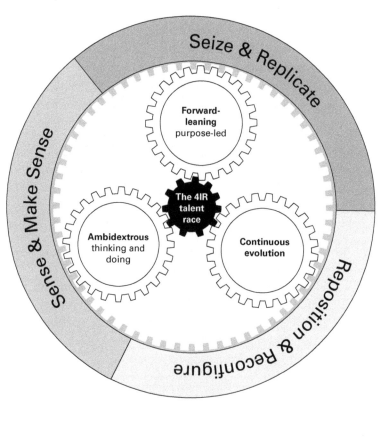

that those firms that do succeed in developing and leveraging the capacity to compete in 4IR outperform their peers by over 30 per cent (31 per cent over the five-year term). However, those that fail to do so fall behind their peers by approximately 15 per cent over the 5-year period.

Investors, stock holders and the senior leadership team should embrace the management practices and leadership traits required for success in 4IR. However, beyond the financial logic, 4IR firms also tend to be positive, dynamic places to work. They are often purpose-led, addressing a meaningful societal mission; they liberate and mobilize talent to work in teams on exciting and important projects. They strive to stay ahead of the competition (traditional and non-traditional) – and they attract the best talent. They move from one position of transient competitive advantage to the next, maintaining and building momentum. They confidently face the ambiguity and uncertainty of the future, relishing the new possibilities and opportunities that will be revealed.

My best wishes to you for your journey into the future...

Endnote

1   https://sustainabledevelopment.un.org/post2015/transformingourworld (archived at https://perma.cc/6N36-MJ42)

APPENDIX

Many thanks to friends and supporters from the following companies, without whose input and guidance this book could not have been written. Many of the executives spoke on the condition of anonymity, expressing their own personal opinions and not speaking as representatives of the companies – inclusion in the list below does not indicate or imply endorsement of this work by these organizations.

Company	Industry descriptor
3 Telecom	Telecoms
ABB	Industrial products
AgriProtein	Agricultural products
Ahold	Retail
Airbus Defence	Defence, aerospace, marine
Alibaba	Platform provider
Amazon	Platform provider
Bain	Consultancy
Barclays	Financial services
Bayer Medical Devices	Life-sciences
BCG	Consultancy
BD (Becton Dickinson)	Life sciences
BNP-Paribas	Financial services
Cargill	Agricultural products
Caterpillar	Industrial products
Cathay Pacific	Airline
Claremont Graduate University	University
Coca-Cola	Beverages

(continued)

(Continued)

Corning	Industrial products
Credit Suisse	Financial services
Danaher	Life sciences
DBS Bank	Financial services
Deloitte - Monitor	Consultancy
DHL	Logistics
Diageo	Alcoholic beverages
Dischem	Pharmaceuticals
Disney	Media and entertainment
Egon Zehnder	Executive search
Fuji-Xerox	Platform provider
Google	Media and entertainment
Heineken	Alcoholic beverages
Heraeus	Industrial products
Honeywell	Industrial products
IBM	Platform provider
Indian School of Business	University
Infineon	Semiconductors
Ingersoll-Rand	Industrial products
IXL-Center	Consultancy
J&J	Pharmaceuticals
JAL	Airline
Jardines	Conglomerate
Mars Group	FMCG
Mondelez International	FMCG
Nestle	FMCG

(continued)

(Continued)

P&G	FMCG
PCCW	Telecoms
Pernod Ricard	Alcoholic beverages
Philips	Consumer products
PSA Corporation	Logistics and marine
PWC	Consultancy
Rolls-Royce	Defence, aerospace, marine
SC Global	Real estate
Sembcorp Marine	Marine
Singapore Airlines	Airline
Singapore Management University	University
StateStreet	Financial services
Swire Group	Conglomerate
Syngenta	Life sciences
Tata Communications	Telecoms
TCS	Platform provider
Thales	Defence, aerospace, marine
Uber	Platform provider
Unilever	FMCG
University of Bath	University
University of Cambridge	University
UOB Bank	Financial services
UTC-BIS	Industrial products
Vodafone	Telecoms
WingTai	Real estate
Zuellig Pharma	Pharmaceuticals

INDEX

CPSIA information can be obtained
at www.ICGtesting.com
Printed in the USA
LVHW022336281020
669988LV00004B/4